*For fellow journeyers, as we walk together
through the Bible's pages.*

Walking Through the Bible

A Journey Guide

Marshall Holtvluwer and Nelson Miller

Walking through the Bible—a journey guide.

Holtvluwer, Marshall, and Nelson Miller.

Published by:

Crown Management LLC – July 2020

1527 Pineridge Drive
Grand Haven, MI 49417
USA
millern57@gmail.com

ISBN-13: 978-1-64945-017-3

Table of Contents

Table of Reading Guides

Timeline

B.C.

> 4000	God creates the world
> 2500	Flood destroys nearly all living things
2100	Abraham called from what is now Iraq to the promised land
1440	Moses leads the Israelite exodus from Egypt (traditional date)
1275	Alternate exodus date many scholars prefer
1050	Saul becomes Israel's first king
1000	David declares Jerusalem Israel's capital
960	Solomon builds the first Jewish temple
930	Israel divides into two nations
722	Assyria conquers the Northern Kingdom
586	Babylon conquers Southern Kingdom, exiling the survivors
470	Esther, the Jewish queen of Persia, halts a holocaust
37	Rome appoints Herod the Great king over the Jews
6	Mary bears Jesus
4	Herod the Great dies

A.D.

27	Jesus begins his public ministry
30	Jesus crucified and resurrected
35	Paul becomes a Christian
43	Paul begins 10,000 miles of missionary trips
50	Paul writes likely first New Testament book 1 Thessalonians
64	Rome executes Paul
66	Jews rebel against Rome, driving them from parts of Israel
70	Rome destroys Jerusalem and its temple, never rebuilt
95	John writes the Bible's last book Revelation

Themes

Book (Theme)	Key Verse
Genesis (beginnings)	In the beginning God created the heavens and the earth. 1:1.
Exodus (deliverance)	"I am the Lord your God, who brought you out of Egypt, out of the land of slavery." 20:2.
Leviticus (instruction)	"The fire on the alter must be kept burning; it must not go out." 6:12.
Numbers (wandering)	"In this wilderness your bodies will fall—every one of you twenty years old or more who was counted in the census and who has grumbled against me." 14:29.
Deuteronomy (obedience)	"Love the Lord your God with all your heart and with all your soul and with all your strength." 6:5.
Joshua (victory)	"No one will be able to stand against you all the days of your life. As I was with Moses, so I will be with you; I will never leave you nor forsake you." 1:5.
Judges (deterioration)	In those days Israel had no king; everyone did as they saw fit. 21:25
Ruth (redemption)	"Don't urge me to leave you or to turn back from you. Where you go, I will go, and where you stay, I will stay. Your people will be my people and your God my God." 1:16.
1 Samuel (leadership)	"The Lord does not look at the things people look at. People look at the outward appearance, but the Lord looks at the heart." 16:7.
2 Samuel (kingship)	"Your house and your kingdom will endure forever before me; your throne will be established forever." 7:16.
1 Kings (disobedience)	"Since this is your attitude and you have not kept my covenant and my decrees, which I commanded you, I will most certainly tear the kingdom away from you and give it to one of your subordinates." 11:11.
2 Kings (captivity)	So, Judah went into captivity, away from her land. 25:21.

1 Chronicles (remembrance)	Remember the wonders he has done, his miracles, and the judgments he pronounced.... 6:12.
2 Chronicles (inheritance)	"[I]f my people ... will humble themselves and pray and seek my face and turn from their wicked ways, then I will hear from heaven, and I will forgive their sin and will heal their land." 7:14.
Ezra (restoration)	For Ezra had devoted himself to the study and observance of the Law of the Lord, and to teaching its decrees and laws in Israel. 7:10.
Nehemiah (rebuilding)	"[W]e are powerless, because our fields and our vineyards belong to others." 5:5.
Esther (providence)	"And who knows but that you have come to your royal position for such a time as this?" 4:14.
Job (suffering)	"I know that my redeemer lives, and that in the end he will stand on the earth." 19:25.
Psalms (intimacy)	Your word is a lamp for my feet, a light on my path. 119:105.
Proverbs (wisdom)	Trust in the Lord with all your heart and lean not on your own understanding; in all your ways submit to him, and he will make your paths straight. 3:5-6.
Ecclesiastes (vanity)	Now all has been heard; here is the conclusion of the matter: fear God and keep his commandments, for this is the duty of all mankind. 12:13.
Song of Songs (love)	Let him lead me to the banquet hall, and let his banner over me be love. 2:4.
Isaiah (salvation)	Therefore, the Lord himself will give you a sign: the virgin will conceive and give birth to a son and will call him Immanuel. 7:14.
Jeremiah (exile)	"For I know the plans I have for you," declares the Lord, "plans to prosper you and not to harm you, plans to give you hope and a future." 29:11.
Lamentations (weeping)	Yet this I call to mind and therefore I have hope: Because of the Lord's great love we are not consumed, for his compassions never fail. They are new every morning; great is your faithfulness. 3:21-23.
Ezekiel (glory)	The Spirit lifted me up and brought me to the exiles in Babylonia in the vision given by the Spirit of God. Then the vision I had seen went up from me, and I told the exiles everything the Lord had shown me. 11:24-25.

Daniel (ability)	"My God sent his angel, and he shut the mouths of the lions." 6:22.
Hosea (faithlessness)	"Go, marry a promiscuous woman and have children with her, for like an adulterous wife this land is guilty of unfaithfulness to the LORD." 1:2.
Joel (destruction)	Alas for that day! For the day of the Lord is near; it will come like destruction from the Almighty. 1:15.
Amos (justice)	Away with the noise of your songs! I will not listen to the music of your harps. But let justice roll on like a river, righteousness like a never-failing stream! 5:23.
Obadiah (indifference)	"The day of the Lord is near for all nations. As you have done, it will be done to you; your deeds will return upon your own head." 15.
Jonah (grace)	"In my distress I called to the Lord, and he answered me. From deep in the realm of the dead I called for help, and you listened to my cry." 2:2.
Micah (judgment)	What does the Lord require of you? To act justly and to love mercy and to walk humbly with your God. 6:8.
Nahum (refuge)	The Lord is good, a refuge in times of trouble. 1:7.
Habakkuk (faithfulness)	"See, the enemy is puffed up; his desires are not upright—but the righteous person will live by his faithfulness...." 2:4.
Zephaniah (coming)	The great day of the Lord is near—near and coming quickly. 1:14.
Haggai (priorities)	Now this is what the Lord Almighty says: "Give careful thought to your ways." 1:5.
Zechariah (deliverance)	"Not by might nor by power, but by my Spirit," says the Lord Almighty. 4:6.
Malachi (refinement)	But who can endure the day of his coming? Who can stand when he appears? For he will be like a refiner's fire or a launderer's soap. 3:2.
Matthew (kingdom)	From that time on Jesus began to preach, "Repent, for the kingdom of heaven has come near." 4:17.
Mark (servant)	"Anyone who wants to be first must be the very last, and the servant of all." 9:35.
Luke (perfection)	Then Pilate announced to the chief priests and the crowd, "I find no basis for a charge against this man." 23:4.

John **(word)**	"For God so loved the world that he gave his one and only Son, that whoever believes in him shall not perish but have eternal life." 3:16.
Acts **(gospel)**	In this way the word of the Lord spread widely and grew in power. 19:20.
Romans **(faith)**	For in the gospel the righteousness of God is revealed—a righteousness that is by faith from first to last, just as it is written: "The righteous will live by faith." 1:17.
1 Corinthians **(striving)**	Do you not know that in a race all the runners run, but only one gets the prize? Run in such a way as to get the prize. 9:24.
2 Corinthians **(apostleship)**	He has made us competent as ministers of a new covenant—not of the letter but of the Spirit; for the letter kills, but the Spirit gives life. 3:6.
Galatians **(freedom)**	It is for freedom that Christ has set us free. 5:1.
Ephesians **(blessings)**	Praise be to the God and Father of our Lord Jesus Christ, who has blessed us in the heavenly realms with every spiritual blessing in Christ. 1:3.
Philippians **(joy)**	In all my prayers for all of you, I always pray with joy because of your partnership in the gospel from the first day until now…. 1:4-5.
Colossians **(supreme)**	The Son is the image of the invisible God, the firstborn over all creation. 1:15.
1 Thessalonians **(fellowship)**	Now about your love for one another we do not need to write to you, for you yourselves have been taught by God to love each other. 4:9.
2 Thessalonians **(resolve)**	So then, brothers and sisters, stand firm and hold fast to the teachings we passed on to you, whether by word of mouth or by letter. 2:15.
1 Timothy **(leadership)**	I am writing you these instructions so that … you will know how people ought to conduct themselves in God's household…. 3:14-15.
2 Timothy **(endurance)**	I have fought the good fight, I have finished the race, I have kept the faith. 4:7.
Titus **(teaching)**	These, then, are the things you should teach. Encourage and rebuke with all authority. 2:15.
Philemon **(forgiveness)**	Perhaps the reason he was separated from you for a little while was that you might have him back forever—no longer as a slave, but better than a slave, as a dear brother. 1:15.

Hebrews (superior)	[T]he ministry Jesus has received is as superior to theirs as the covenant of which he is mediator is superior to the old one 8:6.
James (authenticity)	Show me your faith without deeds, and I will show you my faith by my deeds. 2:18.
1 Peter (hope)	For Christ also suffered once for sins, the righteous for the unrighteous, to bring you to God. 3:18.
2 Peter (warning)	Therefore, dear friends, since you have been forewarned, be on your guard so that you may not be carried away by the error of the lawless and fall from your secure position. 3:17.
1 John (fellowship)	Anyone who claims to be in the light but hates a brother or sister is still in the darkness. 2:9.
2 John (discernment)	Watch out that you do not lose what we have worked for, but that you may be rewarded fully. 8.
3 John (hospitality)	We ought therefore to show hospitality to such people so that we may work together for the truth. 8.
Jude (perseverance)	[K]eep yourselves in God's love as you wait for the mercy of our Lord Jesus Christ to bring you to eternal life. 21.
Revelation (unveiling)	[T]he voice I had first heard speaking to me like a trumpet said, "Come up here, and I will show you what must take place after this." 4:1.

Reading the Bible

Reading the Bible, God's word revealed to a humankind whom he loves so exquisitely, is an unprecedented privilege and pleasure. The Bible is not a book that one reads just once, although a first end-to-end reading should be stunningly profound, indeed life changing. Reading the Bible, though, should continue through a lifetime of discovery. The Bible, although a grand narrative, is also meditation literature, meant for the reader to return, read, question, review, and consider again, for the mind to continually mull. The Bible, read properly, wisely, in the right Spirit and frame, with a soft heart and open eyes and ears, feeds and transforms the soul into what God intended for it, which is a vessel in which he can dwell so surely that the reader flourishes in his intimacy, now and eternally. To promote that open heart and foster that keen mind for the Bible, under the Spirit's influence, is this book's goal.

Yet reading the Bible can also be difficult. God plainly desires that readers work for at least some of what he wishes the Bible to give us. Jesus told parables for precisely that reason. Handing truths to us on a silver platter somehow doesn't always serve their value and purpose. The Bible reveals many truths as plainly as one could serve them. But the Bible weaves other truths within stories, histories, songs, and patterns, there to discover but only with the right tools and discipline, passionate heart, and reasonable effort. God does not just use people and events to form us. He also uses reading the Bible to shape in us the heart attitude, mental clarity, and righteous character that attract him.

The interested or curious person, or the intellectual explorer, has many ways to read the Bible, whether historically, critically, or as literature or philosophy. Followers of Christ, though, read the Bible differently. We read the Bible as a unified story, from start to finish, of the unimaginably good news of eternal life in Jesus Christ. You may read the Bible any way that you wish and in doing so still find it profitable. But if you wish to read the Bible as God intended it, as his Spirit guides a

Christ follower, then read for its repeating events, figures, and references, marvelously arranged across the span of a millennium and a half, to offer us the best possible news that we need not die but may live and flourish eternally in intimacy with Christ Jesus.

Thus, read the Bible for the subtle and profound ways in which God creates all things, arranges all things, and intervenes in the natural order. Know the beauty and benefit of God's natural order, while knowing more the beauty and benefit of its one Creator. Read the Bible, as Romans 12:2 tell us, so that it transforms you in renewal of your mind. Resolve, as 1 Corinthians 12:2 urges, to know Jesus Christ through the Bible's holy word. The words of Jesus, those that the Bible records, fill with God's Spirit and life, John 6:63 records Jesus himself telling us. The Bible lights our path, Psalm 119:105 declares. When we walk in that light, 1 John 1:7 assures us, Jesus's blood purifies us of sin. Read the Bible with due sense of wonder for its account of Christ, his power and majesty.

As to how to use this book, consider reading about each Bible book here, just before you read the book, and perhaps again after reading it. Or you may wish to skim through this book, looking for a Bible book that would especially pique your interest. You may also just wish to read this whole book before picking up the Bible again, to get the Bible's structure, patterns, and purpose firmly in mind. A good read here may refresh your interest in the Bible and renew your ability to benefit from it. Watch, too, for the reading guides interspersed throughout the text. They may provide you with clues or reminders of how to get the most from your reading. Above all, may God's Spirit lead you.

The Old Testament

The Old Testament, or as some prefer the *Hebrew Bible*, is the collection of writings that Jews recognize as their scripture. Christians do, too, although they complete those scriptures with the New Testament, Old and New Testaments together making up the Christian Bible. Muslims may also recognize portions of the Old Testament, especially its first five books the Torah and then also the Psalms, even some accounts of Jesus. The Old Testament spans thirty-nine books, while the New Testament twenty-seven more books, of the Bible's total sixty-six in number.

To refer to the Old Testament, originally recorded in Hebrew, as *old* is historically accurate. The writings are ancient, many of them older, for instance, than Homer's *Odyssey* and *Iliad,* books that the world celebrates for their antiquity. The Old Testament's many human authors, Spirit guided, recorded it from about 1,500 B.C. to 400 B.C., over more than one-thousand years. The Bible's history begins thousands of years earlier with God's creation of the world and of the first human, later to trace that first human's ancestors, listed in Luke 3, down seventy-seven generations to Jesus.

Yet to call the Hebrew Bible's collection *old* may mislead the reader into thinking that the writings are outdated, overturned, or surpassed, when they are not at all so. Together, the Hebrew Bible and New Testament together stand as a single story, the former anticipating and foreshadowing the latter in every significant respect. Christians view the Bible, both Old and New Testaments together, as a single unified story pointing to the Lord Jesus Christ. Read the Old Testament, the Hebrew Bible, as establishing the people and patterns that would usher in the world's Savior.

The Hebrew Bible has a definite structure. It begins with five books we know as the *Torah*, also called the *Pentateuch*. Those five books describe God's creation of the world, humankind's fall from his Eden garden, and a cycle of restorations and falls from Noah through Abraham, to Moses and Joshua. Those five books also show how God established his covenant people Israel, giving them laws they were to follow in an obedience that they could never quite manage and sometimes grossly rejected.

The Torah gives way to twelve history books describing how the nation Israel regained the promised land, rose to world prominence, but then divided, eventually falling into exile before making a tentative return. The first seven history books extend the Torah's chronology, the next two summarize that extension, and the last three extend the chronology farther into the nation's post-exile malaise. The histories end four centuries short of the birth of the Messiah Jesus Christ, where the New Testament begins, breaking those centuries of silence.

The Old Testament, though, does not end with history. Five books we know as the *writings* or *wisdom literature* develop underlying themes that the Old Testament introduces in its opening five Torah books and repeats throughout its dozen histories. These writings may seem an odd collection, from the suffering of Job to the emotion of the Psalms, and the sayings of Proverbs, ending with the despair of Ecclesiastes and love affair of the Song of Songs. Yet read properly, the writings profoundly deepen and enrich the Old Testament narrative.

The Old Testament's last two sections, the five books of the major prophets and twelve books of the minor prophets, further deepen, enrich, and extend the narrative. These books include significant history, repeating descriptions of some events that the histories already describe, while amplifying many of those descriptions and providing abundant other detail. Their greater contribution, though, is prophetic, drawing out God's perspective on the machinations of Israel's leaders and people, and the nations and people who support and oppose them. They make a spectacular introduction to the New Testament that follows.

The Torah

The first five books of the Old Testament, including Genesis, Exodus, Leviticus, Numbers, and Deuteronomy, we know as the Torah, Pentateuch, or books of Moses. The Torah is spectacular standing alone, describing as it does thousands of years of history from God's creation of the world to his recalling his chosen people into his promised land. After Genesis and the first part of Exodus, though, many readers find the Torah's laws daunting to follow, unless having a supportive understanding in which to read them.

The word *Torah* refers to the Jewish written law, although not using *law* in the narrow legislative or judicial sense that we give the word today. A better translation would refer to revealed teaching or commands constituting the people Israel. Indeed, Jews continue to place Torah readings at the center of synagogue Sabbath services. Synagogue officials remove the Torah parchment scrolls from their special storage, unroll them on the ceremonial lectern to the planned reading, and chant or read them aloud. Commentary follows. The Torah is thus more than a collection of histories, poetry, and laws from which to draw lessons. It constitutes the Jewish community and continues to define and shape its culture.

Followers of Christ also treasure the Torah, for many of the same reasons that Jews treasure it, but also for its heralding the Messiah. The Torah's herald of Christ, though, is not like the overt pleas of Isaiah and other prophets, appearing much later in the Old Testament, for the Savior. The Torah's prefiguring of the coming Christ is more subtle, in stories like the ram caught in the bush and in the people's repeated falls from which God's grace must rescue them. Read the Torah for how it constituted God's chosen people Israel, while also reading it for how God would need to rescue those people and, in so doing, rescue the world.

Genesis

In the beginning, God created the heavens and the earth.
1:1.

Theme. The theme of the Bible's first book Genesis is, naturally, *beginning*, just as the word *genesis* implies. Genesis begins at the earliest beginning with God creating heavens, earth, and all earth contains, including humankind. But Genesis also describes the beginning of relationship between God and humans, and then between God and the nation of humans he would form to restore that relationship after humans had broken it. One beginning, though, Genesis does not describe, that of our uncreated, always-existent God. God has neither beginning nor end. Genesis instead reveals God as pre-existent creator of all things, both sovereign in his rule and singular in his form as the one true God. Genesis also introduces our one true God as a lover of human beings, whom he made in his own image for relationship with him.

Author. Scriptural reference and tradition credit Moses with authoring Genesis, under the Spirit's inspiration. Raised in Pharaoh's palace as an adopted member of the Egyptian royal family, and later leader of Israel in its exodus from Egypt, Moses surely had the education, standing, information, time, reason, and experience to write or compile, and to transmit, Genesis. Moses died at age one hundred twenty, on a date variously attributed between 1407 B.C. and 1271 B.C. If Moses wrote the book near his death, then Genesis would have been extant for hundreds of years before Israel's unification under David and his son Solomon, and well over a thousand years before Christ's birth. Genesis does not name its author, and some modern scholarship dates Genesis's compilation to a significantly later date. But numerous Old Testament and New Testament verses, including statements by Jesus, attribute the book to Moses. Mark 12:26, for instance, records Jesus attributing Genesis's account of the burning bush as from "the book of Moses," while John 5:46 records Jesus saying that if you believe Moses, you believe Jesus, "for he wrote about me."

Context. Reading the Bible accurately and richly depends on knowing the context for what we read. The obvious canonical context for Genesis is that it is the Bible's opening book. In that place, Genesis sets the stage, rather than appearing within an existing historical, spiritual, and narrative context. Genesis creates the context for everything that follows in the Bible. It reveals the Bible's focus, introduces the Bible's narrative structure, and foreshadows its goal and theme, from its first page forward. One cannot truly appreciate the context of any other Bible book without grasping Genesis's storyline proceeding from God creating heavens, earth, and humankind, through humankind's fall and a gradual unfolding of God's gracious plan for humankind's redemption. Genesis is the Bible's foundation, from which its narrative, theme, and goal build.

Structure. Genesis indeed has a narrative structure. Genesis begins a grand story, the grandest story of them all. The first part of that story involves four major events, while the second part of that story, as it further unfolds, involves four leading figures. The four events begin with God creating heaven, earth, and all living beings on earth, including humankind in his own image. In a second seminal event, humankind then falls from God's Eden garden, when Adam and Eve heed Satan, disobey God, and eat the forbidden fruit of the tree of knowing good and evil. God offers the fallen family covering and guidance. Yet a violent humankind instead pursues such evil that in a third great event, God brings the flood on all but Noah, his family, and the animals taking shelter in his ark. Humans return through Noah's line, but God must again strike them down from building Babel's tower to heaven, in a fourth great event. Genesis's story then turns to the four figures Abraham, whom God calls out from Babel to form his chosen nation, and Abraham's progeny Isaac, Jacob, and Joseph, who in succession lead that nation.

Key Events. As just indicated, key Genesis events include God's creating Adam and Eve, Eve's eating and sharing with Adam the forbidden fruit, their banishment from Eden, the later flood from which Noah's labors saved his family and the animals, and God demolishing Babel's tower to spread humankind across the face of the earth. Yet Genesis fills itself with extraordinary events beyond those just mentioned. These other events include Cain's murder of Abel resulting in Cain's further banishment, God's promise to make a great nation out of the childless Abram, God's destruction of the wicked Sodom and Gomorrah, Lot's wife looking back to become a pillar of salt, Abraham's near sacrifice of Isaac, Esau selling his birthright to Jacob, Jacob stealing Esau's blessing, Jacob wrestling with God all night, Jacob's sons selling their brother Joseph into slavery, Joseph rising to lead Egypt, and Joseph's family joining him in Egypt, among many others. Read Genesis for its grand narrative, whom millions worldwide know and embrace.

Key Locations. Genesis unfolds across three regions: (1) an unknown location but one sometimes associated with Babylonia (modern-day Iraq) around the Tigris and Euphrates Rivers, both of which the Bible names but may have been different rivers than their modern counterparts; (2) Palestine (modern-day Israel) at the eastern end of the Great (Mediterranean) Sea; and (3) Egypt around the Nile River and its delta region west of Palestine. Genesis's first eleven chapters develop in or near Babylonia, although Eden's precise location remains unknown. God then calls Abraham (then Abram) out of Babylonia to the promised land of Palestine, later Israel, where Genesis chapters twelve through thirty-six unfold. Slave traders then take Joseph to Egypt, where his father, brothers, and family eventually join him, as Genesis chapters thirty-seven to fifty record. More-specific key locations include: Shechem in Israel's northern region, where God promised Abraham the land, Jacob bought his plot of land, and Joseph found his brothers tending sheep; Bethel in Israel's central region, where God promises Jacob the blessing of Abraham; Hebron where God again promised Abraham the land and Abraham buried Sarah; and Peniel, where Jacob wrestled with God. Genesis begins to introduce the geography of the promised land.

Revelation of Christ. Genesis foreshadows the Savior Jesus Christ from its beginning to its end. When God speaks humankind into creation, recorded in Genesis 1:26, he says, "Let *us* make mankind in *our* image, in *our* likeness," reflecting his trinitarian nature as Father, Son Jesus Christ, and Holy Spirit, just as three figures of the Lord appeared to Abram at his tent, recorded in Genesis 18. Genesis 3:9 records that God placed the tree of life in Eden's middle, from which Adam was free to eat, prefiguring Christ's own life, tree sacrificed. Genesis 3:15 announces a veiled gospel in that the fallen woman Eve's offspring would someday crush the serpent's head. Genesis 3:21 records God shedding an animal's blood to cover his disobedient and ashamed Adam and Eve, prefiguring the cleansing blood of his sacrificed Son Jesus Christ. Likewise, Genesis 4:4 records Abel bringing God a blood sacrifice of his firstborn from his flock, as God would accept his own firstborn Jesus's sacrifice to bring humankind back to him. The ancestral line Genesis traces from Adam through Abraham, Jacob, and Judah, ends many generations later in the birth of Jesus Christ. Genesis 49 records Jacob's prophecy that nations would bow to the ruling lion of Judah whom we know as Jesus Christ. These are but a few of Genesis's prophecies and figures of Christ. Genesis sets the pattern of God's covenant, human breach of that covenant, the necessary banishment in disobedience, and God's blood rescue in new covenant.

Application. Genesis shows that God creates each of us for relationship with him. Genesis teaches us about God's power, authority, and sovereignty but also his love for humankind and his desire for our intimacy. We learn how fatal is grasping what we see and desire, when God commands us not to do so. Genesis teaches us that God knows better than we can know and that we must therefore trust him. God, who created all things including us, calls us each to trust him not only for our rescue from sin and death but also for the flourishing life that we desire for ourselves and one another. Genesis points us back to God's Eden garden.

Memory Verses. 1:1: In the beginning God created the heavens and the earth. 1:27: God created mankind in his own image; in the image of God he created them; male and female he created them. 2:16-17: And the Lord God commanded the man, "You are free to eat from any tree in the garden; but you must not eat from the tree of the knowledge of good and evil, for when you eat from it you will certainly die." 3:1: Now the serpent was more crafty than any of the wild animals the Lord God had made. He said to the woman, "Did God really say, 'You must not eat from any tree in the garden'?" 4:9: Then the Lord said to Cain, "Where is your brother Abel?" "I don't know," he replied. "Am I my brother's keeper?" 22:9: "God himself will provide the lamb for the burnt offering, my son." 22:16-17: "I swear by myself, declares the Lord, that because you have done this and have not withheld your son, your only son, I will surely bless you and make your descendants as numerous as the stars in the sky and as the sand on the seashore." 28:16: "Surely the Lord is in this place, and I was not aware of it." 50:20: "You intended to harm me, but God intended it for good to accomplish what is now being done, the saving of many lives."

Exodus

"I am the Lord your God, who brought you out of Egypt, out of the land of slavery." 20:2.

Theme. The theme of Exodus, the Bible's second book, is leaving, as in departure, exit, just as its name implies. The historical event that Exodus describes is the Israelites leaving Egypt after hundreds of years. The kind of exit, though, that Exodus makes it theme is not just leaving but instead obtaining one's liberty, one's freedom from slavery. Freedom is a powerful and dominant Bible theme, indeed a central aspect of the good news of Jesus Christ that the Bible brings. Salvation's freedom is not so much from a literal slavery, though it can entail throwing off real bonds, but more so from the spiritual bondage that comes with sin, a bondage that brings not simply suffering but ultimately death. Exodus's historical movement from literal slavery into literal freedom reflects the Bible's spiritual theme of movement from eternal death to eternal life and liberty.

Author. What one concludes of Genesis's authorship one might also apply to Exodus. Scriptural reference and tradition credit Moses with also authoring Exodus, under the Spirit's inspiration. Moses would have had the basis for doing so, perhaps shortly before his death somewhere between 1407 B.C. and 1271 B.C., making Exodus extant for well over a thousand years before Christ's birth. As in the case of Genesis, some modern scholars date Exodus's compilation to a significantly later date. Yet numerous Old Testament and New Testament verses attribute the collection of books we know as the Torah, or the book or law of Moses, to Moses, fitting in that series both Exodus and other books of the Torah recording God's words to Moses. Exodus itself attributes Moses with authorship, in verses 17:14 ("Then the Lord said, 'Write this on a scroll as something to be remembered'"), 24:4 ("Moses then wrote down everything the Lord said"), and 34:27 ("Then the Lord said, 'Write down these words'"). And Mark 7:10 records Jesus quoting Exodus 20:12 and 21:17 with the introduction, "For Moses said...."

Context. Exodus's canonical context, following Genesis and preceding the law book Leviticus, is important to its structure and theme. Genesis's conclusion poses a narrative problem. Genesis ends with God's chosen people Israel serving the Egyptians, who worshipped many gods. God had not called the Israelites to make them servants in a polytheistic nation. God's people were to be obedient to him while free of the world, not slaves of the world while free of him. Thus, Exodus opens with the Egyptian's oppression of the Israelites, to the point of Pharaoh's ordering the murder all newborn Jewish males. Israel needed escape from its earthly bondage to resume its spiritual inheritance. Hence, Exodus's title and narrative structure involving escape. Escape, though, poses the next problem of confirming new identity. To address that problem, Exodus moves from the story of Israel's Egypt departure to God's constitution of Israelite society and culture, under law and command at Mount Horeb. Read Exodus within that context.

Structure. Knowing Exodus's larger structure can help much with reading Exodus's forty chapters profitably. Exodus's first eighteen chapters describe Israel's literal exodus from Egypt, a story celebrated so widely and grandly as to reach popular cinema and lore. Everyone, it seems, knows the story of Moses, Pharaoh, and the ten great plagues through which God freed Israel. Exodus, though, offers much more. Chapters nineteen through twenty-four record God speaking the law to his freed people. Freedom resides in God's caring relationship, sound structure, and just order, not in the deadly consequences of licentiousness. The final chapters of Exodus from twenty-five through forty record God's design for his tabernacle, a pattern of his presence, magnificence, design, and care, reflecting both the former Eden and the future heaven. Enjoy Exodus's grand freedom narrative, but don't miss the marvel of its laws and tabernacle.

Key Events. Like Genesis, Exodus brims with seminal events. Moses's mother had to set him adrift in a papyrus basket because of Pharaoh's edict to kill all male Jewish infants. Pharaoh's daughter discovered the infant Moses, drawing him from the water to raise and educate in Pharaoh's palace. Yet the adult Moses, after interceding for his Jewish people, had to flee from Pharaoh to the faraway Midian desert. Then, after decades of humble shepherding, Moses encountered God's burning bush, out of which God sent Moses back to call ten plagues on Egypt to convince a stubborn Pharaoh to free the enslaved Jewish people. In the last plague, the angel of death passed over the Jewish households marked with the blood of sacrifice, to strike down all

Egypt's firstborn. Pharaoh's army nonetheless pursued the freed Israelites across the divided Red Sea, where God drowned the pursuing army. God fed the wandering Israelites with manna, and Moses met God on Mount Sinai to receive the Ten Commandments. These events are but a few of Exodus's wonders Jews and Christians make their signposts.

Key Locations. Exodus sets its narrative accounts in the settled northeast delta region of Egypt and the vast Sinai Peninsula to Egypt's east. The early narrative begins around Pharaoh's palace, the Jewish settlements in Goshen just to the east, and the far-away land of Midian all the way across Sinai and its eastern Gulf of Araba, where Moses fled to shepherd Jethro's flocks. On Moses's return, and in consequence of the ten plagues, the Jews' fled from Goshen across the Red Sea dividing Egypt from Sinai. They then journeyed southeast through Sinai, all the way to Mount Horeb (Mount Sinai) in Sinai's southern region, where unfolded the great drama of God giving Moses the law, while the Israelites fashioned a golden calf below. Exodus is a book of locations, where place names and attributes accentuate its phenomenal liberty theme. Appreciate how the geography of Exodus informs its grand narrative.

Revelation of Christ. Exodus, like Genesis and every other Bible book, reveals Christ. Moses is himself a type of the savior Christ, drawn in infancy from deadly waters, later to save and liberate his people, themselves drawn through and out of the deadly Red Sea. The liberator Moses anticipates the savior Christ. Christ is equally present in Exodus's Passover lamb that God had the Israelites sacrifice, the blood of which saved them from the avenging angel of death. Exodus's Passover lamb represents the sacrificed Christ. Likewise, Christ's cross was the stick Moses threw into Marah's bitter water to make it fit for life, and Christ Exodus's manna, the genuine bread of life come down from heaven. Christ was also the rock Moses struck to gush living water in the desert. Exodus's tabernacle, shrouding God's holy presence, pointed to the righteous Christ whose sacrificial death would open the temple's curtain. The priesthood that Exodus elevated points to Jesus as the great high priest who leads a kingdom of priests in holy assembly. Above all, though, Exodus confirms the great pattern of a humankind so ready to reject God's love to pursue their own comforts and passions, saved by a God so ready to love a humankind made in his own image. Exodus builds magnificently on Genesis's extraordinary foundation.

Application. What we draw from Exodus is the revelation of Christ as our rescue from the slavery of sin and its toil, hardship, hunger, thirst, and death. No matter our oppression, no matter our enemy's deadly pursuit, no matter our hunger and thirst in our wilderness, we always find Christ at hand, ready to rescue. He draws us from the waters, not only securing us but also satisfying our hunger and thirst. We have no need of anything other than him, his rescue, his intimacy, for he and his Father created us for them. Exodus teaches that we must turn to Christ at every challenge and with every opportunity. Our struggle is not with flesh and blood but with spiritual forces because we are also spiritual beings, not just flesh-and-blood mortals. We make that choice every moment of every day, whether to mistakenly conceive ourselves as destined for dust and thus only here to slake our senses, or to properly perceive ourselves as destined for eternal grandeur in the presence of Christ.

Memory Verses. 2:10: She named him Moses, saying, "I drew him out of the water." 3:14 God said to Moses, "I am who I am. This is what you are to say to the Israelites: 'I am has sent me to you.'" 6:6: "I am the Lord, and I will bring you out from under the yoke of the Egyptians. I will free you from being slaves to them, and I will redeem you with an outstretched arm and with mighty acts of judgment." 12:13: "The blood will be a sign for you on the houses where you are, and when I see the blood, I will pass over you." 16:4: Then the Lord said to Moses, "I will rain down bread from heaven for you." 17:6: "Strike the rock, and water will come out of it for the people to drink." 20:1-17: The Ten Commandments. 33:22: "When my glory passes by, I will put you in a cleft in the rock and cover you with my hand until I have passed by."

Reading Guide

Meaning

A great challenge in reading the Bible well, aptly, fairly, properly, is to understand the nature of meaning. Of course, we want to know what the Bible authors mean from their writings. Yet consider what meaning itself means. When we think of meaning, we think of what the author intended to convey. We do not get to assign our own meaning. We must consider instead what the author meant. Otherwise, text would have whatever meaning readers wished to assign it, making the text wholly unreliable as a basis for sharing understanding. Communication works best when we agree that the author's intention determines the meaning. Yet, authors also concern themselves with the significance of their writings to their readers. Meaning is one thing, mattering is another. And writings, carrying one intended meaning, can have differing significance to different readers.

Reading the Bible carefully, productively, wisely, as its inspired writers intended, thus involves assessing accurately the authors' meaning and then separately, as a second step, considering how the authors believed their meaning would be significant to different readers. What the writing's significance is to you may be quite different from the significance to someone else, such as an ancient Israelite. Or the significance may be the same. Don't assume that the ancient author expected the same significance to the modern reader as to the ancient audience. Get the meaning first, using other reading guides beginning with what the words and phrases meant to the author, the context in which the author wrote, to whom the author wrote, the patterns that the author followed, and the imagery and symbols the author used. Then consider how and why the meaning matters to you or others. Read for meaning, and then read for mattering.

Leviticus

"The fire on the altar must be kept burning; it must not go out." 6:12.

Theme. The theme of Leviticus, the Bible's third book, is worship, interpreted broadly to include how to live righteously before the Lord as he prescribes, for relationship with his people. Leviticus establishes specific offering and worship forms. It also commands more-general practices, in forms that we might think of as moral rules or laws but are more properly specific examples of how to live holy before the Lord. The name Leviticus refers to the Levites, that tribe of Israelites whom God charged with the care first of his tabernacle and later his temple. The title Leviticus literally means *about Levites*, which the book surely is. Leviticus fills with instructions on how the Levites specifically, and the Israelites more generally, were to conduct themselves with respect to God's tabernacle, his holy place that the Israelites carried among them in their wilderness wanderings between their rescue from Egypt and promised land Israel. Leviticus begins a series of three books that many readers find especially difficult. Yet read Leviticus as a worship manual, for the patterns, dispositions, and stances we must hold in awe of a righteous God, and you will have read Leviticus well. We, too, are priests in God's holy kingdom. See in Leviticus commands, forms, attitudes, and intimations of how a priest is to conduct worship.

Author. What one concludes of the authorship of both Genesis and Exodus one might also apply to Leviticus. Scriptural reference and tradition credit Moses with authoring Leviticus, under the Spirit's inspiration. Moses would have had the basis for writing, either well or shortly before his death somewhere between 1407 B.C. and 1271 B.C., making Leviticus extant for well over a thousand years before Christ. As with Genesis and Exodus, some modern scholars date Leviticus's final compilation to a significantly later date, though still hundreds of years before Christ. The fact that many Old and New Testament verses attribute the Bible's first five books, the Torah or Law of Moses, to Moses, is consistent with those books recording God's words to Moses, as Leviticus does throughout. The New Testament in Luke 2:22 and Hebrews 8:5, including Jesus himself in Matthew 8:4, refers to Moses when quoting passages from Leviticus. Leviticus records the details of worship forms and holiness practices that the Israelites followed from Moses until Jerusalem fell centuries later. Whether Moses literally wrote Leviticus, or much-later writers compiled what Moses heard, experienced, and successfully transmitted, may not be critical to your effective reading of Leviticus.

Context. Appropriately, Leviticus is at the center of the five books of the Pentateuch or Torah. The context for its detailed worship rules and ritual laws is that God gave these commands in Mount Sinai's covenant. They thus express his grace in choosing and setting apart Israel for himself from among the nations, a grace that God extends to Christians today. Leviticus's worship rules and ritual laws also express God's holy conditions for covenant, conditions that Christians satisfy not by impossibly strict observance but instead under the blood of their savior Jesus Christ. Leviticus's rules and rituals reinforce that God is present in his people's lives, which means that his people must be holy as God is holy. Leviticus's many rules for offerings demonstrate that humankind's holiness, impossible in our broken condition, only comes with atonement, prefiguring the sacrifice of the savior Jesus Christ. Leviticus's context places presence, holiness, and atonement at the center of God's calling and constituting his people.

Structure. Leviticus's structure reinforces its theme. Its first ten chapters articulate the way to God, while its remaining chapters eleven through twenty-seven articulate how to walk with God. Chapters one and two show burnt offerings of defect-free male animals as the path to God, as the perfect life of the sacrificed Jesus is that path. Chapter three shows fellowship and peace offerings as God's way, as Jesus's blood brings us peace. Chapter four illustrates sin offerings, as Jesus's offer of himself took the world's sin away. Chapter five illustrates guilt offerings, as Jesus offers to take our guilt away. Leviticus's second part, beginning at chapter eleven, has the people bring regular sacrifices, as we dwell in Jesus's sacrifice to draw close to God. Chapter seventeen shows how humankind meets God at the altar's place of sacrifice, just as Christ's cross is that meeting place of sacrifice. See in Leviticus's successive offerings, festivals, and feasts both a path to God and way forward with him.

Key Events. Leviticus's entirety involves God communicating covenant terms to Moses on Mount Sinai. God's announcing to Moses detailed and lengthy terms for guilt, fellowship, grain, sin, and burnt offerings are a single key event spanning Leviticus's first seven chapters, confirming God's holy nature. In chapter eight, God directs Moses to ordain the Levitical priesthood of Aaron and his sons, following which the priests begin their centuries of tabernacle and temple ministry. Chapter ten shows Aaron's sons Nadab and Abihu offering unauthorized fire to the Lord and dying for it. Only God, not humankind, determines the way to approach him, on the day of atonement, as chapter sixteen describes. Chapter twenty-two confirms that God does not accept unauthorized, defective, or blemished sacrifices. In chapter twenty-three God announces to Moses the appointed feasts, offerings, days, and festivals of unleavened bread, firstfruits, weeks, trumpets, tabernacles, and atonement, and in chapter twenty-five the years of sabbath and jubilee.

Key Locations. As just indicated, Mount Sinai is the geographic locus of Leviticus's entirety. Yet Leviticus features other figurative, if not literal geographic, locations. Leviticus's key figurative or symbolic location is the tabernacle, traveling as it did with the Israelites' wilderness wanderings recorded in the Bible's following books. The tabernacle was the place of God's presence, where Moses heard from God and where the priesthood of Aaron and his sons ministered. The tabernacle also represented the lost garden where Adam and Eve had walked with God, foreshadowed the temple Solomon would build for God on Jerusalem's mount, and prefigured the body of Christ through whom believers have God's access. Leviticus is thus very much a book of location, even though it reads as a set of commands and instructions. Those commands and instructions are all about preparing for God's presence, which is the book's primary figurative location. Read Leviticus as a book of God's holy location.

Revelation of Christ. In the same sense of illustrating the approach to God in his utter holiness, Leviticus is also a book revealing Christ. The sacrifices that Leviticus details, whether of sin, guilt, offering, or fellowship, point us to Christ whose sacrifice satisfied every such offering. Leviticus's tabernacle that God designed for his presence, revelation, and atonement, Christ fulfills in the same three dimensions. The priesthood that Leviticus established, Christ fulfills as great high priest, so that we, too, can enter the most holy place as priests. Jesus is the scapegoat that Leviticus 16:21-22 describes. And the holiness that Leviticus everywhere commands, Christ fulfilled in his perfect righteousness and utter redemption. Read Leviticus for its revelation of Christ.

Application. Though often described as the Bible's hardest book for the casual reader, Leviticus offers critical lessons for the reader who sees its larger context and purpose. Leviticus proves that God, through sacrifice, can make anyone and anything clean. Leviticus's trumpets call us to him in that recognition. Those same trumpets call us apart to be his, distinct from the world. We must, though, see how soiled we appear to him without the sacrifices that he first commands and then, in the person and blood of Jesus, offers. Leviticus is a call for us to be holy in the transformed, set apart, and sanctified life of Jesus Christ. We are God's people, spiritual beings existing through and for him.

Memory Verses. 4:35: "In this way the priest will make atonement for them for the sin they have committed, and they will be forgiven." 8:30: Then Moses took some of the anointing oil and some of the blood from the altar and sprinkled them on Aaron and his garments and on his sons and their garments. 10:1-2: [T]hey offered unauthorized fire before the Lord, contrary to his command. So, fire came out from the presence of the Lord and consumed them, and they died before the Lord. 11:45: I am the Lord, who brought you up out of Egypt to be your God; therefore, be holy, because I am holy. 16:10: "But the goat chosen by lot as the scapegoat shall be presented alive before the Lord to be used for making atonement by sending it into the wilderness as a scapegoat." 19:37: "Keep all my decrees and all my laws and follow them. I am the Lord."

Numbers

"In this wilderness your bodies will fall—every one of you twenty years old or more who was counted in the census and who has grumbled against me." 14:29.

Theme. The theme of the Bible's fourth book Numbers is not numbers or numbering, although the book does record many counts of the Israelites in their wilderness wanderings. Rather, Numbers' theme is wandering. To wander is not to stroll, nor to explore, nor to pass time pleasurably. The wandering of Numbers refers instead to Israel's lost time in Sinai's wilderness. Indeed, while the Greek title for the book translates as Numbers, the Hebrew word for Numbers, bemidbar, instead means *in the wilderness.* Wandering is aimless, purposeless, dangerous, especially in the wilderness where people die, as Israel's whole adult population, save for the heroic Joshua and Caleb, died in Israel's Sinai wandering. In its record of counting and wandering, counting again and wandering some more, Numbers documents humankind's lost condition, even while pointing to humankind's rescuer. The Israelites failed repeatedly in their wandering, but God never failed and was instead ever-present. Numbers' theme is thus not simply wandering but trusting in the leading, provision, and plan of God.

Author. What one concludes of the authorship of Genesis, Exodus, and Leviticus, one also concludes about the authorship of Numbers. Scriptural reference and tradition credit Moses with authoring Numbers, too, under the Spirit's inspiration. As with the Torah's other books, Moses would have had the basis for writing, by the time of his death somewhere between 1407 B.C. and 1271 B.C., making Numbers extant for well over a thousand years before Christ. As with Genesis, Exodus, and Leviticus, some modern scholars date Numbers' compilation to a significantly later date, though still hundreds of years before Christ. The fact that many Old and New Testament verses attribute the Bible's first five books, the Torah or Law of Moses, to Moses, is consistent with those books recording God's words to Moses, as Numbers also does. Indeed, in two instances, at verses 33:2 and 36:13, Numbers records

God's command that Moses write down events. Numbers counts the wandering Israelite tribes and records details of their leadership and makeup, under Moses' leadership. Whether Moses literally wrote Numbers or much-later writers compiled what Moses heard, experienced, and successfully transmitted may not be critical to your effective reading of Numbers.

Context. Numbers sets its wanderings between the Israelites' receiving of the law at Mount Sinai shortly after its exodus, and the Israelites' arrival at the Jordan River opposite Jericho thirty-eight years later. Numbers thus spans most of the Israelites' notorious forty years of wilderness wandering. The exodus's liberty and Mount Sinai's law precede Numbers, while the promised land beyond Jericho's walls follows it. Numbers' bracketing of wilderness between rescue and relationship informs every step of the wandering Israelites. Every numbering of every tribe, every naming of every ancestor, each to fall in their wandering, reminds the reader that God counts every hair on our head, numbering our own wilderness days in our mortal bodies before our eternal spirits rise to him in intimacy. Numbers might make little sense to anyone other than a genealogist if the Spirit had not set it in such precious context.

Structure. Numbers' structure serves its theme and context. Its first part prepares the Israelites for their wandering. In chapters one through four, God first consecrates from among them his priests. In chapters four through six, God then teaches the Israelites about purity, before returning in chapters seven and eight to how his priests must model that purity. After this instruction, in chapters nine and ten God blesses the Israelites with his presence. His visible cloud would guide them, and the ark of his covenant would go before them. Numbers' second part, from chapters eleven through sixteen, shows the Israelites failing to trust God, instead complaining when the journey grew difficult. Chapter thirteen sees the Israelite spies exploring the promised land but fearing the giants there, leading in chapter fourteen to Israel's rebellion from God and forty-year banishment to the wilderness. Numbers' third part shows God persevering with the wandering Israelites despite their rebellion. Numbers is thus a pattern for our own journey, prepared but stumbling in disbelief and yet finding that God persists with us.

Key Events. While Numbers is much about counting and wandering, it does include several key events, a first of which set the Israelites to their forty years of Sinai wandering. Numbers 13-14 records the sad account of Moses sending spies into the promised land. The spies come

20

back bearing the land's fruit but warning that the Israelites had no chance of defeating the giants there. Only Joshua and Caleb advocated that the Israelites take possession of the promised land, in consequence of which all Israelite adults other than those two must fall in the wilderness. Even Moses's own family members Miriam and Aaron opposed Moses. A group led by the Levite Korah grumbled at Moses and rebelled, until God struck down the rebels and then had Aaron's staff sprout, bud, and bear almonds, to prove Aaron their chief priest.

In another key event, Moses himself fell victim to his own sudden rebel streak. Numbers 20 records a second account, after the first in Exodus, of Moses striking the rock to bring forth water for the Israelites, but this time when God had instead instructed Moses to speak to the rock, the consequence of his disobedience being that he would not enter the promised land. Numbers 21:6-9 records the account of Moses lifting a bronze serpent on a pole so that all Israelites who looked on it received healing from their snake bites, a seemingly odd but importantly prefiguring event. Numbers 22:21-34 records the extraordinary account of Balaam's donkey rebuking the prophet for striking him, when the donkey had saved Balaam from an angel blocking the road and ready to kill him. Hired to curse Israel, Balaam would instead bless it, as God would only allow. For all its counting and genealogies, Numbers has its seminal events to add to the Bible's grand narrative.

Key Locations. Numbers doesn't have key locations as much as wandering routes. Chapter thirty-three records the details of those wanderings. Numbers begins, though, at Mount Sinai in the south of the vast Sinai Peninsula, the Israelites having just received God's law there. Moses counts the Israelite men, 603,550 strong omitting the Levite tribe, in the Desert of Sinai, where Moses also struck the rock to gain water for the Israelites, at the waters of Meribah. The Israelites headed north from Mount Sinai, all the way to Kadesh Barnea in the Peninsula's northeast, from where Moses sent the spies further north through the Wilderness of Zin to explore the promised land. The Israelites having rebelled from God in fear of the giants in the promised land, God sent them wandering south to Ezion Geber at the tip of the Gulf of Arabah dividing Sinai from Midian. They then wandered north again in circuitous routes to Punon and Oboth until, their forty years complete, their then-adult children camped in Moab's plains east of the Jordan River, looking across the river to Jericho. The false prophet Balaam would stand in the mountains of Moab at Kiriath Huzoth, blessing the encamped Israelites.

Revelation of Christ. Even in Numbers' wilderness wandering, the Bible reveals symbols and patterns of Christ. Christ spent forty wilderness days after his Jordan River baptism, just like the Israelites spent forty years in the wilderness after their baptism through the divided Red Sea. God let his Son Jesus perfect God's purpose in his Son's own wilderness test on the cross. In Israel's Sinai wanderings, Moses raised a bronze serpent on a stick to save the stricken Israelites who looked on it, just as Christ took sin to the cross so that he might save all who look to him. The serpent Satan bites, even striking Christ's heel, but Christ crushes him on the cross. Numbers magnificently sets the stage for Christ to come well over a millennium later.

Application. Numbers teaches us that although we receive God's new covenant in Jesus Christ, we, too, somehow nonetheless wander, facing our own wilderness test. We choose whether to live in faith or fear. The apostle Paul in 1 Corinthians 10:7-10 tells us what, then, to do with wilderness testing. Hearkening back to the Israelites' Numbers wandering, when the grumbling people died in the wilderness, Paul warns us against idolatry, immorality, testing Christ, and, above all, grumbling. We learn from Numbers the harsh consequences of complaining, that doubting God courts disaster. Paul writes in 1 Corinthians 10:11-13 that Numbers preserved this history for us to warn us against temptation, especially when we believe that we stand firm. When temptation comes upon us, we are to remember that God remains faithful, even to the point of giving us a way out that we might endure it. God provides for us in the wilderness. Numbers stands testament to God's faithfulness in the face of our grumbling and as warning against that grumbling.

Memory Verses. 6:24-26: *"The Lord bless you and keep you; the Lord make his face shine on you and be gracious to you; the Lord turn his face toward you and give you peace."* 9:23: *At the Lord's command they encamped, and at the Lord's command they set out. 11:1: Now the people complained about their hardships in the hearing of the Lord, and when he heard them his anger was aroused. 11:29: "I wish that all the Lord's people were prophets and that the Lord would put his Spirit on them!" 13:27: "We went into the land to which you sent us, and it does flow with milk and honey!" 21:8: The Lord said to Moses, "Make a snake and put it up on a pole; anyone who is bitten can look at it and live." 33:55: "But if you do not drive out the inhabitants of the land, those you allow to remain will become barbs in your eyes and thorns in your sides."*

Deuteronomy

"Love the Lord your God with all your heart and with all your soul and with all your strength." 6:5.

Theme. Deuteronomy's theme, indicated by its title meaning *second law*, is reiteration, explanation, renewal, recommitment. We often need to go back to our vows, rekindle our passion, renew our covenant, and rediscover our commitment. Spiritual growth, our instruction in the word and the way of God, is not always forward, if indeed it is ever forward. It is instead often back, perhaps even always back, to the Ancient of Days. God does not issue new edict after new principle after new command. His Word was instead with him at the beginning. His instruction is thus always a reminder of who he was, who he is, and who he will always be. God calls us back to him out of our wandering, so that we can walk with him into his promised land. Deuteronomy is that kind of call back, a return to roots that have always been there and that go so deep as never to leave us nor forsake us.

Author. Deuteronomy 1:1 begins, "These are the words that Moses spoke to all Israel," while Deuteronomy 31:24 ends that "Moses finished writing in a book this law from beginning to end" before commanding the Israelites to place the book beside the ark of the covenant as a witness against them. In between, Deuteronomy 4:44 and 29:1 confirm Moses as Deuteronomy's author or at least the one who related the book's words. Thus, what one concludes of the authorship of the Torah's first four books, one may also conclude about Deuteronomy's authorship. Scriptural reference, content, and tradition credit Moses with authoring Deuteronomy under the Spirit's inspiration, excepting of course its last section describing Moses' demise. As with the Torah's other books, Moses had the strongest basis for writing Deuteronomy, his own speech, just before the time of his death somewhere between 1407 B.C. and 1271 B.C., making Deuteronomy extant for well over a thousand years before Christ. As with the Torah's other four books, some modern scholars date Deuteronomy's compilation to a significantly later date, though still hundreds of years before Christ. That Old and New Testament verses attribute Deuteronomy's laws to Moses, including Matthew 19:7 recording Jesus's own attribution of one such command specifically to Moses, makes sensible attributing Deuteronomy to Moses. Whether Moses literally wrote Deuteronomy or later writers compiled what Moses heard from God and spoke to the Israelites should not greatly affect your reading of Deuteronomy. Tradition ascribes to Joshua's authorship Moses' obituary at the end of Deuteronomy, although Aaron's son Eleazar the high priest, the prophet Samuel, and even the much-later scribe Ezra are other candidates, and Moses himself may even have dictated it nearing his demise.

Context. As the Torah's last of five books, Deuteronomy summarizes and restates what God has taught the Israelites at Mount Sinai and in their wilderness wanderings. The adult generation that rebelled against God, when God had led them to the promised land, had died off in their forty-year banishment to the wilderness. The children of that generation then stood again at the promised land's entrance, this time wilderness-hardened, ready to take the promised land. But before they did so, God recommitted them to do what their parents had failed to do. They needed God's instruction, as every generation needs God's instruction. Deuteronomy thus stands between the test and the reward of wilderness wandering. Read its law summary in that rich context of the Bible's grand narrative.

Structure. Deuteronomy's form is an exhortation by Moses to the Israelites as they prepare to enter the promised land under his successor Joshua's command. Moses' speech takes three parts: past, present, and future. In Deuteronomy's first four chapters, Moses encouraged the Israelites to remember God's faithfulness in the past. God had demonstrated, not just promised, his loving care. Moses then spent the greater part of Deuteronomy, chapters five through twenty-six, warning the Israelites to respect God's holiness in the present, keeping his decrees to enjoy life. Moses organized that warning around the Shema's four pillars, recorded in Deuteronomy 6:4-9, that God is one, we are to love God with all our heart, we are to impress his love on our children, and we must not forget these things. For his last exhortation, recorded in Deuteronomy's chapters twenty-seven to thirty-four, Moses admonished the Israelites as to the future. First, the promised land belongs to God's people, but second, his people must obey God alone. Recall Deuteronomy's structure, even as you explore its detail.

Key Events. Deuteronomy's central event is Moses' one long address to Israel, in which a dozen times Moses repeats that *all Israel* must hear and heed his words. Embedded within that address at Deuteronomy 6:4 is an especially important moment when Moses begins, "Hear, O Israel: the Lord is our God, the Lord is one. Love the Lord with all your heart and with all your soul and with all your strength." This passage, known as the *Shema*, meaning not just to hear but to embrace and obey, remains the Jews' core confession of faith, one repeated countless times while kept on one's mind throughout one's day. Another key moment occurs in Deuteronomy 5 when Moses repeats the Ten Commandments. Moses begins to wind up his long address in chapters twenty-seven and twenty-eight with blessings for obedience and curses for disobedience, renewing the covenant in chapter thirty, designating Joshua as his successor in chapter thirty-one, and singing Israel a long song in chapter thirty-two. Deuteronomy 34 records its last key event, the death of Moses within sight of the promised land.

Key Locations. Deuteronomy has one primary location, where Moses' gave his speech to the Israelites on Moab's plains east of the Jordan River, at the northern head of the Dead Sea. Israel's wanderings were done, having taken them north all the way from Mount Sinai in the Peninsula's southern region, through Moab to the Dead Sea's east, up to the plain and mountains east of the Jordan River north of the Dead Sea. Deuteronomy 34 records the death of Moses atop Mount Nebo, in Moab's plains, in view of Jericho. But before Moses' death, the Lord showed Moses from the top of Mount Nebo the whole of the promised land, "all the land of Judah as far as the Mediterranean Sea...." Deuteronomy's panorama is in that sense spectacular, hearkening to God's own mountain-top garden Eden, lost so long ago to humankind but visible once again in God's embrace.

Revelation of Christ. Moses, the rescuer who drew Israel out of its slavery, prefigures Christ. We see Christ in the course, purpose, and accomplishment of Moses' life, leading Israel through the wilderness to the promised land. Yet Christ had to die on a hilltop, in sight of his Father's embrace, to accomplish his profound purpose of delivering his followers into his Father's paradise. And so, Deuteronomy traces the life of Moses to his own death atop a mountaintop in sight of the promised land, as he delivered his people into that land. In Moses' grand exhortation, retracing Israel's history and path while repeating the terms of God's curse and blessing, ending in Moses' deliverance in death, Deuteronomy is a summation of the pattern of Christ's own life. Deuteronomy contains other prophetic Christ references, including Deuteronomy 21:23 that God's curse would someday die on a pole,

Christ's cross. Jesus also quoted Deuteronomy more than any other Bible book. Though a law book, Deuteronomy surrounds its law with God's grace, the gospel message.

Application. Deuteronomy 30:19-20 crystalizes its application. Unlike God's unilateral promise in Genesis to bless Abraham, God's assurance in Deuteronomy of blessing involves a bilateral obligation. Here, we have something to do, even while God surely does his part. And so in that passage, Moses exhorts that having his blessing and curse before us, and the life and death that they contrastingly augur, we must "choose life, so that you and your children may live and that you may love the Lord your God, listen to his voice, and hold fast to him." The Lord is our life, Moses reveals, a God who wants us in his promised land with him. We have one thing to do and one thing only, which is to hold fast to God, cling to God, in whom we have everything. Our obedience to God's laws, as Deuteronomy so thoroughly explicates them, is thus a response to God's gracious embrace. Deuteronomy's application, like the gospel message itself, is to obey a loving and forgiving God rather than to negotiate impossibly with a harsh judge.

Memory Verses. 5:6-21: The Ten Commandments. 6:4-9: "Hear, O Israel: The Lord our God, the Lord is one. Love the Lord your God with all your heart and with all your soul and with all your strength. These commandments that I give you today are to be on your hearts. Impress them on your children. Talk about them when you sit at home and when you walk along the road, when you lie down and when you get up. Tie them as symbols on your hands and bind them on your foreheads. Write them on the doorframes of your houses and on your gates." 9:6: "It is not because of your righteousness that the Lord your God is giving you this good land to possess...." 12:8: "You are not to do as we do here today, everyone doing as they see fit...." 25:4: "Do not muzzle an ox while it is treading out the grain." 29:29: "The secret things belong to the Lord our God, but the things revealed belong to us and to our children forever, that we may follow all the words of this law." 32:39: "See now that I myself am he! There is no god besides me."

Reading Guide

Context

Context, you've already seen from the paragraphs headed by that word in each of the above sections, helps define the author's meaning and the significance the author intended the writing to have to its audience or audiences. Every writing, including a book of the Bible, has a historical context. A certain author or authors recorded the writing in a certain place and time, affected to large or small degree by certain events, experiences, and remembrances of that day. Historical context can include religious events, experiences, and remembrances of the day, not just political, military, social, or other world-historical data, although world history can matter in Bible books, too, right along with religious history.

Yet Bible books have another context that other writings may well lack. Each Bible book is a part of the scriptural canon, discerned, established, and approved by representative action millennia ago under the Spirit's guidance. One does not read non-canonical books, however ancient, interesting, and even informative though they may be, as part of the scriptural canon. Each Bible book also has its own place within the scriptural canon. The books have a certain order, discerned and established across ages. That order does not mean superiority. No minor prophet is any more authoritative than another, simply because one comes first in the canon. The same would be true of the gospel books Matthew, Mark, Luke, and John, that none is subordinate to another. Yet the five books of the Torah share attributes, authors, audiences, and purposes, as do the wisdom writings, as do the gospel books, and so on. Appreciate the canon. Appreciate each book's place within the canon.

History

The Hebrew Bible, indeed, the whole of the Bible including the New Testament, relates abundant history. Every book has a historical context, and nearly every book relates or refers to historical events and details. Yet Bible readers and scholars recognize certain books as belonging to a collection of histories. Those twelve books begin with the book Joshua describing Israel's conquering the promised land. The histories continue with the book Judges recording Israel's early history in that land under successive leaders. The major history books then come in pairs, 1 and 2 Samuel, 1 and 2 Kings, and 1 and 2 Chronicles, the latter pair recapping history just covered. The books Ezra and Nehemiah record events of the Israelites' return after exile. An earlier book Ruth and a late book Esther provide helpful other glimpses into Israel's history, adding significant flourishes to the narrative.

History plays an important role in the Bible. The Bible is not simply a set of religious principles. Indeed, its gospel message is not a formula, nor a ritual, nor a contract to fulfill, perhaps not even quite just a message. The Bible is instead the narrative of all history, describing our relationship with our creator God while revealing his purpose for us in relationship with him. The Bible must include history because it is the course of history and judge of history. The history of Israel is especially significant insofar as God chose to draw humankind out of its fallen state and back to him through a nation, a chosen people Israel. God might instead have issued an edict or revealed a magic formula but did not. God's plan to redeem humankind through Israel's Messiah king was the better plan, the way in which he could love the greatest number of us for our best. A nation Israel needs a history. The Hebrew Bible gives us that history throughout its different parts but especially in these twelve history books.

Followers of Christ embrace that history for the reason just given: God brought Christ out of his people Israel. Jesus knew the Israelites' history and drew on it frequently, even constantly, when teaching. One cannot understand the depth and nuance, or even at times the basic goal, of Jesus's teaching without knowing the history to which he refers.

Those references can be extraordinarily subtle. Inveterate Bible readers, those who know the Bible best, can spend the rest of a lifetime discovering more of them. Christian readers value the Hebrew Bible enormously, including its histories, without which they would miss so much of God's movement among his people and so much of the critical context for the gospel message. Read the histories often, deeply, and joyously, just as you read the rest of the Bible.

Joshua

"No one will be able to stand against you all the days of your life. As I was with Moses, so I will be with you; I will never leave you nor forsake you." 1:5.

Theme. The theme of the first history book Joshua is victory, referring especially to conquering, overcoming, prevailing. *Joshua*, after all, means *God saves*. As Joshua 21:45 states, "Not one of the good promises the Lord had made to the house of Israel failed; all came to pass." The life of faith is not a life of burden, denial, defeat, and depression. Rather, godly life, righteous life, rescued life is a life of joy, flourishing, freedom, and victory. To receive God and for God to receive us is to win and win big. It is to enter God's kingdom, not just for a glimpse but eternally, to defeat death in favor of life everlasting in a paradise garden. To form a reliable historical foundation for our faith, Israel's history must give such glimpses of our ultimate victory. Israel's conquering of the promised land is one such moment in history pointing forward to our own victory. We need to see the life of faith as a prevailing, not a diminishing and defeating, life. The book Joshua shows how walking with God is conquering all enemies.

Author. Tradition and internal reference credit Moses' attendant Joshua, whom Moses designated to take his place to lead the Israelites into the promised land, with writing the book Joshua, up to its record of his death, after which the high priests Eleazar and Phinehas may have completed its narrative. Joshua 24:26 shows Joshua recording the book's events in God's law books. That writing would have taken place in the twenty-five years after Moses' death between 1407 B.C. and 1271 B.C. Facts and inferences also support Joshua's authorship, or at least that contemporaneous writers compiled his words, including eyewitness descriptions, ancient place names, details of ancient boundaries, and accurate references to ancient sources and contexts outside the biblical record. The book's later portions, recording not only Joshua's death but conditions after his death and events in the later time of Israel's judges, were surely the work of other hands, the high priests the logical candidates.

Context. Joshua wrote his book to the Israelites as conquerors, though incomplete conquerors, of the promised land. The book spans the promised land's entry, conquering of its people, and division and settlement of the land. In that sense, the book shows the fulfillment of God's promise to lead his people to the promised land. The book includes in its course several military campaigns, along with disputes, negotiations, and compromises over those campaigns and the land and other spoils that they produced. The book ends with Joshua's exhortation to the Israelites, much like Moses ended Deuteronomy and the Pentateuch with an exhortation. Conquering is special but not conclusive. In one sense, conquering only begins the work of faith. Indeed, the book Joshua reveals several tensions or contradictions. God fulfills while humankind, though striving, does not. God completes while humankind, though intending, does not. God is faithful while humankind is fickle. God possesses sovereignly, in utter victor over enemies, while humankind compromises with and accommodates enemies, to its eventual defeat.

Structure. Joshua's chronological structure begins in its first five chapters with God preparing the Israelites for their first conquest Jericho. The Israelites must cross the Jordan River at flood stage, only with God's miraculous help, which the Israelites memorialize with twelve stones from the river's middle. Joshua must also circumcise the Israelites and then face in utter reverence the commander of the Lord's army. Joshua's second part from chapters six through twelve records the Israelites' victories, beginning with Jericho's fall. Joshua's third and final part, from chapters thirteen to twenty-four, records Israel dividing the conquered promised land, ensuring that every tribe has their due place to claim as their own. Joshua's structure of preparation, conquest, and claim is how the Lord's people proceeded then and, in a spiritual sense, proceed now. The Lord is a God of order, so that his people proceed in his will and order.

Key Events. Readers remember the book Joshua for its account of Jericho's walls coming tumbling down. Joshua had for days marched the Israelites around those walls, until on the day of victory trumpet blows brought the walls down. Joshua embeds within that story the account of Jericho's prostitute Rahab saving her family from destruction, by having hid the Israelite spies. Notably, Rahab later bore the child Boaz, an ancestor of both David and Jesus. Preceding the victory at Jericho, God had stopped the Jordan River's flow for the Israelites to cross, and Joshua had met the commander of the Lord's army, falling face down in reverence. During another battle against five kings, God made the sun stand still for a full day to allow the Israelites to complete their victory. Yet the book also records accounts of defeat, such as when Achan took as spoils some devoted articles, the result of which was Israel's loss at Ai. Joshua himself made a treaty with the deceptive Gibeonites without first consulting the Lord. These and other shortfalls and compromises left Israel's victory incomplete, while setting traps for the nation's future course. The book ends with the burial in the promised land of the bones of Joseph, Joshua, and Eleazar, three Israelites whose lives captivity marked, now free and at rest in the promised land.

Key Locations. Conquest involves geography and tactics. The book Joshua makes clear, in its description of the Israelites' military campaigns, that God directed Israel's victories cognizant of the land's geography and of military tactics. The book begins on the plains of Moab east of the Jordan River, which the Israelites crossed in miraculous fashion for their approach to the fortified city Jericho. Israel next defeated Ai northwest of Jericho, a city not discovered in modern day but from the account in the vicinity of Bethel. The Israelites then proceeded southwest to Gibeon and beyond for continued conquest, before returning, by way of the Jordan River valley, to a conquest of northern kings at the Waters of Merom. Joshua 11 describes further mop-up battles and Israelite victories before concluding that "then the land had rest from war." These victories were incomplete. Joshua 13 lists other lands in the same region that the Israelites failed to conquer. The book, though, takes great pains in following chapters to record the division of the conquered lands. The book ends with Joshua renewing the covenant with Israel at Shechem in the central part of modern-day Israel.

Revelation of Christ. Joshua, like Moses before him, prefigures Christ in various respects beginning with his name. Joshua in Hebrew and Jesus in Greek each signify a savior, as Joshua's military leadership saved the Israelites in their conquests and Jesus's sacrifice saves all who turn to him. Joshua served the lawgiver Moses, as Jesus served and fulfilled the law. As Joshua succeeded the lawgiver Moses, Jesus's salvation of grace satisfied the law. Joshua and Jesus both passed through the Jordan River, Joshua to enter the promised land and Jesus in baptism. Joshua received the Spirit when Moses laid hands on him, while Jesus received the Spirit in John's baptism in the Jordan. Joshua led and commanded his people, as Jesus leads and commands his own. Joshua's trumpets tore down Jericho's fortified walls, while Jesus's word destroys the fortifications of sin. Joshua saved the prostitute Rahab, she later proving to be in the royal ancestral line, while Jesus saved the woman caught in adultery and cleanses us of our own scarlet sins. Joshua ushered the Israelites into the promised land, while Jesus ushers us into his Father's presence. Read Joshua, like the rest of the Bible, for its patterns and types of Christ.

Application. The book Joshua is great encouragement that we stand victorious in Christ, who is our full access to God's promised land. We apply Joshua when we rely on God's promise, our hearts made new to receive the fullness of God's presence in embrace of the glory of his kingdom. God repeatedly urges in Joshua that his people be courageous, and not a foolhardy courageousness but one grounded and rooted in him. In victory, we are to claim our due spoils and then stand as God's testament, living stones paying full tribute to him. Yet Joshua also shows that to appropriate all that God offers us, we must obey all that God commands. Conquering, pursuing the enemy, and prevailing are processes. We take a lifetime to discover and claim for God our hearts' unclaimed, enemy-controlled lands.

Memory Verses. 1:9: "Be strong and courageous. Do not be afraid; do not be discouraged, for the Lord your God will be with you wherever you go." 3:5 "Consecrate yourselves, for tomorrow the Lord will do amazing things among you." 5:15: "Take off your sandals, for the place where you are standing is holy." 6:10: "Do not give a war cry, do not raise your voices, do not say a word until the day I tell you to shout. Then shout!" 7:12: "I will not be with you anymore unless you destroy whatever among you is devoted to destruction." 23:14: "You know with all your heart and soul that not one of all the good promises the Lord your God gave you has failed. Every promise has been fulfilled; not one has failed."

Judges

In those days Israel had no king; everyone did as they saw fit. 21:25

Theme. The theme of the history book Judges is surely in its cycles. The people forget the Lord, then the nation of Israel sins, then God brings due punishment, and finally the nation repents, restoring relationship, until the people forget again. Judges illustrates the human condition without a savior, without rescue: try as we might, we cannot sustain the kind of holiness that a just and perfect God rightly demands. Our hearts bend instead toward compromise, sensuality, indulgence, until we find no character within ourselves with which to stop the cycle. Without salvation, the weary cycle simply continues, except that the cycle is more of a downward spiral than merely a repeated circle. Each cycle adds depth and breadth to human depravity until humankind has no hope of recovery. God, it seems, must wipe humankind from the earth's face, as he did with Noah's flood, except that then God promised never again to do so. The cycle theme of Judges is cautionary, even depressing, except that its flawed deliverers, styled as *judges*, point forward to our perfect Savior.

Author. Judges covers a span of approximately two- to three-hundred years from Joshua's death forward, and so from sometime in the 1300s or 1200s B.C. to Saul's anointing as king, attributed to 1051 B.C. The book Judges does not identify its author, but the Talmud credits the prophet Samuel, who was the last judge, to be the book's author, up to the book's account of Samuel's death. The prophets Nathan and Gad may have written the latter part of Judges recording events following Samuel's death. Choosing an author like Samuel, who lived during the book's latter events into the early reign of Israel's first king, makes sense because of Judges' indirect contrasts, repeated several times, of Israel under the judges to Israel under a king, that "in those days Israel had no king." In any case, Judges was surely extant more than a thousand years before Christ, leaving no question of its ancient authorship during or near the events it records.

Context. Judges serves as a narrative bridge from Joshua's conquering leadership to Israel's first kings Saul and then David. Joshua, of course, led Israel into possession of the promised land, a glorious time in Israel's history. On the other side of Judges, kings Saul, David, and his son Solomon similarly led Israel to a high point in its national history, dominating the Middle East if not also the world's stage. What Judges records in between is a very different but equally or more significant national history, one that the prior and subsequent high points only accentuate, which is Israel's cycles of increasing depravity. Israel would continue that pattern of depravity-to-repentance-to-depravity in the centuries following the time of the judges, until the hundreds of years of post-exile silence awaiting the coming of Israel's one true King, the King of kings. Read the increasing horrors of Judges as confirmation of Israel's need and our need for the Messiah, our Lord and Savior Jesus.

Structure. Judges first introduces the book's theme that Israel would respond to God's blessing not with obedience but with forgetfulness and sin, then suffering punishment, leading to repentance. Judges 2:10 begins that "another generation grew up, who knew neither the Lord nor what he had done." Verse 2:14 follows that God handed Israel over to their enemies, as a result of which, verse 3:9 shows, Israel "cried out to the Lord," and "he raised up for them a deliverer." From chapters three through sixteen, Judges then documents twelve imperfect but effective deliverers, or judges, whom the Lord raised to rescue and restore Israel. Among them are Deborah, Gideon, Jephthah, and Samson. Judges' narrative is likely not strictly chronological. Various judges' tenures may have coincided in different regions of Israel or overlapped, and passages in Judges likely reflect on the culture of earlier tenures. The book's last five chapters, though, show Israel in yet further moral decline. No judge had succeeded in rallying the nation for more than temporary restoration, and no judge had broken the cyclical pattern nor reversed its downward spiral. Israel needed a perfect Savior, not a series of flawed leaders.

Key Events. Key events occur at Judges' beginning and end, initiating and then putting an exclamation point on Israel's troubling history during that period. Joshua's death opens Judges in a passage repeated from the prior book. Judges also opens with an ominous warning from the angel of the Lord that the Israelites had not destroyed their enemies' places of worship, so that now their gods would trap the Israelites. Judges ends with the prophet Samuel's anointing of Israel's first king Saul. In between, Judges records remarkable stories of deliverance. The left-handed Ehud killed the fat oppressing king of

Moab. The prophet Deborah led a reluctant Israelite commander into victory over Sisera, whom a woman killed, confirming the commander's weakness. Gideon emerged from hiding in a winepress to conquer the oppressing Midianites with his trumpets. The angel of the Lord appeared to Samson's parents, announcing the coming conception and birth of the incredibly strong, long-haired deliverer. In a last fatal show of tremendous strength, Samson avenged his Philistine defeat at the hands of his betrayer Delilah. Horrific depravity, such as the murder of the Levite's concubine and distribution across Israel of her body parts, intersperses these rescues. Read these and other remarkable accounts in Judges for their stark illustrations of human despair, when apart from God.

Key Locations. The up-and-down accounts in Judges occur across the breadth of Israel. The book takes the reader to many locations, none of them of significantly greater import than any other. Indeed, the wide distribution of battle and rescue locations is Judges' point. In conquering the promised land, the Israelites had failed to do as God had commanded, which was to rid the land of its altars to other gods and the people with whom the Israelites would inevitably intermarry. The story of Judges is thus temptation from all quarters, not a single high place, with falls, depravity, and battles everywhere, not at a special strategic location. Locations that Judges mention are nonetheless of interest, like Bokim, a lost location thought perhaps to be Bethel, where the angel of the Lord appeared to Israel. The angel of the Lord appeared to Gideon under the oak at Ophrah, northwest of Bethel, where Gideon's son Abimelek would later kill all but one of his seventy brothers. The Levite coaxed his concubine back to him from her home in Bethlehem. Judges sets its accounts in many well-known and little-known or even lost locations, consistent with its theme of despairing cycles everywhere.

Revelation of Christ. One might see the prefigured Christ, our one Savior, in Judges' many heroic-but-flawed deliverers like Othniel, Gideon, Shamgar, Ehud, and Samson. Yet the flaws of those deliverer heroes, violent form of their deliverance, and brevity of their deliverance, discourage such comparisons. Instead, Judges may reveal Christ more in its dramatic demonstration of the need for his transformative deliverance. Judges points to the urgent need for Israel to break its cycles. The period of the judges proved to Israel that it needed a king. While Israel would later anoint flawed king after flawed king, much as it had accepted one after another flawed judges, Judges turned Israel's history toward the

King of kings. Read Judges as that turning point, as proof of our need for the true Savior Jesus.

Application. Judges makes no pretense of hiding its life lessons. Judges 2:10 makes clear that we must remember the Lord always, if we are to remain in his gracious protection and blessing. To forget God is to fall into temptation leading to depravity, when God disciplines and, if they fail to repent, rejects the depraved. God disciplines those whom he loves, Hebrews 12:5-11 reassures us. And so, we should set down markers, create memorials, to foster remembrances of God's actions, comforts, blessings, rescues, and provisions. Let our focus be on the Lord, relying on him, trusting him, honoring him, and above all following him in embrace of his kingdom. Let us look, too, to the Lord's return, for the full deliverance of his people and the redemption of all things. Judges shows us our despair without him, when we have no need of despairing, instead embracing his gracious invitation.

Memory Verses. 2:3: *"I will not drive them out before you; they will become traps for you, and their gods will become snares to you." 2:10: After that whole generation had been gathered to their ancestors, another generation grew up who knew neither the Lord nor what he had done for Israel. 6:17: "If now I have found favor in your eyes, give me a sign that it is really you talking to me." 13:18: "Why do you ask my name? It is beyond understanding." 21:25: In those days Israel had no king; everyone did as they saw fit.*

Reading Guide

Author

One doesn't have to know who wrote the Bible book that one is reading, but it sure can help. The sixty-six books of the Bible may have had approximately forty different authors. But who knows? Scholars find at least some disagreement on who wrote most of the Bible's books. Put another way, fewer Bible books have undisputed authors. Tradition, though, assigns authorship to most books and does so with good reason. Traditionally assigned authors may not have written those books, but in many cases they very probably contributed writings or accounts, even though later authors compiled, edited, and transmitted their writings. It may not matter much to the lay reader if a certain author who experienced the described event wrote the description that the reader reads or merely related the description to another author or wrote something on which the later author drew.

The point is that having a probable or even possible author in mind can help to understand the author's meaning, that which the author intended. Judges, lawyers, and other readers do a similar thing with legislation, which typically has several or many authors, or has staff authors whose writings legislators would claim. We still read the legislation, which after all we know that *someone* wrote in a certain era and circumstance, with a theoretical author's intent in mind, to help us understand the meaning and significance of what we are reading. Who the author was, when the author wrote, where the author wrote, and the circumstances of the writing all influence interpretation of the author's meaning. Read the Bible with an idea of the author in mind, especially as the Bible's own text identifies or suggests the author.

Ruth

"Don't urge me to leave you or to turn back from you.
Where you go, I will go, and where you stay, I will stay. Your
people will be my people and your God my God." 1:16.

Theme. Ruth's theme is redemption, more specifically, to have a
redeemer who at the perfect moment acts in rescue, drawing one back
from despair's precipice. To redeem is to pay, to give, to relinquish
something of value with the purpose of recovering something, taking
back what was once one's own. While redemption is also a legal term
and procedure, describing the recovery of foreclosed lands, the
redemption in the book Ruth is of the person Ruth by a kinsman Boaz of
Ruth's mother-in-law Naomi. The book illustrates the personal rescue of
a desperate widow Ruth, without hope of offspring, and even more-
desolate mother-in-law Naomi, even as it suggests the rescue of a family,
community, nation, and world by the one great redeemer Christ. Ruth is
thus a book of hope, and not hope prolonged, but hope realized.

Author. Jewish tradition, reflected in the Talmud, identifies the
prophet Samuel as the author of Ruth, even though the book does not
name its author, and certain references to David indicate a later author or
addition. The book may indeed have been written around the time of
David's anointing as Israel's king because it traces Ruth's offspring to
David but not beyond to Solomon. The setting for Ruth is during the late
period of judges, around 1160 to 1100 B.C., which would have been a
dark time of famine and war. Famine drove Naomi's family from Israel's
Bethlehem to the foreign land of Moab, where her son married Ruth
before dying. Naomi and Ruth returned to Israel in hopes of food, for the
Lord's provision. The book Ruth is thus unusual among the Bible's
sixty-six books in its perspective told so clearly through the eyes and
experiences of women, whether that perspective suggests anything about
the author's identity or not.

Context. In one sense, the cyclical events of Ruth, showing a family
driven from the promised land only to return for rescue, reflect their
context within the time of the judges. Yet Ruth's narrative stands apart

from Judges as a beacon of hope. Not apparent from Ruth's narrative is that its kinsman redeemer Boaz is the son of the prostitute Rahab whom Joshua rescued when conquering Jericho. Boaz was also the great-grandfather of David. The genealogy of Matthew 1 further confirms that the redeemer Boaz and his mother Rahab are ancestors in the direct line of Christ. Ruth's redeemer theme thus rescues the reader from Judges' wearying cycles, pointing forward to David and Christ. The book's family love affairs are tender, intimate, and deeply personal, and thus the opposite of Ruth's predecessor book Judges. Yet Ruth's redemption theme, set against the sordid decline shown in Judges, suggests not only that God is our personal redeemer, that God redeems only the saved and sanctified individual, but that God also sends his Savior Son to redeem all things honoring him in his creation. Read Ruth not just for its tender story of hope but also for this broader context.

Structure. Ruth's short four-chapter length in no way diminishes, and instead accentuates, its highest-quality organization and writing. Effective stories require character development. Ruth's first chapter introduces Naomi, who having moved to a foreign land to escape famine promptly loses her husband and sons, and Ruth, the devoted daughter in law who despite her husband's death insists on following Naomi back to Israel. The second chapter introduces Ruth's about-to-be kinsman-redeemer Boaz, whom the text reveals to be of high reputation, godly, and righteous. The third chapter tells the climactic moment when Ruth offers Boaz her most-tender devotion, to which the honorable Boaz responds with an indication of Ruth's coming redemption. The final chapter tells of Boaz's arrangement to marry Ruth and of the offspring Obed whom they produce, who becomes the grandfather of David.

Key Events. Ruth's key events each involve intimate family relationships. Ruth's mother-in-law Naomi first loses her husband and sons in Moab. A second key turn occurs when Naomi resolves to return to Israel and Ruth insists on accompanying her, against her mother-in-law's advice. For their survival, Ruth must glean behind the barley fields' harvesters, where Ruth meets her redeemer Boaz. Boaz invites Ruth to remain in his fields under his protection, rewarded by his generous kindness. At Naomi's urging that she seek Boaz as her redeemer husband, Ruth secretly returns to sleep at Boaz's feet, where Boaz again protects and rewards her. Boaz subsequently negotiates with another relative for the right to marry Ruth, so that they bring forth the offspring of which Naomi had despaired, in the very line of David.

Key Locations. The book Ruth opens in Bethlehem but shifts briefly to the foreign land of Moab east of the Dead Sea and Jordan River before returning to Bethlehem, where the story unfolds. One tender scene, that of Ruth's commitment to follow Naomi back to Bethlehem, occurs on that road back to Bethlehem. Scenes back in Bethlehem switch between Naomi's residence and Boaz's barley fields, until Ruth joins Boaz overnight at the threshing floor. In the last scene with a specific setting, Boaz negotiates with a relative at the town gate, for Ruth's hand. While the reader may simply enjoy the intimacy of these scenes and their settings, also consider what these locations may echo or symbolize. Bible accounts place several events on, in, and around, and make lessons and parables out of, roads back to the promised land and its harvest fields and threshing floors.

Revelation of Christ. The redeemer Boaz, in the ancestral line of Christ, is surely a type of Christ. Boaz's care for the widows Naomi and Ruth, indeed for the Moabite foreigner Ruth, prefigures Christ's care for the outcast and powerless, just as Boaz's adoption of Ruth points to the Christian's adoption in Christ. Christ recognized and ministered to foreigners, women, widows, the powerless, and the poor, with a tenderness that Boaz's gentle and generous measures, protecting and honoring Ruth, so well reflected. Note, too, though, how the figure Ruth, so devoted first to her Israelite mother-in-law Naomi and then to her redeemer Boaz, prefigures Christ's church, looking always to its splendid redeemer. The story's setting in Christ's birthplace Bethlehem, the name of which means *house of bread*, adds parallels that turn the Christian's thoughts to Jesus, the author and bread of life. Ruth points forward to Christ as surely as the Bible's other books, although uniquely in its intimacy and tenderness.

Application. Ruth teaches, indeed intimately assures, that God has a plan for each of us, as he had a most-extraordinary plan for a hungry old widow and her bereaved foreigner daughter-in-law. We must trust God's plan even when we cannot imagine it. If Naomi and Ruth were without apparent rescue, and yet God came to their aid so graciously and generously, then he is able and willing to rescue us. We need only trust, hoping for that which we cannot see, which means to show our faith. Ruth also shows that God is the lasting redeemer, not the temporary fix. We should seek God, the true redeemer, not the crutch with which idols tempt. Ruth also teaches that God's rescue can be intimate, precious, warm, fulfilling, as a hen covers her chicks with her wing, or a landowner Boaz covers a young woman Ruth with his garment. Ruth invites us to dwell and rest in the grace of Christ's magnificent redemption.

Memory Verses. *1:16: "Don't urge me to leave you or to turn back from you. Where you go, I will go, and where you stay, I will stay. Your people will be my people and your God my God." 2:12: "May you be richly rewarded by the Lord, the God of Israel, under whose wings you have come to take refuge."*

1 Samuel

"The Lord does not look at the things people look at. People look at the outward appearance, but the Lord looks at the heart." 16:7.

Theme. Leadership is the theme of the history book 1 Samuel, covering a period when Israel's leadership transitioned from loosely associated tribes to a highly centralized monarchy. The book centers on Israel's last judge, the prophet Samuel whose name the book bears, then on Israel's call for and choice of a first king Saul, and finally the contrast of that first king to the heir apparent David. The book contrasts accounts of Saul's elevation and actions to the Lord's identification of David who will replace him, revealing both how the Lord chooses and values leaders, and how the Lord himself leads. The lessons of 1 Samuel in leadership, though, are not just for leaders. They are also for followers, for all of us. Indeed, the core theme of 1 Samuel is not how to lead but instead how to identify, trust, and follow leaders. We are all followers, while few of us also lead. More important to every one of us than leadership is whom we choose to follow. To follow wisely, one needs to identify the true leader, a personal lesson that 1 Samuel illustrates within Israel's national history.

Author. Given that 1 Samuel bears the prophet Samuel's name, and the narrative of its first twenty-four chapters follow the course of his life, Jewish tradition naturally attributes to Samuel the book's authorship up to his death. Hannah bore Samuel in about 1120 B.C., while 1 Samuel records events up to Saul's death in about 1010 B.C., giving the book that hundred-and-ten-year span. The prophets Nathan and Gad may have completed the book, especially those parts after Samuel's death, given their equivalent positions to Samuel. Later authorship than Samuel would especially have been necessary considering that 1 Samuel formed one book with 2 Samuel until its Septuagint translation from Hebrew to Greek in the few hundred years before Christ. First Samuel 27:6 mentions Israel's divided monarchy, while 2 Samuel records other history occurring decades after Samuel's death. Modern scholarship attributes the six history books beginning with 1 Samuel to unidentified members of the prophetic school around the time of Israel's exile in 597 B.C., although they surely would have worked from much-earlier writings, perhaps including writings by Samuel, Nathan, and Gad. The latter history book 1 Chronicles 29:29 notes that Samuel recorded the acts of king David.

Context. First Samuel begins six books in three pairs (three books until divided in the Greek Septuagint), all chronicling Israel's history in the promised land under its many kings, up to its 597 B.C. exile. The period of the judges precedes 1 Samuel, which together with 2 Samuel documents the reigns of Saul and David. The history books 1 Kings and 2 Kings, chronicling the reigns of the rest of Israel's kings, come after 1 Samuel and 2 Samuel in the Hebrew Bible. The prophet Samuel is the last of the judges and thus the one who anointed Israel's first king. First Samuel's context, then, is one of transition from the cyclical period of Israel's judge deliverers to the at-times-spectacular and at-times-abysmal reigns of Israel's kings. That transition explains 1 Samuel's focus on the process of choosing leaders and the qualities they should possess, most significantly, their relationship to the Lord. Those explanations underscore Israel's later failures. First Samuel is thus all at once a book of transition, launch, and foreboding, having a special place in the Bible and in Israel's history.

Structure. The structure of 1 Samuel serves its leadership theme and its transition context. Its first eight chapters record the times of the last judges including Samuel. Its next chapters nine to fifteen record the rise and leadership of its first king Saul. Its last chapters sixteen to thirty-one then record the growing conflict between Saul, as king, and his estranged lieutenant David, who will rise to lead Israel. The chronological structure of 1 Samuel lends itself well to the contrast of its three leaders Samuel, then Saul, then David. Samuel is a man of God's word whom obedience marks as God's own. In contrast, self-reliance marks Saul, an outwardly impressive but inwardly needy and limited man. In contrast again, faith marked David, not an impressive but rather an impressed man whose heart remained after God. First Samuel is an orderly book, one that modern readers can readily embrace for its narrative, theme, action, and contrasts.

Key Events. Key events in 1 Samuel begin with the tender story of the childless Hannah whom the priest Eli blessed that God would give her a child, Samuel. Hannah dedicated Samuel from infancy to serve in the Lord's house at Shiloh, where the Lord spoke to Samuel as a boy and continued to reveal himself to Samuel as a prophet. When the Philistines capture the ark, the priest Eli and his sons die. The ark returns to Israel, led then by God's word through Samuel. As Samuel grows old, Israel demands a king, and so Samuel anoints Saul, even though Saul hides among the baggage and then cannot find Samuel. Saul succeeds in battle, but Samuel must rebuke Saul for acting without the Lord. The Lord rejects Saul as king and directs Samuel to anoint David, who serves Saul loyally but over whom Saul grows jealous and fearful, especially after David defeats Goliath. David must flee, while Saul pursues in attempts to kill him, even as David spares Saul's life on two occasions. During these events, 1 Samuel records poignant moments such as David's intimate friendship with Saul's son Jonathan and Abigail's rescue of David from her foolish husband Nabal. First Samuel also records instructive moments, like when God chooses the youngest David from among Jesse's sons, and dramatic moments, like when Saul consults the witch of Endor. The book fills with other memorable events contrasting the leadership and character of Samuel, Saul, and David, ending with Saul taking his life.

Key Locations. Other peoples surrounded Israel in the time of king Saul. To the west between Israel and the Great (Mediterranean) Sea were Philistia in the south and Canaan and Phoenicia in the north. Syria bounded Israel to the north, while Ammon and Moab bounded Israel to the east. Edom and the Amalekites bounded Israel to the south. Many of 1 Samuel's key locations were in central Israel or nearby, like Samuel's birthplace Shiloh, Ramah where the Israelites demanded a king, Ephes Dammim where David defeated Goliath, Adullam where David hid from Saul, and Mount Gilboa where Saul died at his own hand. Samuel anointed the Benjamite Saul in that tribe's ancestral lands in central Israel. Key battles that 1 Samuel records occurred throughout central and north-central Israel. For examples, the Philistines captured the ark in battle between Ebenezer and Aphek, at Philistia's northwest boundary with Israel, and Samuel subdued the Philistines in nearby Mizpah toward central Israel. The Lord rejected Saul, though, after battles to Israel's south, and other battles that 1 Samuel records occurred throughout the region. First Samuel is indeed a book of action, centering in central Israel but moving swiftly around the region.

Revelation of Christ. In recording the call and anointing of David as Israel's coming king, 1 Samuel introduces the reader to one of the Bible's primary figures of Christ. David was, 1 Samuel 13:14 intimates and Acts 13:22 confirms, a man after God's own heart. David had full faith in God, whether in trusting God to deliver him as a shepherd from lion and bear, or when carrying God's battle to the giant Goliath. David also delighted in God's law and word, as Psalm 119 and so many other of David's psalms witness. Unlike Saul, David repeatedly demonstrated that he would wait on the Lord, at critical junctures like when he could have killed or been killed by king Saul or the dangerous fool Nabal. David's heart for God, and David's celebrated royal tenure, gave many other reasons for Matthew's gospel six times to call Jesus, born in the City of David in David's ancestral line, the *Son of David*. God promised David that one of his offspring would rule forever, making Christ the fulfillment of God's covenant with David.

Application. In story after story of Hannah, Samuel, Saul, Jonathan, Abigail, David, and others, 1 Samuel shows us God's providence, when we have the faith to wait on the Lord. Who, having in 1 Samuel seen God give children to the barren, defeat giants, and elevate shepherds to king, would not ask for the faith to wait on the Lord? First Samuel also reminds us of God's kingship, not just his Son Jesus's priesthood but also his power and authority, referenced in his royalty. Israel should indeed have a king, as we have our King of kings Jesus. With royalty comes sovereignty, that we respect God's full will in absolute obedience and trust. What God decides God accomplishes, with or without us, making far better that we obey and participate rather than reject and rebel. We should, too, reevaluate what and who impress us, ensuring that we rely on the righteous godly rather than worldly things. First Samuel fills with sound lessons, though its greatest lesson, like every other Bible book, is to point us firmly to the eternally wise King.

Memory Verses. 2:2: *"There is no one holy like the Lord; there is no one besides you; there is no Rock like our God."* 3:10: *"Speak, for your servant is listening."* 12:16: *"Now then, stand still and see this great thing the Lord is about to do before your eyes!"* 12:24: *"Be sure to fear the Lord and serve him faithfully with all your heart; consider what great things he has done for you."* 13:14: *"The Lord has sought out a man after his own heart...."* 15:22: *"To obey is better than sacrifice, and to heed is better than the fat of rams."* 16:7: *"People look at the outward appearance, but God looks at the heart."* 17:37: *"The Lord who rescued me from the paw of the lion and the paw of the bear will rescue me from the hand of this Philistine."* 24:6: *"The Lord forbid that I should do such a thing to my master, the Lord's anointed, or lay my hand on him; for he is the anointed of the Lord."*

Reading Guide

Structure

The structure of a book, meaning how its author organizes the text and material to best accomplish the book's purpose, informs its reader. Structure can have both large scale and small scale. The large-scale structure of some of the Bible's books is clear, such as those, like the book of Acts, that follow events in chronological order. If you know the author is tracing events chronologically in connected sequence, then you expect to evaluate passages for their chronological relationship and continuity or discontinuity. But not all Bible books are chronological. Some skip ahead and then circle back. Reading those books assuming chronological order can confuse the reader. Other books are chronological only in part while organizing other parts thematically. Some books have no chronology, only thematic structure.

Even within these large scales, though, authors may also be organizing material in small-scale ways. Authors may move back and forth between poetry and prose, each such movement cluing the reader to a shift in the author's intention. Authors may shift from figure-centered narratives to event-centered narratives in which the figures are less significant. Bible authors also often use shifts in locale, such as from northern to southern kingdom or from Israel to enemy of Israel, to structure narratives and clue the reader to significant shifts in meaning. Multiple different large-scale and small-scale structures, shifting back and forth across books and within books, can make reading the Bible more difficult than reading simpler works. Recognizing those shifts can also make reading the Bible far more rewarding.

2 Samuel

"Your house and your kingdom will endure forever before me; your throne will be established forever." 7:16.

Theme. The theme of 2 Samuel is kingship, rule, royalty. God called, as his premier king of Israel, a person David after God's own heart. Second Samuel records David's ascension to the throne, his largely beneficent rule, and his preparation for building God's temple, a glorious time in Israel's history. In that record, the reader sees how one like David who pursues God's heart can, through challenge, lead a blessed and victorious life, while contributing mightily to the flourishing of others. When God rules the heart, the person rules the world, whether as a literal king like David or simply a humble member of God's own kingdom. Genesis 1:28 records that God made humankind to rule with him. When residing in his person to carry out his will, we are God's co-rulers of all we encounter, bringing peace, order, and flourishing in this chaotic and troubled world. Nowhere in the Bible does one see the benefit of godly kingship, godly rule, more so than in 1 Samuel. Read the book for the glorious record of God's coming and emerging rule, in which we take part.

Author. The prior section on 1 Samuel indicates that it formed one book with 2 Samuel until their Septuagint translation from Hebrew to Greek in the few hundred years before Christ. Second Samuel records history starting not long after Samuel's death, account of which appears at 1 Samuel 25:1, and for decades afterward. Thus, the prophet and last judge Samuel did not author 2 Samuel. As the prior section indicates, modern scholarship attributes the several history books beginning with 1 and 2 Samuel to unidentified members of the prophetic school around the time of Israel's exile in 597 B.C., although they surely would have worked from much-earlier writings, likely including writings by David's contemporaries the prophets Nathan and Gad, whom tradition credits with the book's authorship. Given that 2 Samuel records the events of David's kingship from 1011 B.C. to 971 B.C., those early writings of Nathan, Gad, and perhaps others would date to that period.

Context. Second Samuel's core context, as just indicated, is David's rule as Israel's king. After hundreds of years led by the deliverer judges and then under Saul's rule, the nation was still consolidating, still gathering and constituting itself on the regional stage, and still rising toward world prominence, an influence that it first achieved under David. Yet one does not have 2 Samuel's full context without also considering what follows it. After David's death, recorded just after 2 Samuel ends, Israel rose in power and glory still further under David's son Solomon. That subsequent history, though, did not supplant David's place as Israel's beloved king after God's heart, but instead cemented it, because of Solomon's extraordinary defect, displayed in his seven-hundred wives, through which he led Israel into disastrous alliances that soon split the kingdom. Though Israel's history in 2 Samuel was turbulent, as the book also shows David's character to clearly be imperfect, 2 Samuel nonetheless displays Israel led by its beloved king. Read 2 Samuel for the sweetness and delicacy of that relationship.

Structure. Inside of that context, 2 Samuel has a powerfully dynamic structure, one that follows a dominant Bible pattern of blessing, sin, and repentance. The book's first part accentuates David's virtue and God's blessing that follow it. As 2 Samuel 8:15 records, David reigned "doing what was just and right for all his people," while regularly inquiring of the Lord. The Lord accordingly gave David victory wherever he went, 2 Samuel 8:6 confirms. Yet in the security of victory, David did as humankind does, which is to turn from the Lord, first in 2 Samuel 11's record of David's adultery and murder, and later in 2 Samuel 24 when David counted his troops against the Lord's will. The Lord rebuked David, seen in chapters 14, 19, and 24, with David and the nation suffering harsh consequences. Unlike other leaders, though, David confessed, took responsibility, and repented, giving God grounds to forgive and restore. Second Samuel teaches even as it records. We learn much from the life of David, and not just that God desires and pursues our co-rule.

Key Events. Second Samuel begins with David's surprising lament over the death of Saul, who had pursued David to kill him, and unsurprising lament over the death of David's friend Jonathan, Saul's son. The Lord then made David the leader first of his tribe Judah and soon of the whole of Israel, uniting the nation under their beloved king, while David exhibited his generosity, justice, and grace. David brought the ark of the covenant up to his conquered Jerusalem, pausing at Obed-Edom's house when Uzzah died touching the ark. David's wife Michal, daughter of Saul, despised David for dancing half-naked in celebration before the whole nation. David brought calamity on himself when he committed adultery with his lieutenant Uriah's wife Bathsheba and then arranged Uriah's murder. David's son Amnon raped David's daughter Tamar, Amnon died at the hands of another of David's sons Absalom, and Absalom conspired to overthrow David. David fled from Jerusalem as the nation devolved into civil war, ending in Absalom's defeat and death. Second Samuel nears its end, though, with David in victorious song of praise, followed by one last episode of David disobeying the Lord by counting the troops, requiring that David build an altar to the Lord on the Jerusalem site of the future temple to stop the avenging plague. Second Samuel, like its predecessor, fills with action in which the reader sees the strong hand of the Lord.

Key Locations. A first central location in 2 Samuel is the land of Judah, from the Dead Sea's northern-to-southern length west to the land of the Philistines, where David first ruled, after anointing at Hebron in Judah's center, with Jerusalem at Judah's northern border. God then brought all Israel under David's reign at Hebron, Israel then reaching much further north and south, west to the Great (Mediterranean) Sea, and east across the Jordan River to Ammon and Moab. David then promptly conquered the Jebusites in Jerusalem, making it his home, the City of David, to which David brought the ark of the covenant, and the future site of God's temple. David's other wars of conquest included battles with the Philistines to the west, the Arameans to the northeast, Ammonites and Moabites to the east across the Jordan River, and the Edomites south of the Dead Sea. David fled his son Absalom to Mahanaim across the Jordan River in Israel's northeast. Second Samuel ends with David building the altar on Araunah's threshing floor in Jerusalem, where David's son Solomon would build God's temple. Overall, 2 Samuel's action circles first around Hebron and then Jerusalem, David's first and final homes.

Revelation of Christ. The Davidic covenant, recorded at 2 Samuel 7:16, that God would establish David's house, kingdom, and throne before him forever, grants Christ his position as God's King of kings. More than a type of Christ, David received God's promise that his line would bring the Messiah as King. At the same time, David also served as a type of Christ, whose name after all indicated God's beloved. David was also God's elect to firmly establish Israel's kingdom, as Christ would bring God's kingdom. David was a shepherd when called, as Christ would shepherd God's people, and received God's Spirit when anointed, as Christ received the Spirit when baptized. David also exhibited Christ-like attributes, even beyond his celebrated heart for God. David had a humble and meek spirit, as Christ came a servant, and cared deeply for the poor and outcast, as Christ served the hungry and poor. David brought to his table Jonathan's disabled son Mephibosheth, lame in both feet since an injury at Jonathan's death. David was both wise and courageous, as was Christ. David was a musician whose play could soothe Saul, while Christ brought the people's praise of God. David saved Israel from Goliath and the Philistines, while Christ saved his people of the world's sin. The revelations of 2 Samuel are many more, for the discerning reader to discover.

Application. David's life teaches more than how to wait and rely on God to overcome, to kill the giant. The lessons of David's life may be even more acute and helpful in teaching us how to manage success. David's fall with Bathsheba, involving both adultery and murder, began when he should have gone out to battle, when kings go to war. We must continue our struggles, being wary of laurels' rest. David fell victim to his own wandering eyes, as we must guard our eyes lest we, too, fall to temptation. Yet once David fell, he did as one should, which was to admit the fall, turn from the sin, take responsibility, and seek God's forgiveness. Second Samuel 12:13 records David admitting, "I have sinned against the Lord," while verse 14:21 records David turning from sin, saying, "Very well, I will do it." David asked the Lord in 2 Samuel 24:17, "Let your hand fall upon me and my family," and saw in 2 Samuel 24:25 that "the Lord answered prayer." David's restoration sets a pattern for the follower of Christ, we who are sure to fall but also sure to receive God's grace and forgiveness.

Memory Verses. 6:21-22: "I will celebrate before the Lord. I will become even more undignified than this, and I will be humiliated in my own eyes." 7:16: "Your house and your kingdom will endure forever before me, your throne will be established forever." 7:18: "Who am I, Sovereign Lord, and what is my family, that you have brought me this far?" 9:8: "What is your servant, that you should notice a dead dog like me?" 12:13: "I have sinned against the Lord." 14:14: "God ... devises ways so that a banished person does not remain banished from him." 16:12: "It may be that the Lord will look upon my misery and restore to me his covenant blessing instead of his curse today." 22:2-3: ""The Lord is my rock, my fortress and my deliverer; my God is my rock, in whom I take refuge, my shield and the horn of my salvation." 22:31: "As for God, his way is perfect: The Lord's word is flawless...."

1 Kings

"Since this is your attitude and you have not kept my covenant and my decrees, which I commanded you, I will most certainly tear the kingdom away from you and give it to one of your subordinates." 11:11.

Theme. The theme of 1 Kings is disobedience and the awful consequences that follow it. That the book begins not with disobedience but Solomon's display of great character, one that God sumptuously rewards, simply heightens the message of 1 Kings: even the great, even those whom God elevates to the heights, can disobey with disastrous consequence. The higher one rises, the greater one's fall. First Kings is a fascinating book the panoramic action of which mesmerizes readers, but despite the presence of heroic figures like Solomon and Elijah, its core motif of figure after royal figure turning from God to apostasy is dark, even dismal. Read 1 Kings instructively. Do not disobey. Hold fast to God.

Author. Some tradition holds Jeremiah to be 1 Kings' author, while other tradition prefers Ezekiel or even Ezra. Because 1 Kings was originally a single book with its 2 Kings sister, like 1 and 2 Samuel, and the two books 1 and 2 Kings record four-hundred years of history, whoever authored it surely worked from other writings to compile its abundant details. The book and its sequel do, however, have a single literary style and integrated themes, indicating a single author. That author would have written in the middle or latter half of Israel's exile to Babylon, around 560 B.C., the year that Israel's exiled king Jehoiachin gained release from his Babylonian prison. First Kings records history from just before David's death in about 971 B.C. until 853 B.C., a point deep into the history of a divided northern Israel and southern Judah.

Context. First Kings' context richly informs its disobedience theme. Second Samuel's record of David's reign precedes 1 Kings, highlighting David's godly character and beneficent actions, and Israel's consequent rich rewards. The opening chapters of 1 Kings, filled with political intrigue over who would succeed David and whether that successor could survive, stand in stark contrast to the generally upward course of 2 Samuel. When 1 Kings soon devolves to division and warfare between northern and southern Israelite kingdoms, the reader sees that 1 Kings is plainly a different book than 2 Samuel. That 2 Kings follows 1 Kings with an even greater decline, all the way to Israel's Babylonian exile, simply confirms the nature of 1 Kings as a witness to disobedience's destructive forces. Read 1 Kings in its transitional setting, taking the reader from Israel's glory days down its dark path toward its eventual destruction in exile.

Structure. First King's structure makes obvious Israel's extraordinary decline. The book's first ten chapters document the height of Solomon's reign, when God rewarded Solomon's humble prayer for wisdom with both that critical leadership attribute and with unprecedented riches. Solomon at first sought the welfare of others, exhibiting God's own servant heart. First Kings then turns swiftly, in its chapters eleven through sixteen, to the record of Solomon's seven-hundred-wives decline and, at Solomon's death, the kingdom's division under two idolatrous successors. The third part of 1 Kings documents Israel's further decline, through the lens of the great prophet Elijah's dispute with Ahab and the prophets of Baal. That latter part of 1 Kings records one of the most dramatic moments in Israel's history, showing the enduring power of a godly witness even during idolatry's calamity, giving 1 Kings a fitting conclusion, pointing the reader firmly forward and up to God.

Key Events. The intrigue of royal succession surrounds David's death at 1 Kings' beginning. David's wife Bathsheba intercedes for their son Solomon, who takes the throne, wisely wary of his competition, whom he must cull from leadership. The Lord appears to Solomon at Gibeon, granting him one wish. Solomon pleads for discernment, and God gives him that and riches. Solomon displays his wisdom in ruling to divide a disputed baby, revealing the love of the baby's true mother. Solomon builds the Lord's temple in Jerusalem from the supplies his father David had accumulated. He then takes nearly twice as long to build an even greater palace for himself. Solomon brings the ark to the new temple, and God again appears to Solomon. Sheba's queen visits Solomon to witness his wisdom, bringing a great caravan of riches. Solomon, however, loved many wives, the account tells us at 1 Kings 11:1, who turned his heart to foreign gods. Solomon's own officials rebelled. When Solomon died and his son Rehoboam took the throne, Israel revolted, and the kingdom divided. Egypt attacked, carrying off the temple's treasures. King succeeded king in the divided northern and southern kingdoms, all sinning to greater and lesser degrees, until the great prophet Elijah, whose miracles adorn 1 Kings, announced a famine. Elijah lured the corrupt king Ahab to assemble his prophets of Baal at the top of Mount Carmel, where Elijah called down fire from heaven in a sacrifice to God, and the people slaughtered Baal's prophets. Elijah fled to God's mountain Horeb, where God whispered to Elijah to return. Elijah called Elisha. First Kings ends its roller-coaster history in another succession of sordid kings.

Key Locations. Much of the political intrigue in 1 Kings occurs in Jerusalem, where David reigned, died, and was buried, and Solomon built the temple and his palace. The priest Zadok anointed Solomon king in Gihon, just east of Jerusalem. When the northern kingdom Israel divided from the southern kingdom Judah, it did so just to the north of Jerusalem, which lay near Judah's northern border. Solomon offered sacrifices and saw the Lord at the high place in Gibeon, northwest of Jerusalem, but brought the ark to Jerusalem's temple, where Solomon saw the Lord a second time. Sheba's queen visited Solomon in Jerusalem. The northern king Jeroboam met the man of God at Bethel, well north of Jerusalem, well beyond Gibeon. Farther north along the Mediterranean coastline lies Mount Carmel, where Elijah lured the prophets of Baal. Mount Horeb, to which Elijah fled, lies far to the southwest in the southern region of the vast Sinai Peninsula.

Revelation of Christ. First Kings shows a nation, and by extension a world and humankind, without Christ. Humankind may attain victories of a sort, through complex alliances among nations. But those victories without God are always tenuous, shallow, and temporary, fraught with mistrust and peril, expensive in the extreme, and not made to last. Without a heart for God, transformed of the Spirit gifted from Christ, leaders flounder in their flaws and foibles, their corruptions exposed as surely as rain washes a tombstone of its glitter. First Kings, though, also introduces the reader to a herald of Christ in the prophet Elijah, with whom Christ would famously visit in his magnificent transfiguration. Malachi 4:5 prophecies that the Lord would send Elijah before the Lord's day comes. Matthew 11:14 records Jesus saying that John the Baptist was the Elijah to come. As a first of the great prophets, and the only prophet taken into heaven without dying, in a prefiguring of Jesus's own ascension, Elijah bears a special relationship to Christ. First Kings reveals Christ in its own way.

Application. Although a history book, 1 Kings makes its life lessons crystal clear. How each successive king treated the Lord's law judged the king, whether evil or righteous. We rely on the Lord, not, as Psalm 20:7 warns, chariots and horses. First Kings also reveals the temptation that can pull us away from the Lord's law, whether in wealth or wives, the latter warning against intimate association with others who do not share our faith. First Kings also shows that we must pursue the Lord until our earthly end, running the race God marks out for us. As much as the Lord blessed Solomon for his humble prayer for discernment, when later in his life Solomon's wives turned his heart from the Lord, the Lord turned from him. God loves generously and in full grace but deserves our full and enduring devotion. Finally, we hue to the Lord's law not solely for our own salvation but also that the world might know the love of the Lord.

Memory Verses. *2:2-3: "I am about to go the way of all the earth," he said. "So be strong, act like a man, and observe what the Lord your God requires: Walk in obedience to him, and keep his decrees and commands, his laws and regulations, as written in the Law of Moses. 3:9: "[G]ive your servant a discerning heart to govern your people and to distinguish between right and wrong." 8:27: "But will God really dwell on earth? The heavens, even the highest heaven, cannot contain you." 8:39: "Forgive and act; deal with everyone according to all they do, since you know their hearts (for you alone know every human heart)...." 18:24: "Then you call on the name of your god, and I will call on the name of the Lord. The god who answers by fire—he is God." 19:12: After the earthquake came a fire, but the Lord was not in the fire. And after the fire came a gentle whisper.*

Reading Guide

Revelation

The single most-remarkable aspect of the Bible, attributable entirely to the work of God's Holy Spirit, is that despite the Bible's large number of authors writing over as much as fifteen-hundred years, the Bible nonetheless tells the integrated story of our Lord and Savior Jesus Christ. At times, Jesus's presence in the described events is obvious, such as in the four gospel books describing directly, in abundant and marvelous detail, his earthly ministry. Other times, though, the Bible's books and passages do not make clear to all readers that they refer to the Lord Jesus. The Bible's first thirty-nine books, comprising the Hebrew Bible, certainly refer at times to the coming Christ or Messiah, Son of David, and Son of Man, all titles the New Testament would recognize as referring explicitly to Jesus. Yet the reader must acquire some familiarity even to recognize those references, not to mention other messianic signifiers.

The modern reader unfamiliar with the Hebrew Bible's Jewish culture and religion would miss those signifiers, even when Jews, well-read Christians, and other informed readers generally would not. The challenge of seeing Christ in every book of the Bible grows even greater when one considers how often the Bible uses figures, types, symbols, and imagery of Christ. Not every lion in the Bible symbolizes Christ, but some lion features or references plainly do, as tradition affords those references and trained readers generally accept the authors' intentions. The same is true with other figures and imagery, that sometimes they do signify a reference to the Lord Jesus while other times they may not. And certainly, scholars can disagree about the number and location of such references. A sound approach, then, is to accept the aid of informed sources when trying to discern but also to seek the Spirit's guidance. God is sovereign. He may give different revelations to different readers at different times.

2 Kings

So, Judah went into captivity, away from her land. 25:21.

Theme. The theme of 2 Kings is captivity, and not just sudden, inexplicable captivity but rather the deep corruption, weakness, capture, and exile that comes from a long disobedience toward God. While on its surface, 2 Kings is a history of the divided kingdom Israel's long creep toward annihilation and exile to Babylon, its spiritual theme is certainly the utter degradation, loss, and enslavement that comes with the deep embrace of sin. If 2 Kings is a record of humankind without God, on national and regional if not also world scale, then it is also a witness to the depravity of the individual human soul without Christ's transformation. The Bible must have a book that despairs of individual hope without God. Though written as national history, 2 Kings is that book, the author of which knew well how hopeless humankind is without a healthy relationship with the Lord.

Author. As indicated in the prior section, some tradition holds Jeremiah to be 1 and 2 Kings' author, while other tradition prefers Ezekiel or even Ezra. Because 2 Kings records hundreds of years of history, whoever authored it surely worked from other writings to compile its details. The book and its predecessor 1 Kings do have a single literary style and integrated themes, indicating a single author who would have written in the middle or latter half of Israel's exile to Babylon, around 560 B.C., the year that Israel's exiled king Jehoiachin gained release from his Babylonian prison, the last event that 2 Kings records. Second Kings records history from 850 B.C. to 560 B.C. including the northern kingdom Israel's exile in 722 B.C. and the southern kingdom Judah's exile in that later year 586 B.C.

Context. Second Kings has two contexts, one external and one internal, each important to the book's place and appreciation. Its external context lies in the long history of Israel's sure decline to the point of exile. First Kings introduced that decline, beginning with the glory of Solomon's reign leading directly to his embrace of idolatry and rejection by God, followed by the kingdom's division and civil wars. Second

Kings doesn't just continue that history but perfects it, in all its awfulness, leading to not just one but two terrible annihilations and exiles. True, subsequent history books Ezra and Nehemiah show Israel's return, but that tentative return leads only to hundreds of years of God's silence before Christ bursts on the scene. Second Kings' internal context involves a continuation from 1 Kings of the story of Elijah, his lieutenant Elisha, and following prophets who pronounce the cause and predict the disastrous result of Israel's decline.

Structure. Second Kings divides itself neatly into three parts. Its first part, from chapters one through ten, records the story of Elisha's ministry within the northern kingdom Israel, beginning with Elijah's ascension, passing Elisha his mantle. Second Kings' second part, from chapters eleven through seventeen, documents the interaction of the northern and southern kingdoms, Israel and Judah, and the exile of the northern Israel. Both kingdoms disobeyed the uncreated God, not just in small actions but in openly worshiping false created gods. Second Kings' third part, from chapters eighteen to its end at chapter twenty-five, record the last hundred-plus years of the southern kingdom Judah, beginning with promise in the reign of Hezekiah but succumbing as Israel succumbed, ending likewise in Judah's exile.

Key Events. Second Kings opens with Elijah still prophesying, in this instance to the northern kingdom Israel's errant king Ahaziah, calling down fire on Ahaziah's captains. Elisha, introduced in 1 Kings, continued to attend Elijah, whom Elisha dramatically witnessed God taking straight to heaven. Elisha picked up where Elijah left off, including in performing multiple miracles, healing a foreign commander Namaan of leprosy, floating a lost ax head, and bringing a rich widow's dead son back to life. Northern-kingdom king succeeded corrupt king, as Israel fell into warring with, and under siege by, its emboldened neighbors. Israel also battled Judah, Jehu killing Judah's king. The seven-year-old Joash took Judah's throne, later as an adult repairing the temple. The book's middle narrative proceeds with alternating lines of kings of Judah and Israel, until 2 Kings 17 records the exile of Israel to Assyria, whose later king also threatened Judah. But Judah's king Hezekiah prayed to the Lord, and the prophet Isaiah foresaw Judah's deliverance. Hezekiah's successor king Manasseh, though, placed carved idols in Jerusalem's temple. A later king Josiah had his high priest Hilkiah discover the Book of the Law in the temple, causing Josiah to renew the covenant and cleanse the temple. Josiah's successors, though, returned to evil, until Judah, like Israel, fell into captivity, Judah to the Babylonian Nebuchadnezzar.

Key Locations. Second Kings focuses its action on the divided northern and southern kingdoms of Israel, the boundary of which was north of Jerusalem roughly at the united kingdom's center. That line ran from Gilgal at the northern tip of the Dead Sea west to Joppa on the Great (Mediterranean) Sea, also forming the northern boundary of Philistia along the sea. Jericho and Bethel, where companies of prophets told Elisha that God was going to take Elijah that day, were just north of the boundary, in Israel. Shunem, where Elisha restored the Shunammite's son, Samaria where Israel's kings ruled, and Megiddo were also in Israel. Hebron, Lachish, Beersheba, and Bethlehem were in Judah, as of course was Jerusalem where Judah's kings ruled, Josiah brought the book of the law out of the temple, and Babylon brought its sieges. Battles occurred with Aram to the northeast of Israel and Moab to the east of Judah across the Dead Sea. Israel's exile to Assyria took the Israelites due north to that land, while Judah's exile to Babylon took the people far to the east.

Revelation of Christ. Elijah's ascension, witnessed by his protege Elisha, points toward Christ's own ascension from the Mount of Olives, witnessed by the disciples. Elisha received Elijah's spirit, as we receive the Holy Spirit from Christ. Elijah's mantle remained for Elisha to pick up, as Christ left the church to carry forward in gospel ministry. Elisha struck the Jordan River with Elijah's mantle, parting the waters so that he could proceed in ministry, as we carry Christ's Spirit into the world's waters to part them for ministry. Elisha cleansed the Assyrian commander Namaan of leprosy, as Christ cleanses not just God's chosen Israelites but also the Gentiles, meaning all of us, of our sin. Every movement of the Spirit in 2 Kings is a movement of Christ, without whom we are in exile, as Israel and Judah ended 2 Kings in exile.

Application. Second Kings offers precious lessons in Elisha's devotion to Elijah, from whom Elisha inherited a double portion of his spirit. Though Elijah seemed at times indifferent to Elisha's company, even urging Elisha to stay behind as Elijah approached his end on earth, Elisha pursued Elijah's company and, as Elijah's ministry ended, attended Elijah in a miracle crossing of the Jordan River to witness Elijah's ascension in a chariot of fire. And so likewise, we cling to Christ, following him wherever his travels take us, praying for his Spirit, and then sharing his Spirit richly, as Elisha did, to feed widows and restore life. We also mentor others, as Elijah mentored Elisha, and not reluctantly but as a privilege, opportunity, and duty. We also learn lessons from the contrasting lives of the kings whose legacies, either awful or admirable, teach us to do what is right in the Lord's eyes, fleeing from the temptation to do evil. Each day, we repeat our commitment, and through our selfless actions confirm, that we pursue God alone. Second Kings reminds us to persevere in God's way to our own earthly end, that we would rise in victory with him.

Memory Verses. *2:9: "Let me inherit a double portion of your spirit." 2:12: "My father! My father! The chariots and horsemen of Israel!" 2:13: He picked up the cloak that had fallen from Elijah. 4:6: "There is not a jar left." Then the oil stopped flowing. 5:10: "Go, wash yourself seven times in the Jordan, and your flesh will be restored, and you will be cleansed." 6:17: "Open his eyes, Lord, so that he may see." Then the Lord opened the servant's eyes, and he looked and saw the hills full of horses and chariots of fire all around Elisha. 17:15: They followed worthless idols and themselves became worthless. 17:38-39: "Do not forget the covenant I have made with you, and do not worship other gods. Rather, worship the Lord your God; it is he who will deliver you from the hand of all your enemies." 18:3: He did what was right in the eyes of the Lord. 19:19: "[D]eliver us ... so that all kingdoms on earth may know that you alone, O Lord, are God."*

1 Chronicles

Remember the wonders he has done, his miracles, and the judgments he pronounced.... 6:12.

Theme. The theme of 1 Chronicles is remembrance. Because 1 and 2 Chronicles review history that prior books already addressed, their perspective on that history must be different. The two Chronicles view the same history not from the perspective of sin, judgment, and captivity, as 1 and 2 Kings recorded that history, but from the standpoint of God's mercy. In 1 and 2 Chronicles, we remember how patient God was with Israel's worsening sins, how many times God forgave Israel as God forgives us. The Spirit constructed the prior history books 1 and 2 Kings for a nation in exile, as we have found ourselves in exile, while the Spirit constructed 1 and 2 Chronicles for a nation restored, as we find ourselves restored. God wants us to remember our history, whether national, tribal, family, or individual. First Chronicles has us look back across that history, as we look back across our own history, to remember God and draw from his mercy.

Author. Neither 1 Chronicles nor 2 Chronicles, which like 1 and 2 Samuel and 1 and 2 Kings were one book before their Septuagint translation, tell us who was their author. Tradition credits Ezra, who wrote the following history book carrying his name. What 1 Chronicles does make clear from its own text is that its author relied on annals, books, and records that the author regarded as reliable. The author was a meticulous historian who researched 1 Chronicles' history through official documents supported by other writings outside the official record. The author also took a priestly perspective, showing greater concern for the details of worship and observance than other history authors. From the final passage of 2 Chronicles, referring to Israel's restoration and the rebuilding of Jerusalem's temple, the author of 1 and 2 Chronicles would have been writing at the dawn of Israel's post-exile period. As to the period of history that 1 Chronicles records, it begins its history with a genealogy from Adam to Abraham and on down to David but focuses its history on David's reign from 970 B.C. to 853 B.C.

Context. The post-exile, early restoration authorship of 1 and 2 Chronicles gives the most-important clue to 1 Chronicles' context. Israel had just suffered horrific defeat, more like annihilation, after centuries of desultory divided rule. Judah had, though, survived in exile, even prospered, to the point that its Babylonian and later Persian rulers looked with favor on it. Judah's leaders in exile had not only access to the Babylonian and Persian kings but also such favor as to draw on their treasuries to return to Jerusalem to rebuild the temple. First Chronicles' author could thus write convincingly from the perspective of God's mercy. Even in Judah's deserved exile, God would do the miraculous in preserving, showing favor to, and then restoring his people. The God who had drawn the Israelites out of Egyptian captivity, through the waters, and out of the wilderness would also draw his people out of a crushing foreign captivity. Read 1 Chronicles in its restoration context, revealing once again God's extravagant mercy.

Structure. First Chronicles' genealogies, covering the book's first nine chapters, serve its purpose of documenting Israel's continuity and God's unending mercy. Chapters twenty-three to twenty-five, near 1 Chronicles' conclusion, return to genealogies of musicians and gatekeepers, and in the army. In between, 1 Chronicles records the history of David's reign, deemphasizing the corruption that 2 Samuel and 1 Kings record, while emphasizing instead aspects of Israel's history that glorify God. In exile, Israel knew its corruption. It now needed to remember other things. Its leaders in exile and post-exile were more religious leaders than political leaders, given Israel's tenuous military and political position. Israel needed to celebrate its spiritual history, not its political or military history. First Chronicles ends recording David's plans and gifts for the temple that his son Solomon would build. First Chronicles is a heartening history, far more easily digested than the already-documented history of Israel's despairing corruption.

Key Events. The key events of 1 Chronicles, repeating history in 2 Samuel and 1 Kings, begin with Saul taking his life in losing battle with the Philistines, David becoming Israel's king at Hebron, and David conquering Jerusalem. The account of David bringing the ark up to Jerusalem details the elaborate preparations and extravagant display. David then appointed Levites to minister before the ark, again accentuating how the Israelites glorified God. God gave the prophet Nathan a promise to share with David that God would establish his throne, the line of David, forever. David subdued surrounding powers, leaving a strong and united kingdom for his son Solomon, for whom

David also purchased the Jebusite's threshing floor and assembled the materials for Solomon to build Jerusalem's temple. First Chronicles ends with David sharing elaborate plans for that temple while naming its ministers, making for a resounding history of Israel glorifying God.

Key Locations. Appropriate to its restoration theme, the history of 1 Chronicles centers on Jerusalem, the City of David, where the restored Israelites would rebuild God's temple. First Chronicles also briefly records Saul's death on Mount Gilboa to Israel's far north, David's anointing at Hebron deep to the south in Judah, the defeat of Philistines garrisoned at Bethlehem for the waters of which David thirsted, the assembly of David's fighting men at Ziklag farther to the southwest at the border of Philistia and Judah, and David's defeat of surrounding foreign powers, giving the book a broader location context. Yet 1 Chronicles devotes its narrative details to such events as David bringing the ark to Jerusalem and David planning and providing for the temple's Jerusalem construction, not to mention detailing the temple's staffing in Jerusalem. The author of 1 Chronicles clearly intended readers to focus on God's glorious presence among his chosen people, with the coming temple as his dwelling place.

Revelation of Christ. First Chronicles prepared an exiled Israel not just for restoration to Jerusalem but also to anticipate once again the coming Messiah, both priest and king, from the line of David. The Israelites knew God's Davidic covenant that David's line would establish the throne forever. Yet at the time of their restoration to Jerusalem, the Israelites had no recognized king, whether of David's line or any other. They thus needed from 1 Chronicles the reminder that God keeps his promises, meaning that they should indeed once again expect the Messiah to arise from David's line to reign from his throne in Jerusalem. David had the heart for Christ and so supplied richly for God's Jerusalem temple. First Chronicles points forward to Jesus Christ as the Messiah whose throne, a wooden cross, he would indeed take in Jerusalem's environs.

Application. First Chronicles pushes the reader to discern, memorialize, celebrate, and remember the reader's own spiritual inheritance. The book encourages the reader to think beyond the reader's own salvation to the flourishing and salvation of future generations. What legacy do you wish to leave your own family and community? How must we each behave today to influence future generations? We each contribute to the nation's course, too, not only the course of our own family and local community. How ought we each to behave, for our nation to remain or become one of godly individuals each responsible to account to Christ? God honors the righteous, those whom his Spirit forms in his Son's image. Remember who you are. Remember where you are. And let your identity and location represent well the glorious Father and Son whose Spirit guides and sustains you.

Memory Verses. 9:1: They were taken captive to Babylon because of their unfaithfulness. 11:17: David longed for water and said, "Oh, that someone would get me a drink of water from the well near the gate of Bethlehem!" 14:11: "As waters break out, God has broken out against my enemies by my hand." 16:23: "Sing to the Lord, all the earth; proclaim his salvation day after day." 16:34: Give thanks to the Lord, for he is good; his love endures forever. 17:14: "I will set him over my house and my kingdom forever; his throne will be established forever." 21:13: "Let me fall into the hands of the Lord, for his mercy is very great; but do not let me fall into human hands." 21:24: "I will not take for the Lord what is yours, or sacrifice a burnt offering that costs me nothing." 28:8: "Be careful to follow all the commands of the Lord your God, that you may possess this good land and pass it on as an inheritance to your descendants forever." 29:14: "But who am I, and who are my people, that we should be able to give as generously as this? Everything comes from you, and we have given you only what comes from your hand."

2 Chronicles

"[I]f my people ... will humble themselves and pray and seek my face and turn from their wicked ways, then I will hear from heaven, and I will forgive their sin and will heal their land." 7:14.

Theme. The theme of 2 Chronicles is inheritance. Like its sister book 1 Chronicles, of which 2 Chronicles was originally a part, 2 Chronicles looks back across the history of Israel's kings. Like 1 Chronicles, 2 Chronicles views that history through rose-colored glasses, and not because Israel had anything to hide, for the Israelites were just emerging from long exile and knew the reasons for their captivity. Rather, 2 Chronicles casts a hopeful light, as 1 Chronicles glorified God, to give the returning Israelites confidence in their inheritance. An inheritance is something bequeathed, gifted out of relationship, not something earned. The Israelites could see in their return from exile to Jerusalem that they would indeed receive their coming Messiah, the Son of David. They had every reason for great hope in that course of history and prophetic word. And now, if they'd previously had any doubt, they knew that he would rescue them by his Father's grace, which is 2 Chronicles' subtle but still-evident theme.

Author. As the prior section on 1 Chronicles indicates, neither 1 Chronicles nor 2 Chronicles, one book before their Septuagint translation, tell us who was their author, although Jewish tradition credits Ezra, who wrote the following history book carrying his name. The whole of 1 and 2 Chronicles does show from its text that its meticulous historian-author relied on official annals and records backed by unofficial writings. Whether a priest or not, 2 Chronicles' author also took a priest's perspective, showing great concern for the details of worship and observance. From the final passage of 2 Chronicles, referring to the returned exiles' rebuilding of Jerusalem's temple, 2 Chronicles' author would have been writing at the dawn of Israel's post-exile period. As to the period of history that 2 Chronicles records, it begins in 853 B.C. with Solomon taking the throne and concludes with

Judah's exile in 586 B.C., with a concluding note of the Israelites' return from exile seventy years later.

Context. Second Chronicles shares the early restoration context of 1 Chronicles, its sister book. Israel had recently suffered annihilation defeat, after centuries of declining and divided rule. Yet Israel had then survived in exile, to a degree even prospered, to the point that its Babylonian and Persian captors looked with such favor on it as to draw on their treasuries to return the exiles to Jerusalem to rebuild the temple. In the face of that merciful, too-good-to-be-true return, 2 Chronicles' author could point convincingly to Israel's extraordinary inheritance. The Israelites did not know that hundreds of years would pass before that inheritance appeared in a Bethlehem manger. Nor did they know much of the upside-down nature of God's humble entry into the world. Neither did they know that he would lead his people far beyond a temporal, political kingdom to his eternal heavenly kingdom. But their restoration context urged them to trust 2 Chronicles' inheritance narrative. Read 2 Chronicles as confirming God's Davidic covenant and merciful will.

Structure. Second Chronicles devotes its first quarter, chapters one through nine, to Solomon's reign. Solomon first consolidates his power before building the temple. Second Chronicles devotes six chapters alone to the temple's construction and dedication, making clear the book's interest in conveying the glory of Israel's inheritance. No other people had such privilege as to construct and maintain God's temple home. Unlike 1 Kings, which revealed Solomon to be a deeply flawed ruler in his extravagances and dalliances, 2 Chronicles mentions barely a few words of Solomon building his palace and nothing of the corrupting distraction of his hundreds of wives. Second Chronicles' last three quarters, chapters ten through thirty-six, record the history of Judah's kings. Note 2 Chronicles' different focus, not on both lines of kings of the competing and at times warring northern and southern kingdoms, Israel and Judah, as 2 Kings documented, but instead on Judah's kings alone. The reason for 2 Chronicles' unique focus and structure is, of course, that God's covenant was with David, meaning the Messiah would come from Judah, not from the northern kingdom Israel.

Key Events. Second Chronicles naturally focuses its key events on the actions of Judah's kings in David's line, pointing toward God's eternal throne. Solomon asked for wisdom rather than wealth, and so God gave him both. Solomon conscripted all foreigners in Judah to build God's temple, although 2 Chronicles pointedly and repeatedly attributed to Solomon, not those laborers, the construction of the temple and its furnishings. When Solomon brought the ark of the covenant to the temple, the Lord's glory filled the temple so that the priests could not perform their service. Solomon's son Rehoboam succeeded Solomon as king, leading to the northern kingdom's revolt. Second Chronicles continues its description of each of Judah's successive kings, highlighting how although they at times turned from God, those who humbled themselves God restored to his favor. The book shows how righteous kings like Asa would remove Judah's high places, his son Jehoshaphat would follow God's laws, and Hezekiah would purify the temple, so that God would accordingly give Judah peace and rest. Second Chronicles also shows how God would reject wicked kings like Ahaziah, Ahaz, and Manasseh, who pursued other gods and idols. Second Chronicles ends with brief mention of Jerusalem's fall, the exile, and the Persian king Cyrus's offer to restore Judah to rebuild its temple.

Key Locations. Second Chronicles has one primary location: Jerusalem, where Solomon builds God's temple, Judah's kings reign, Assyria and then Babylon lay siege, Babylon defeats Judah, and to which the exiles return at book's end. Yet while Judah's kings rule and war from Jerusalem, 2 Chronicles' more-precise focus is on the temple within Jerusalem. Second Chronicles, like its predecessor 1 Chronicles, focuses on the glory of God. Its high point is not the exiles' return, which barely warrants an afterthought mention. The high point of 2 Chronicles is when God's glory fills the temple to the point that the priests must stand in awe rather than serve. The temple is 2 Chronicles' location focus because 2 Chronicles intends to highlight God's relationship with his people, and not just God as king and judge but as highest priest, prepared to establish Judah's throne in heaven forever. The temple *as a building* is not even 2 Chronicles' focus, as Christ would soon make clear, but instead the temple as the locus of the presence of God, as God's Eden garden for his people to see again in his returning celestial city.

Revelation of Christ. One could say that the so-called good kings of Judah, those whose reigns 2 Chronicles especially celebrates, prefigured Christ, as they surely did in their reverence of God and his holy law. Second Chronicles' greater revelation of Christ, though, was not in those kings' representative character or actions but in their preserving the Davidic line ruling Judah, through whom God's promised Messiah would soon come. When God covenanted with David to establish his throne forever, and then carried David's line through the succession of Judah's alternately righteous-and-wicked kings, God did not mean that a temporal king in David's line would always be on the earthly throne of a political Judah. God instead pointed to the one eternal Messiah Jesus whose birth, life, sacrifice, and resurrection would place the Lamb of God Jesus on God's heavenly, eternal throne. Second Chronicles points the reader to that eternal inheritance of salvation in Jesus Christ, the one who forever reigns in heaven.

Application. Second Chronicles' kingship history teaches us to reject evil while pursuing righteousness. No reader needs to do any more than survey the dramatic ups and downs of Judah's kings to, from that lesson, recommit to righteous living. Yet we draw much more from 2 Chronicles than lessons in good living. Second Chronicles turns our hope once again to the returning King Jesus. Second Chronicles reminds us to place our hope in things eternal, the glory of God on his heavenly throne, the God whose presence is our one true desire. Second Chronicles has us turn from worldly ambitions, even as we do as we ought, to heavenly ambitions, to do God's will, glorify God, and embrace his Son's salvation. The world wearies, while heaven restores. The world offers but brief pleasures and yet no escape but death, while the Son offers us paradise in bodies resurrected, life made whole, and relationship restored. See in 2 Chronicles' record of God's glory filling the temple, the glory of God filling your soul.

Memory Verses. 1:12: "I will also give you wealth, possessions and honor, such as no king who was before you ever had and none after you will have." 5:13-14: Then the temple of the Lord was filled with the cloud, and the priests could not perform their service because of the cloud, for the glory of the Lord filled the temple of God. 15:2: "The Lord is with you when you are with him. If you seek him, he will be found by you, but if you forsake him, he will forsake you." 19:9: "You must serve faithfully and wholeheartedly in the fear of the Lord." 20:15: "Do not be afraid or discouraged because of this vast army. For the battle is not yours, but God's." 24:13: The men in charge of the work were diligent, and the repairs progressed under them. They rebuilt the temple of God according to its original design and reinforced it. 29:2: He did what was right in the eyes of the Lord, just as his father David had done. 30:7: "Do not be like your parents and your fellow Israelites, who were unfaithful to the Lord, the God of their ancestors, so that he made them an object of horror, as you see. Do not be stiff-necked, as your ancestors were; submit to the Lord." 31:21: In everything that he undertook in the service of God's temple and in obedience to the law and the commands, he sought his God and worked wholeheartedly. And so he prospered.

Reading Guide

Translations

The Bible has many English translations. Translation is necessary for the reader in English because the original Bible was written in Hebrew, as to the Old Testament (with small portions of Daniel and Ezra in Aramaic), and Greek, as to the New Testament. The further translation and preservation of original Bible texts down through the centuries and millennia is a fascinating topic, one worthy of its own study, for the dedication, interests, skill, and challenges of the translators, as well as the reliability of the texts they produced. The much-narrower question here is which English version to read? Readers tend to find their own favorite translation, each to his own. Yet knowing something of the categories of translations and differing goals of translations may help you make wise choices.

Bible translations fall into two or three main categories. Some versions attempt literal translations. Those translations are still not entirely word for word, given the frequent absence of parallel words, but they try to reflect in English just what the original authors wrote. Other versions instead attempt to interpret and convey the meaning rather than the literal words. Expressions and idioms change from culture to culture, robbing them of translated meaning. Although it takes interpretation, adept scholars can preserve meaning while changing expressions to fit the modern English context. Still other versions choose a middle course, hewing more toward literal translations but shifting some expressions so that they make sense to the modern reader. Nothing says that one must choose a single translation. To the contrary, many Bible readers go back and forth between multiple translations, learning from the different ways that they translate or interpret the words and meanings of the original Hebrew and Greek texts. Take an interest, though, in the nature of the translation you are reading, even as you explore different versions.

Ezra

For Ezra had devoted himself to the study and observance
of the Law of the Lord, and to teaching its decrees and laws in
Israel. 7:10.

Theme. Ezra's theme is restoration. The prior history books 1 and 2
Chronicles have already shown how Israel needed first to remember its
history and then to embrace its inheritance. Ezra records how that
restoration of the exiles to Jerusalem occurred. Ezra, though, needed to
do more than record details of the exiles' departure from Babylon, trek to
Jerusalem, and challenges in resettlement. Ezra had also to remind the
Israelites of that to which God was restoring them, which was not
primarily a geographic homeland but instead a relationship of adoption
and inheritance. Ezra is not political history, although one sees how God
worked in politics. Ezra is spiritual history, spiritual restoration to a place
where God could once again accept Israel's devotion. Nothing created
remains as it was before exile. Israel had changed as a people. Yet God
restored them to the Davidic covenant, which means God restored
Israel's hope for a divine rather than worldly future. Israel would not
again reign over the region as Solomon had reigned, but Israel would
once again embrace its true glory, which was God's inheritance, a
heavenly future.

Author. Tradition names the priest, scholar, and scribe Ezra the
author of the history book bearing his name, supported by first-person
references in Ezra 8:15-28. The Hebrew Bible places the books Ezra and
Nehemiah together, although the accounts suggest separate authorship, as
English translations afford them. Ezra held such high position in the
exiled community that he led the second group of Jewish returnees to
Jerusalem, as the second half of the book and its sequel Nehemiah
document. Ezra was a direct descendant of Moses' brother Aaron, whose
anointing established Israel's priest line. If Ezra was indeed the book's
author, writing as events occurred, then Ezra would have written the
book between 458 B.C., when he led the second group of exiles to return,
and 450 B.C., the date of the book's last events.

Context. The six history books preceding Ezra tell the chronological story of the decline and exile of Israel and Judah. Those six books carry the Bible's narrative forward hundreds of years to the exile of God's chosen people. Ezra, written around the exile's end, after two successive returns that decades separated, doesn't so much carry the Bible's narrative forward as instead has the narrative look back. When Ezra tells the story of return, it begs the reader to consider that which the returning Israelites were attempting to recapture and restore. Ezra's context encourages the reader to remember the temple's glory under Solomon and Israel's former military power and great wealth. Yet the comparison quickly becomes a stark contrast. The returnees utterly lack the resources, position, and power to even begin to replicate Israel's former glory. The context demands that one see Israel's return as meaning something less but also something more than restoring its prior glory.

Structure. Ezra describes two exile returns. The book's first six chapters describe the first return in 583 B.C. that Zerubbabel led under Persian king Cyrus's edict, together with twenty-five years of history to 515 B.C., as the returnees rebuilt the temple. The book's last three chapters describe the sixty-year-later return that Ezra led in 458 B.C. Ezra's first six chapters, describing the exiles' first return in which they struggled to rebuild the decimated temple, address the physical challenges the exiles faced and overcame. Ezra's last three chapters, describing the exiles' second return that Ezra led, address Israel's spiritual restoration, how God's word reveals sin. The final chapter ten also illustrates the necessity of confession and repentance, that seeing our sin, we must change so that we do God's will. The book's structure thus teaches the practical lesson that a person or people may first have to obtain a degree of physical security, safe and at liberty enough to join and form a spiritual community, to fully embrace their spiritual destiny.

Key Events. Ezra's key events begin with the Persian king Cyrus authorizing the exiles to return to Jerusalem, incredibly, with extravagant gold-and-silver items that the Babylonian king Nebuchadnezzar had pillaged from the temple. The Persian empire had replaced the Babylonians as the Israelites' captors in exiles. Ezra records no reason why Cyrus sent the exiles back other than that the Lord moved his heart, to fulfill Jeremiah's prophecy. The book then mentions briefly that those exiles rebuilt the altar and then the temple in Jerusalem, although Ezra 3:12 records that many of the older exiles wept aloud when they saw the temple's foundation laid, one readily presumes because the restored temple would bear little resemblance to the former temple's glory.

Subsequent passages record opposition to the rebuilding, overcome with edicts not just from the originator Cyrus but also from Darius and Artaxerxes. The narrative then takes up the course of the second return under Ezra, beginning with the returnees' departure from Babylon under Artaxerxes. Upon his arrival at Jerusalem, Ezra confronted the already-established returnees with their sins of intermarriage and unfaithfulness. The book ends there, taken up with the following Nehemiah narrative.

Key Locations. Although the returnees settled in surrounding towns, too, Ezra focuses its narrative and events on Jerusalem, where the returnees rebuilt first the altar and then the temple. The accounts make occasional references to discussions, investigations, negotiations, work stoppages, and work authorizations from far away Babylon, which Ezra also mentions when he describes the second returnees' departure from Babylon. The Israelites and their opposition each sought the favor of Cyrus, Xerxes, Artaxerxes, and Darius, earning competing edicts dramatizing the returnees' tenuous situation. Ezra thus has a world-historic, secular, and political cast to it, even though its focused action occurred around the temple in Jerusalem. Historians would especially appreciate Ezra for those broader world contexts.

Revelation of Christ. The priest and scholar Ezra carried Christ's Spirit, in the clear sense of Ezra's devotion to observing the law and to teaching its authentic meaning. Ezra was not a legalist but instead one concerned with the hearts of his people, as Jesus seeks the heart. Ezra soaked himself in God's word, prayed in fervor, sought God's kingdom on earth, and exhibited passion for his people's purity, all as Jesus did in his own earthly ministry and continues to do for us through his Spirit. Ezra's broader focus on rebuilding the temple and restoring a godly people to its renewed service, further reflects Christ both in his own passion for God's temple and as that temple. God allowed men to destroy that temple, the body of Christ, whom God promptly raised from the dead so that all humankind might live through him. As Ezra points to the temple, the book also points to Christ. Ezra's returnees need not have worried that the restored temple bore little likeness to Jerusalem's first temple because both temples were but shadows of the temple we have in Christ.

Application. In showing the striving of a people to live up to their covenant heritage, Ezra offers valuable lessons. God watches. Actions matter. We measure our actions against God's eternal, righteous standard, not in the way that the world measures success. When we do as God warrants, we worship and sing in celebration that we have honored him. Ezra teaches us how richly God has blessed us, no matter our exiled or tenuous-return status. God's covenant far outshines and outlasts our circumstances, no matter how desperate those circumstances. The priest-scholar Ezra studied, knew, practiced, and above all taught God's word, as we should embrace God's word, wherein lies our only authentic hope for a future. God's word also makes us distinct as a people, unlike the people who reject God to pursue things of the world. Ezra, though a history book and a brief one at that, holds valuable lessons for any reader.

Memory Verses. 1:2: *"The Lord, the God of heaven, has given me all the kingdoms of the earth and he has appointed me to build a temple for him at Jerusalem in Judah." 3:11: With praise and thanksgiving they sang to the Lord: "He is good; his love toward Israel endures forever." 5:17: "[L]et a search be made in the royal archives of Babylon to see if King Cyrus did in fact issue a decree to rebuild this house of God in Jerusalem." 7:6: He was a teacher well versed in the Law of Moses, which the Lord, the God of Israel, had given. The king had granted him everything he asked, for the hand of the Lord his God was on him. 7:10: For Ezra had devoted himself to the study and observance of the Law of the Lord, and to teaching its decrees and laws in Israel. 9:6: "I am too ashamed and disgraced, my God, to lift up my face to you, because our sins are higher than our heads and our guilt has reached to the heavens." 9:13: "What has happened to us is a result of our evil deeds and our great guilt, and yet, our God, you have punished us less than our sins deserved and have given us a remnant like this." 10:11: "Separate yourselves from the peoples around you and from your foreign wives."*

Nehemiah

"[W]e are powerless, because our fields and our vineyards belong to others." 5:5.

Theme. Nehemiah's theme is rebuilding, and not rebuilding just any useless edifice, but rebuilding important markers and memorials, and protective walls. We stumble, and in the embarrassment and struggle, we momentarily forget our faith. Standing again, restored, we wonder at how weak our grasp is on the gospel that we hold so dear. In those moments of recovery, we feel the need to rebuild, not the foundation of our faith that we know as fully secure, but instead faith's boundaries, the borders and perimeters that in challenging times keep our faith strong and secure. And so, we seek to rebuild those perimeters, to restore the walls. As we do so, block upon block, our enemies see our progress and bring the fight. Rebuilding requires more than engineering prowess. It requires more than materials and resolve. It also requires strategic responses to the enemy's advances. One must be not only strong and resourceful to rebuild, but also discerning of the enemy's wiles.

Author. Significant to Nehemiah's rebuilding theme is that its tradition-afforded author, the Jewish-exile court-official Nehemiah, was not a priest, prophet, scribe, nor scholar. Nehemiah wasn't even a historian. He instead served the Persian king as cupbearer, which may sound menial but was a position of both privilege and influence. Nehemiah had the king's trust, meaning that he had high character, and he thus had the king's ear, meaning that he had close and constant access to power and resources. Nehemiah also had administrative and political skills. If Nehemiah did not write his book, its frequent use of the first person in his name, describing details of his own thoughts and actions, suggests that its author compiled it from Nehemiah's communications. Given that Nehemiah's narrative relates details of his thoughts and actions seemingly as they occur, the author may have written the accounts between 444 B.C. and about 430 B.C., the period of those narrated events. Nehemiah is thus not only the most-recent of the history narratives, succeeded in the canon only by Esther, which described an earlier rather than later period, but also the latest book in the Hebrew Bible, along with Malachi, whose author was Nehemiah's contemporary.

Context. After history books showing exiled Israel's remembrance of its history, pursuit of its inheritance, and restoration to the promised land, the Bible would naturally want to show Israel rebuilding. Ezra had already described how the first returnees had rebuilt Jerusalem's altar and temple, and the second returnees had brought spiritual reform. Yet Ezra had also shown that the returned Israelites' military and political position, among the powers that had filled Israel's vacuum since exile, was weak, fragile. Israel had not yet rebuilt its military power and political relationships, at least not to have reasonable security. Nehemiah's third-wave return to rebuild the wall was more than an architectural and engineering effort. His goal was not just to rebuild Jerusalem's physical wall but to demonstrate to the Israelites and their enemies that Israel had returned to stay, to firmly claim its inheritance. Nehemiah's wall surely had a military purpose, but its figurative and political purposes may have been far greater. As Nehemiah 6:16 states, when the people finished the wall, all their enemies were afraid and lost their self-confidence. Israel had risen again.

Structure. Nehemiah's rebuilding narrative reveals a structure for leadership. Nehemiah first prayed for God's discernment, passionately, and with fasting, seen in verse 1:4. Nehemiah then acted, answering the Persian king's request, seen in verse 2:4. Nehemiah then expected and resolutely faced down opposition to his action. Nehemiah simultaneously showed consistent care for those whom he led, care that caused him to turn his people to God's word for life and instruction. Having succeeded in his actions, Nehemiah did not claim credit but instead confessed sin, seen in verse 9:37, after giving God full credit for their victory, seen in verse 9:6. Verse 9:38 then shows Nehemiah committing his people to the covenant that formed and bound them together as a people. The whole of Nehemiah, right down to its conclusion, confirms the primary attribute of leadership, which is to lead. Any leader's course may not always be exact, but the people need a godly leader to lead.

Key Events. The book Nehemiah opens with the cupbearer learning that those of his Jewish people who had returned to Jerusalem were in distress, beset by surrounding opposition. Noticing Nehemiah's sadness, and learning of its cause, king Artaxerxes offered Nehemiah what he wanted, which was to travel to Jerusalem to inspect its protective walls. On arrival, Nehemiah discovered the wall's broken-down condition, leading him to organize and orchestrate the wall's systematic repair.

Opposition to the work built, requiring Nehemiah to post sentries to protect the workers. In the course of the work, Nehemiah arranged to help the people's poor, who had lost ownership of their fields and vineyards. The rebuilding ended with Nehemiah and the priest Ezra gathering the people for celebration, worship, and instruction, and to seal their agreement to pursue God's covenant. Nehemiah then arranged to populate Jerusalem from surrounding towns. The book ends with Nehemiah reciting final reforms. Read Nehemiah for a spectacular history of an effective and godly leader in passionate action.

Key Locations. Nehemiah begins in a most-interesting location for a Bible book: the citadel in Persia's capitol city Susa, north of the Persian Gulf and far to the east of God's temple in Jerusalem. Persia was the dominant regional power at the time, while Jerusalem was only a political and military backwater. Nehemiah delivered the king's safe-passage letters to the governors of Trans-Euphrates, that fertile crescent that travelers from Susa to Jerusalem would have followed. Remarkably, the book details many gates and features of Jerusalem's walls, like the Tower of the Hundred, Fish Gate, Dung Gate, and King's Garden, adding much color to the long narrative listing the individuals, families, trades, and towns whom Nehemiah organized to rebuild the wall. As the rebuilding concluded, the people came together in the square before the Water Gate to celebrate. The book shows Nehemiah's concerns not just for Jerusalem but also for its surrounding villages and towns, naming many such as Kiriath Arba, Dibon, Jekabzeel, Beersheba, and Ziklag. Nehemiah is very much a book of place, as God's people are a people of place, that place God's kingdom, wherever it may take them.

Revelation of Christ. Nehemiah reflects the active-leadership character of Christ. Every prominent feature of Nehemiah's story reflects the position, purpose, and passion of Christ. Like Nehemiah, Christ has intimate access to great power, in Christ's case the ultimate power, our holy Father. The rebuilding challenge that Nehemiah assumed, Christ also faced. Christ would form of himself a new wall and the true temple, of which Jerusalem's temple was but a shadow. Like Nehemiah, Christ faced fierce opposition, and like Nehemiah, Christ dealt with the opposition strategically. Christ protected his disciples, as Nehemiah protected his workers, both turning them to the word of God. And when Christ succeeded, he credited his holy Father, as Nehemiah confessed his people's sin and credited God. The leadership that Nehemiah exhibited was Christ-like leadership because Nehemiah was formed of Christ, dedicated with passion to the God-honoring purpose of his people.

Application. Nehemiah holds all the above leadership lessons: to pray fervently, act firmly, face down opposition, care for one's people, turn them to God, confess sin, commit one another to God's covenant, and lead, lead, lead. Nehemiah, though, is also a book of warning. While Nehemiah prayed, he also posted guards at night and sentries to protect the workers. We learn to take our own protective measures, even as we find refuge in the Lord. Nehemiah also teaches the value of ownership, that we are largely powerless when others control our figurative fields and vineyards. Take ownership and control when able, that you may reap and share the fruits of your labors. Nehemiah is also a book of prayer, especially instructive because Nehemiah was not a priest, scholar, or scribe. His prayers may sound more like our own: earnest, heartfelt, original. Read Nehemiah for its rich lessons, embedded not just in his words but in his adroit actions.

Memory Verses. *1:4: For some days I mourned and fasted and prayed before the God of heaven. 1:11: "Lord, let your ear be attentive to the prayer of this your servant and to the prayer of your servants who delight in revering your name." 2:8: And because the gracious hand of my God was on me, the king granted my requests. 2:17: "Come, let us rebuild the wall of Jerusalem, and we will no longer be in disgrace." 4:9: But we prayed to our God and posted a guard day and night to meet this threat. 4:23: Neither I nor my brothers nor my men nor the guards with me took off our clothes; each had his weapon, even when he went for water. 5:5: "[W]e are powerless, because our fields and our vineyards belong to others." 5:19: Remember me with favor, my God, for all I have done for these people. 6:3: ""I am carrying on a great project and cannot go down. Why should the work stop while I leave it and go down to you?" 6:16: When all our enemies heard about this, all the surrounding nations were afraid and lost their self-confidence, because they realized that this work had been done with the help of our God. 8:10: The joy of the Lord is my strength. 9:6: "You alone are the Lord." 9:20: "You gave your good Spirit to instruct them." 9:31: "[I]n your great mercy you did not put an end to them or abandon them, for you are a gracious and merciful God." 13:22: "Remember me for this also, my God, and show mercy to me according to your great love."*

Reading Guide

Names

Names are often signifiers in the Bible. The name that God gives the Bible figure, whether through the parents bringing the person into the world or later, on God's own direct command, refers to the figure's position or attribute fitting God's plan. Unfortunately, translations from the original Hebrew or Greek hide those meanings. Those who read or hear in the original language would instantly or soon see the relevance of a name, while instead we find many of the names not only opaque as to any meaning but also unfamiliar. English-language readers don't notice that Jacob is *deceiver* or *trickster*, or that God's new name for him Israel is to *struggle with God*. Place names can also carry meanings, such as Jerusalem as *city of peace* and Bethel as *house of God*. Names can also rhyme or otherwise signify other words in the original language, if not having the exact-same meaning. The Bible's authors were thus often skilled at either declaring qualities or hinting at qualities through names, all hidden to the English-language reader. Don't hesitate to explore person- and place-name meanings. They certainly can add insight and clarity to the Bible's narrative, and at times humor or irony.

Esther

"And who knows but that you have come to your royal position for such a time as this?" 4:14.

Theme. Esther's theme is God's providence, strange though that theme is for a book that does not mention God. Providence suggests the hidden hand of a wholly beneficent God. Unforeseen circumstances, not of our own making, confront and confuse us, and we suffer loss. We wonder, where is God? It must have been so for the leading figures in Esther who faced execution and the annihilation of their people. And yet God, never mentioned, was nonetheless ever present. God had already arranged every stumble, every risk, every loss, and every fall for the ultimate flourishing of his people, those who kept their faith in him when he most seemed absent. Esther records the Jews' spectacular last-second victory over a most-formidable and pernicious opponent. The fortuitous way that victory occurred was so unpredictable and extraordinary as to have certainly been the work not of chance but of God. God's hand moves when and where we least expect it, which is the nature of faith, to expect his hand when nothing yet gives it any indication.

Author. History does not reveal Esther's author. While some wish to credit one of its principal figures Mordecai, who would have had the knowledge, capability, and interest to record the account, the book's lavish credit to the humble Mordecai augurs against his authorship. Instead, the honor the book gives Mordecai may suggest that a protégé of his wrote and preserved the account. The book served the national purpose of explaining the origin of the Jewish celebration of the feast of Purim, recognizing how close the Jews had come to their extermination on the day that the *pur*, or random lot, cast. The book addresses a period between 483 B.C. and 473 B.C., during the first half of king Xerxes' reign, although its author would have written the book somewhat later, between 470 B.C. and 424 B.C., during the reign of Xerxes' son Artaxerxes.

Context. Esther describes events affecting the Israelite community in its Babylonian-then-Persian exile, after the first wave of Israelites had

79

already returned to Jerusalem. That first return was modest, tentative, followed decades later by the second return led by Ezra and third return led by Nehemiah. Thus, when Esther's events occurred, most, indeed nearly all, Israelites remained in exile, evidently with little thought of return, at least insofar as the book Esther expressed no such thought. Esther focuses on the exiles, not any hope or thought of return. Esther's context is thus more like a treatment of the Jewish diaspora, the chosen people's dispersion around the world, and the question of their survival living in at-times-hostile nations. Imagine again the cause for the Purim feast celebration that the Jewish people were not annihilated while living among others. The lessons we draw from Esther we should thus take in that extraordinary context.

Structure. Esther organizes itself into a first seven chapters of increasing distress ending in sudden deliverance, followed by three chapters of relief concluding in celebration. The book unfolds chapter by chapter in well-drawn, tense scenes. Chapter one sees the king's wife refuse his drunken request, resulting in a chapter-two search for a new queen, surprisingly, the beautiful Jewish woman Esther. Chapter three shows the king's leading noble Haman plotting to kill the Jew Mordecai, Esther's cousin and protector, and all Jews with him. The key chapter four shows Esther displaying necessary courage seeking the king's relief. Chapter five shows God's extraordinary deliverance, leading to the king's restless pursuit of appropriate remedy, as chapters six and seven record. Chapter eight shows Mordecai exercising the king's authority to issue the remedial edict, following which the Jews rejoice in chapters nine and ten. Read Esther as you would a well-crafted drama, but more so read it for God's hidden hand supplying the dramatic deliverance.

Key Events. As the prior paragraph indicates, Esther's key events, reading very much like a well-constructed drama, begin with king Xerxes deposing his wife queen Vashti, opening the competition for a new queen, won by Esther, the account suggests, because she pleased the king's eunuch. Esther's cousin Mordecai saved Xerxes by discovering and disclosing an assassination plot. Xerxes chose to honor his leading noble Haman, before whom Mordecai would not kneel, causing Haman to plot Mordecai's execution along with the extermination of all Jews. Mordecai then beseeched Esther to intervene with Xerxes to save the Jews, which Esther bravely did at risk of her own execution. The king simultaneously decided to honor Mordecai for having earlier saved the king from assassination. In the book's dramatic climax, Esther then revealed to the king her Jewish ancestry, begging relief from Haman's plot for extermination. The king indeed had Haman impaled where Haman had planned to execute Mordecai, further granting the Jews the right to annihilate their opponents wherever they found them. See in these and other events the providential work of God.

Key Locations. Susa, Persia's capitol, is the primary location of Esther's dramatic ascension to queen, near execution, and providential rescue, along with the rescue of her cousin Mordecai and the Jews. The book's other major events occur within and around king Xerxes' palace including his throne room, royal gardens, inner court, harem quarters, and even a private palace couch on which Esther reclined. The book records Xerxes sending dispatches out from his Susa palace across all 127 provinces of his great Persian kingdom, stretching from India to Egypt. The account records other events involving Mordecai and Haman, at the king's gate, Haman's house, and open square and city streets of Susa. Esther's locations add a rich historical context and refreshing cosmopolitan air to an already-dramatic account. Read Esther for how God's providence works in the highest secular places.

Revelation of Christ. Esther reveals that God in his providence comes out of nowhere, as Jesus emerged from hundreds of silent years to enter the world through a manger. Through Jesus, God is always present, Jesus having mediated our path into God's intimacy while also having sent us our great helper, God's own Spirit. Esther conceals these revelations of Christ within its spectacular story of the Jews' salvation from extermination. Mordecai took in the orphan Esther, as Jesus takes us in to give us his Father. Esther offered her royal position to save her people, an orphan saving a nation, as Jesus, one too with only a heavenly Father, offered his throne to save all who looked to him. Jesus, like Esther, was willing to perish to save his people, with Jesus, like Esther, trusting in his Father's full providence. One may find hard seeing revelations of Christ in a book like Esther that never mentions God, but Christ is there, just as he is in every other book of the Bible.

Application. Esther's remarkable story of bravery, to the point that she was willing to perish for the good of her people, should remind us not only of God's providence, that he can deliver from the most dire of situations, but also that God's ultimate promise is to deliver us from our inevitable earthly demise. Esther was willing to die. She must for that courage have had the sense of her ultimate deliverance, even if she perished. Mordecai gives us our corollary lesson, that if we do not stand in the gap as we should, then someone else will do so, and we will perish anyway. The book of Esther adorns these lessons in bravery with related lessons in accepting one's difficult lot, as Esther surely did in being taken, very likely against her will, into the extraordinary queen competition. Mordecai also stood by his own odd post, trying to protect his beautiful cousin Esther whom he had raised as an orphan, while also trying first to save the king and then to save his own people. While the book does not mention their earnest prayers to God, it does record their extended fasting, itself a lesson in devotion. Yet while the book models bravery and devotion, its primary lesson is to act in full trust of God's providence, even in the worst of situations. Esther is a brilliant lesson in that providence.

Memory Verses. *1:18: "[W]omen of the nobility who have heard about the queen's conduct will respond to all the king's nobles in the same way. There will be no end of disrespect and discord." 4:13-14: ""Do not think that because you are in the king's house you alone of all the Jews will escape. For if you remain silent at this time, relief and deliverance for the Jews will arise from another place, but you and your father's family will perish. And who knows but that you have come to your royal position for such a time as this?" 4:16: "I will go to the king, even though it is against the law. And if I perish, I perish."*

Wisdom

The traditional way of referring to the next five Bible books after the dozen history books is to call them *wisdom literature*. The five wisdom books include Job, Psalms, Proverbs, Ecclesiastes, and Song of Songs. They are, in fact, highly diverse writings in their forms, including an extended conversation within an extraordinary narrative, a large collection of poetry, collected sayings following a remarkable introduction of their inspirational figure, a harsh reflection over a most-extraordinary life, and a semi-erotic love song. Yet wisdom indeed unites these diverse writings. The books tell and teach of the way to live life at its best, not to waste it nor to over-indulge in its sensual attractions but to flourish in best health and society, not just to return to dust but to return to God as our loving creator.

The wisdom books, then, are not simply helpful guides, not merely philosophical musings nor self-improvement texts. They instead relate closely to the Bible's deeper narrative, beginning with Genesis's account of God's creation of humankind, humans' fall, and the struggle of humans to regain their relationship with God, to once again enjoy eternally his garden blessing. To read the wisdom books as self-help literature may well provide some benefit but would very much be to miss their larger point, which is the Bible's point. God has a purpose for humankind, which is to love us so extraordinarily as to compel our greatest passion for him in our greatest intimacy. In shorthand, we call that purpose *glorifying God*. Read the wisdom literature to see clearly how one glorifies God.

Job

"I know that my redeemer lives and that in the end he will stand on the earth." 19:25.

Theme. The theme of the book Job is human suffering. Job deals directly, openly, in extended conversational focus, with what every one of us eventually faces and some of us face often, even constantly. We all suffer, yes, some worse and longer than others, but we all suffer. Moreover, suffering, in the hardship that it works, eventually demands explanation or at least some appreciable context for its understanding, especially when we do not perceive the suffering to have its justification. We suffer unfairly at times, even brutally, often chaotically, against what seems like any rationale, gain, or equity. The hardship of suffering lies not only in its excruciating physical pain and mental and emotional distress but in our inability to comprehend its purpose. Extraordinarily, brilliantly, and shockingly, the book Job gives the reader, from the mouth of God himself, context for understanding the worst of suffering.

Author. We have no clear evidence for Job's author. Those who have studied the question speculate that Job himself may have written the book that, after all, focuses on his story and includes so many of his own words. The book refers to Job only in the third person, although doing so would not have been unusual for an ancient author. Job, the book tells us, was a wealthy landowner, husband, father, and employer. Beyond that, we know little of Job, neither when he lived, among what people, with what heritage or as a member of what tribe. Other speculation is that one of Job's four visiting friends, each of whom would have witnessed the full discourse, was the book's author. The most-likely friend may have been the last friend to speak, and wiser of them, which was Elihu. Some tradition credits Moses as the author. Modern scholars tend to date the book in its canonical form well after Moses, as late as the sixth or fifth centuries before Christ, during Israel's exile, although much earlier versions of Job stories surely exist, well back into antiquity, as early as 2000 B.C. Several references support such an early date, including Job's long life, form of wealth, El Shaddai (God Almighty) honorific for God, and equal treatment of male and female offspring, inappropriate under the later Mosaic law, of which the book makes no mention. Insoluble questions over authorship and date probably add to, rather than detract from, the book's value.

Context. Job is a perfect first wisdom book in that it deals directly with humankind's greatest obstacle to understanding anything. Wisdom is applied understanding, knowledge in fitting action. Who can act, with any confidence, without first knowing how to countenance suffering? We all have our trite and dismissive explanations until—bang!—suffering clobbers us in the face. If wisdom is to build a foundation, then it must build that foundation over our worst fear, which is inexplicable and irremediable personal disaster. Job accomplishes that formidable feat, sending the reader soberly on to other wisdom books, each with their own function. Job's position following several books documenting Israel's long, declining history, and its final tentative return to a shambles Jerusalem, during which it again faced annihilation, makes further sense of Job's instructive, even remedial purpose. Israel's history, not just our own individual history, is one of suffering, context for which Job also supplies.

Structure. Job's structure is to fit its long and ultimately unproductive discourse (save for a few key points) between a brief but critically important introduction and only a little-longer and highly surprising concluding answer. Job's introduction records an extraordinary exchange between God and Satan as to how to test and treat the figure Job's evident righteousness, as to which God gives Satan permission to inflict disaster on Job. The book then proceeds with four visiting figures trying to justify Job's suffering to Job and one another, as humans generally justify and rationalize things. The friends fail in their long effort to either comfort, counsel, or correct Job, although they draw out of Job key points about his own view of his suffering. God then intervenes with Job, answering Job's questions over his own suffering, in God's utterly distinct fashion. The book ends with a brief denouement in which God restores Job to greater wealth than ever, has three of his friends offer sacrifices, and has Job intervene with God for them, lest God judge them as they judged Job. No book is like Job, its own remarkable treasure within the Bible.

Key Events. Job's key events begin with its extraordinary discourse between God and Satan in which God granted Satan license to mistreat Job as proof of Job's righteousness. Satan promptly destroyed Job's family, health, and wealth. Job's three friends joined him, sitting silently with him in commiseration for a full week. Their long discourse then began, one speaker challenging and correcting another, no speaker satisfying Job whose own speech only further frustrates his friends. The friends intended to console but instead judged and condemned. Job rejected both their consolation and judgment, at times turning his accusations to God. A fourth friend Elihu appears in chapter thirty-two, apparently having been present for the full conversation but, the text tells us, having reserved speaking in deference to his older friends. Elihu was little more successful in rescuing the desultory discourse, the only high point of which is Job's mid-discourse declaration, at verse 19:25, that he knew his redeemer lives. But then the Lord spoke to Job out of the storm, declaring his sovereign role as all-knowing Creator of a majestic creation. God did not answer Job directly, instead setting Job's suffering within the grandeur of God's design. God, though, accepted Job's contention in which Job continued to embrace, rather than reject, God. The book's epilogue records God restoring Job beyond his former wealth, after God accepts his friends' sacrificial offering.

Key Locations. Job's first chapter indicates that Job lived in the land of Uz, as the greatest man among all the people of the East. Geographers cannot say definitively where Uz was, although the text suggests a region outside of Israel's promised home, the land of Canaan. Those familiar with the region and its natural life, husbandry practices, and other features see some evidence from Job's text that its setting may have been in northern Arabia. Again, the inability of readers to rest firmly on a location probably adds to the book's value, rather than detracting from it. Job's message applies outside of time and place.

Revelation of Christ. Think of Job's key verse in which the suffering main figure says that he (1) *knows* that he has a (2) *living redeemer* who (3) *in the end* will (4) *stand on the earth.* What a profound profession of the pre-existent and yet-then-unborn Savior Jesus Christ. The book Job reveals as its central tenet that first we must *know* something specific about our future, even when the worst of times assures our death. Such knowledge in the lack of evidence means to have faith. The one thing we must know is that we have a *living redeemer* Christ. Christ lives, and Christ redeems, which means to bring us back from our precipice of death. Christ not only lives to redeem but does so *in the end*, meaning ultimately, beyond anything else that may confront or delay us. And when the living Christ redeems us, he does not do so into some philosophical force or distant vapor but instead to *stand on the earth.*

Christ came, he conquered, and he will return to earth to bring his redeemed paradise, our eternal home, with him.

Application. Job's application quickly becomes obvious to the discerning reader. We all suffer in ways that we can only sometimes understand. Yet we can always trust that God is our redeemer. We know that Christ rose from crucifixion and that he lives to offer us the same. We further know that Christ's redemption extends beyond our souls to all creation including his earth. God's peace is not something that we always understand. Philippians 4:7 says that his peace transcends understanding and yet that God still guards our hearts and minds in his Son Jesus. Job's lesson, then, is that we turn to God for his comfort in all our troubles so that, as 2 Corinthians 1:4 further states, we can likewise comfort others. We ought, as Job's companions at first did, sit in silence with those who suffer, sharing only our compassion without attempting justifying words. God holds justification. He has the big picture, wholly beneficial purpose, and big plans. The book Job cries out to us: trust God! Trust God! And it does so, in God's grand rejoinder, in gorgeous poetry.

Memory Verses. *1:7: The Lord said to Satan, "Where have you come from?" Satan answered the Lord, "From roaming throughout the earth, going back and forth on it." 1:21: "Naked I came from my mother's womb, and naked I will depart. The Lord gave and the Lord has taken away; may the name of the Lord be praised." 2:10: "Shall we accept good from God, and not trouble?" 7:11: "Therefore, I will not keep silent; I will speak out in the anguish of my spirit, I will complain in the bitterness of my soul." 7:17: ""What is mankind that you make so much of them, that you give them so much attention, that you examine them every morning and test them every moment?" 9:2-3: "how can mere mortals prove their innocence before God? Though they wished to dispute with him, they could not answer him one time out of a thousand." 9:33: "If only there were someone to mediate between us, someone to bring us together, someone to remove God's rod from me, so that his terror would frighten me no more." 13:15: "Though he slay me, yet will I hope in him; I will surely defend my ways to his face." 19:25-26: "I know that my redeemer lives and that in the end he will stand on the earth. And after my skin has been destroyed, yet in my flesh I will see God...." 38:2-4: "Who is this that obscures my plans with words without knowledge? Brace yourself like a man; I will question you, and you shall answer me. Where were you when I laid the earth's foundation? Tell me, if you understand." 42:3: "Surely I spoke of things I did not understand,* *things too wonderful for me to know." 42:5-6: "I have heard of You by the hearing of the ear; but now my eye sees You; therefore I retract, and I repent in dust and ashes."*

Reading Guide

Patterns

The Bible's authors fill it with patterns illustrating God's purpose, pointing to Christ. Its dozens of inspired authors, writing down through the centuries with the Holy Spirit's guidance, recorded these patterns declaring God's intent. God choosing the younger son over the older son, the second over the first, despite the natural order to favor the oldest, is one such pattern. The pattern repeats from God favoring Abel over his elder brother Cain to God choosing Isaac over the elder half-brother Ishmael, Jacob over the elder brother Esau, Joseph over his older brothers, Ephraim over his elder brother Manasseh, Moses over his elder brother Aaron, Gideon over his older brothers, and David over his older brothers. The pattern, enriched by each story's details, suggests that God prefers the supernaturally fit, those who know God's will, over the naturally favored.

Humans looking to a tree for life is another such pattern. God first shows Adam and Eve the garden of Eden's tree of life, from which they never get to eat because they first ate of the prohibited tree of the knowledge of good and evil. God later has Noah build an ark out of trees to save human and animal life. God then has Moses throw a tree branch in bitter waters to quench the thirst of, and to revive and save, the wandering Israelites. God then has Israelites, whom poisonous snakes have bitten, look on a snake lifted on a stick, to save their lives. The pattern repeats itself until men lift Jesus on a tree, saving all those who look to him. Read for these patterns, especially those that most point us to Christ.

Psalms

> Your word is a lamp for my feet, a light on my path.
> 119:105.

Theme. Assigning a single theme to the long book of Psalms risks oversimplifying their diverse entries, which address the full spectrum of human emotions. The Greek word from which we draw *psalms*, like the original Hebrew word translated into Greek, means *praise songs*, although not all the Psalms exhibit praise. The frank emotion of the Psalms may better indicate *intimacy* as the book's singular theme, especially in the form of *worship*. Above all else, the Psalms reveal how fit the human heart is to converse and commune with its Creator. Not every Psalm is a prayer, though many are prayers and many others contain passages of prayer. But all Psalms show how intensely, how closely, how totally we dwell with God as his subordinate and dependent, but nonetheless in-his-image co-rulers of his creation. Whether the Psalms shout in anger, confess in humility, lament in loss, prostrate in awe, or thank in full gratitude, they still show the human heart yearning for God in its deepest reaches. Other Bible books also reveal the intensity that humans show for God relationship, in their longing, but the Psalms leave the longing human heart utterly exposed. He made us for him.

Author. David wrote seventy-three, or just about one-half, of the hundred-and-fifty Psalms, by attribution, with several of those Psalms including numbers 34, 52, 56, and 59 referring to specific events of his life that 1 Samuel documents. Yet some of the Psalms appear to date hundreds of years earlier to Moses' time. Other Psalms appear to have later dates, all the way to Ezra's period of the second return after Israel's Babylonian/Persian exile. If as it appears authors contributed Psalms across all those periods, then the book's reflections cover the span of one-thousand years, collected one by one, and curated over that millennium into their compiled, five-part form. Readers have every reason to value the Psalms not just for their eloquence, inspired content, and antiquity, but also for the number, diversity, and extraordinarily long perspective of their several or many authors.

Context. The Psalms fit well between Job's prior story of God-tested, God-justified, and God-rescued suffering and Proverbs' subsequent collection of wisdom sayings. Job shows God as the inspired, beneficent, participant, and controlling creator, while Proverbs gives detailed lessons in the structure of his paradise-borne design. In between, the book of Psalms forms the beating heart of humankind's cry for what each prior and subsequent book Job and Proverbs offer. The Bible's grand narrative captures many fervent cries for God's intimate relationship and full blessing. By collecting many more such cries in a single spectacular book, Psalms achieves something greater that the Bible's distributed plaints could not. One cannot come away from having read Psalms without marveling at humankind's long, loving, and dependent, but also tumultuous, relationship with God. Psalms has the purpose and function of ensuring that the reader knows the human heart for God. No other book, scriptural or otherwise, comes close to achieving what Psalms so compellingly achieves in fulfilling its essential function.

Structure. Psalms has the structure of five books within its one long book. Each of the five books, including as few as seventeen psalms up to as many as forty-one psalms, suggests a successive theme, within Psalms' larger theme of songs of intimate praise. The first forty-one psalms address our humanity. The next thirty-one psalms address God's deliverance of humanity. The next seventeen psalms address God's sanctuary for humankind. The next seventeen psalms carry the theme of God's reign over the earth. And the last forty-four psalms dwell on God's word. Successive themes of humanity, deliverance, sanctuary, reign, and word suggest both a journey and an ascent, which the Psalms clearly intend to fully illustrate. Readers can dive into and out of the Psalms, drawing inspiration, solace, courage, discernment, and other goods from any one or few of them. Yet reading the Psalms within their structure lends greater meaning consistent with the Bible's grand goal.

Key Events. While Psalms collects poetic song rather than being an event-driven narrative, one nonetheless finds within Psalms evidence of key events. Psalm 34, for instance, bears a subtitle introduction that David wrote it when pretending insanity for rescue from Abimelek. Psalm 52 bears a similar subtitle introduction that David wrote it when Doeg the Edomite betrayed him to Saul. Psalm 56's subtitle states that David wrote it when the Philistines had seized him in Gath. And Psalm 59's subtitle states that David wrote it when Saul sent men to his house to kill him. These psalms do not make these events obvious. Only their subtitles clearly express the events. But one can see how each of these psalms relate to their subtitled events. One readily imagines from these examples that each entry in the book Psalms had similarly stimulating circumstances. One should thus read the Psalms with deep appreciation for those untold circumstances, as each psalm suggests them. The Psalms' authors were real people experiencing real, even historic, events. Those events surely included births, deaths, disease, vanquishing, wars, festivals, pilgrimages, coronations, and victories, among most-everything else that persons might experience.

Key Locations. As the prior paragraph indicates, a few psalms do reveal in subtitles certain events, each of which occurred in a certain location. Odd to say, though, that the more-relevant locus for the Psalms is the interior of the human heart rather than any exterior geographical place. David, for instance, could have written his psalms of fear, courage, protection, revenge, and struggle from any location, from the stronghold cave of Adullam under Saul's attack, to David's own palace under Absalom's revolt. The point of each psalm isn't its exterior context but its interior view of the author's relationship with his Creator. Yet the Psalms do follow place-related patterns. Rocks, trees, seas, rivers, other waters, mountains, hills, fields, pastures, houses, cities, and streets, not to mention sun, moon, and stars, are places to which multiple psalms refer. The Psalms' imagery is thus more significant than the Psalms' geographical locations. Read the Psalms for imagery and pattern, especially to connect the imagery with Genesis's creation-and-fall narrative, as other books likewise do. While geography can lend much to a narrative, the Bible is less a geography book than God's grand narrative for how his creation reveals his character.

Revelation of Christ. That the Psalms reveal the God-centered human heart is itself a witness to Christ, whose ministry of love was to transform hearts. The Psalms show both the intensity and intimacy of which the human heart is capable in its relationship with God, just as Christ showed the far-greater intensity and intimacy of his relationship with the Father. Yet individual psalms also point to Christ. Psalm 2 announces Christ as the Father's Son whom the Father would grant nations as his heritage. Psalm 16 reassured Jesus that his Father would not abandon his soul nor let him see corruption. Psalm 22 is Christ's cry to his Father, prophesying how men would mock and insult him as crucifixion pierced his hands and feet, and pulled his bones out of joint, quoted by Christ on the cross. Psalm 23 is Christ as our shepherd, leading us beside his still waters and through our valley of death's shadow, so that we may dwell with him in the Lord's house forever. Psalm 24 prophecies heaven's celebration when its ancient gates open for the King of kings to return to his throne of glory. Psalm 68 prophecies Christ ascending with his host of captives. Psalm 110 records God's invitation that Christ sit at his right hand while God made his enemies his footstool. Matthew 21:42 records Jesus quoting Psalm 118:22 that he is the builders' rejected stone become the whole structure's cornerstone. One cannot read the Psalms as a whole or individually without recognizing their witness to the glory of our Lord Jesus Christ.

Application. Given the Psalms' focus on the heart, perhaps the best way to apply the Psalms is in meditation. Take any mood, any attitude, any moment's reflection, and you will find a Psalm through which to sing, mourn, celebrate, comfort, console, counsel, or otherwise guide your heart in meditation. No matter the mood, no matter the challenge, no matter the opportunity for worship, the Psalms journey with you. The Psalms lie in wait to capture your heart for God, hold your mind and attention, light your passion, and guide your fleeting and whimsical emotions into something so rich that you will treasure more of his relationship. Make the Psalms your well for emotion. Draw from the Psalms deeply, drinking Christ's water of life. Let Psalm 103:3 convince you that God forgives all your sins and Psalms 138:8 and 139:1 that God knows you and has his purpose for you. Let Psalms 22, 23, and 24 point you to Jesus, your shepherd and King of glory.

Memory Verses. 2:12: Kiss his son, or he will be angry and your way will lead to your destruction.... 13:1: How long, Lord? Will you forget me forever? How long will you hide your face from me? 19:7: The law of the Lord is perfect, refreshing the soul. 22:1: My God, my God, why have you forsaken me? 23:4: Even though I walk through the valley of the shadow of death, I will fear no evil, for you are with me.... 27:1: The Lord is my light and my salvation— whom shall I fear? 37:25: I was young and now I am old, yet I have never seen the righteous forsaken or their children begging bread. 46:1: God is our refuge and strength, an ever-present help in trouble. 51:1: Have mercy on me, O God, according to your unfailing love; according to your great compassion blot out my transgressions. 55:22: Cast your cares on the Lord and he will sustain you; he will never let the righteous be shaken. 91:1: Whoever dwells in the shelter of the Most High will rest in the shadow of the Almighty. 147:3: He heals the brokenhearted and binds up their wounds. 100:1-2: Shout for joy to the Lord, all the earth. Worship the Lord with gladness;

come before him with joyful songs. 121:1-2: I lift up my eyes to the mountains—where does my help come from? My help comes from the Lord, the Maker of heaven and earth.

Reading Guide

Inversions

Pattern inversions are a common biblical technique. A pattern repeats itself from story to story, until the pattern reverses itself in the revealed archetype. So, it is with the types of Christ. When God created Adam, the first human, in his image, he revealed a pattern of the Son of Man, Jesus Christ, to come. Adam, though, failed as God's chosen partner, as did his son Cain, Cain's offspring, God's chosen Noah, Abraham, Moses, David, and Solomon. Each figure, supposed to lead God's people to relationship with God, had at most temporary success. Each rebelled and succumbed, the people failing as a result. Christ, though, inverted the pattern. Jesus came as the Son of Man, the perfect human, whose servant leadership would save God's people, indeed all humankind, through perfect sacrifice.

At critical junctures, the Bible inverts patterns, arresting the eye, ear, and mind. The Bible's inversions show that God, the supernatural creator, is not subject to the natural. With every inversion, God breaks through, transforming the human heart, ushering in his kingdom, and bringing new possibilities, even eternal life. God does not act as humans act, nor has he set his creation to naturally work without him. He continues to act, while material, social, political, and economic orders do not constrain him. And so, though, the sun marches across the sky, east to west, for millennia, God once makes the sun stand still. Though women conceive babies only with the natural aid of men, God once sends his Spirit to the virgin Mary to bring forth his perfect Son. As Mary herself sang, God lowers the proud to elevate the humble and impoverishes the rich to bless the poor. Jesus multiplies a few loaves of bread to feed five thousand, inverting human scarcity into abundance, but then withers the fruitless fig tree, inverting the capable but unproductive into scarcity. These reversals are acts of God, revealing his nature and desire. Bible inversions may indeed be necessary to reveal God's action within his created order. How else would God reveal himself acting within his own creation, when his creation already reveals himself?

Proverbs

Trust in the Lord with all your heart and lean not on your own understanding; in all your ways submit to him, and he will make your paths straight. 3:5-6.

Theme. Proverbs' theme is wisdom, the underlying subject of its surrounding books but a theme that Proverbs takes on directly. From start to finish, Proverbs tells the reader that its goal is to help make the reader wise. Yet given its setting within the Bible, and the opening reference Proverbs makes to wisdom finding its foundation in fear of the Lord, Proverbs has a specific idea of what it means to be wise. The worldly might define wise as clever, articulate, smart, entertaining, attractive of mind, or capable. Proverbs, though, instead defines wisdom as the kind of flourishing that humans would have had under God in his Eden garden and yet can still have to degrees if they submit reverently to the Lord. The individual sayings that the book collects show that godly flourishing under wisdom can look like a lot of things. It doesn't, for instance, always mean great wealth. It may generally mean more-secure provision, better relationships, and better health, although it offers no guarantees. Instead, Proverbs assures that respecting its sayings, as one lives a godly life, will foster the humility that one must have to abide and serve under the Lord. Proverbs' goal may seem to be improving one's life, like self-help literature, but its goal is most assuredly not. Rather, its goal is the same goal of every Bible book, which is to draw one closer to the good, good Lord.

Author. Proverbs credits authorship of most of its material to Solomon, although the account admits that Solomon collected some of the book's sayings from other sources. Proverbs also has two sections credited to other authors Agur and Lemuel, neither of whom history identifies. Solomon would have written his proverbs, and collected others, before his death in 931 B.C. Proverbs 25-29 indicates that scribes under Judah's king Hezekiah, who reigned more than two-hundred years later, collected those sayings of Solomon. Thus, the book had a much later final-compilation date than the period of the reign of Solomon. That later compilation does not detract from but rather confirms the book's place as the center of the Jews' practical lessons for living, just as Christians have also now for millennia drawn from it.

Context. Proverbs' wisdom theme is the same theme that constitutes the other four Bible books of which Proverbs is at the center, Job and Psalms before Proverbs and Ecclesiastes and Song of Songs after it. All five books address wisdom from one angle or another, although two of them in narrative form, one in a modified narrative, and one in a love song. Proverbs, though, intends that the reader embrace its wisdom theme practically and directly, much more like instruction, a lesson rather than an allegory or suggestive tale. Yet Proverbs also has significant narrative context in the reign and life of Solomon. Given Proverbs' intimate connection with Israel's renowned king Solomon, who reigned at the height of Israel's worldly wealth and influence, that context should inform readers. Solomon, we know from 1 Kings 3-4, asked God for wisdom, a request that God granted to such a generous degree that Solomon's wisdom drew world renown. Proverbs resonates with that history, including the Queen of Sheba's attesting visit. Read Proverbs knowing how much its sayings have meant to how many in leading a godly life, while also reading it knowing the remarkable life of the one who under the Spirit's inspiration authored it.

Structure. Proverbs is much more than a random collection of sayings. Proverbs instead has a three-part structure. Its remarkable first part, comprised of Proverbs' first nine chapters and including some sayings, is a dramatic warning, demonstration, and justification for wise living. In Proverbs' first part, a father exhorts his sons to heed lady wisdom, contrasting the caution of the wise with the heedless abandon of the fool. Proverbs' first part thus gives the reader compelling reason to heed the book's following advice. Proverbs' first part also serves to connect the book with the Bible's larger narrative, especially Genesis's garden narrative of the fall, when humans first substituted their own judgment of what would be good and bad for them, for the commands and wisdom of God. Proverbs' second part, forming the book's corpus, presents the many couplet sayings, practical principles for the reader to follow for the good life. The book ends in chapter thirty-one with a personification of wise living, using the illustration of a wife of noble character. Savor Proverbs' principles, for which readers pursue the book, but don't miss the marvelous material with which the author bracketed those principles. The eternal message of any Bible book isn't in its small lessons but rather its greater narrative.

Key Events. Proverbs' key events are either contextual or allegorical. Contextual events, mentioned just above, include Solomon's prayer for wisdom, God's generous answer, and the Queen of Sheba's visit attesting to those events. Proverbs' allegorical events occur within its remarkable introduction. Proverbs 1:20 has wisdom calling openly in the public square, crying out at the city gate. Following chapters record a father exhorting his sons to pursue and heed the lady wisdom. Chapter nine says that wisdom has built her house, while folly sits at her own house's door inviting in the fool whose eyes and heart wander. In these and other ways, Proverbs introduces a practical sense of time and place into its lessons, making the book much more than a set of principles and instead more like wisdom's illustration.

Key Locations. As the prior paragraph suggests, Proverbs has symbolic locations that serve its instructive goal quite well. Solomon and the other authors of Proverbs' sayings were not Athenian philosophers. The book makes no pretense of drawing the reader away into abstract constructs. Rather, the sayings embed themselves in the ordinary places and events of life. Wisdom and folly compete in the public square and city streets. Both sit in front of their houses, each beckoning in their own way to passersby, each to opposite ends. These place references adorn the sayings themselves. Proverbs 14:1 has wisdom building a house, one that Proverbs 12:7 says stands firm and Proverbs 15:6 says holds great treasure, these among dozens of other house references. Similarly, Proverbs 24:27 says to get your fields ready before building your house, Proverbs 13:23 and 21:4 warning to be sure to plow your fields, and Proverbs 27:26 and 31: 16 urging to buy such fields out of your earnings. The sayings demonstrate economic and moral principles using actions in ordinary places, making Proverbs highly accessible, even deliberately humorous in places. Thus, better to live on the corner of your roof than in your house with a quarrelsome spouse, Proverbs 21:9 and 25:24 tell us. Delight in the familiarity of Proverbs' places.

Revelation of Christ. As a book of wisdom sayings, one might assume that Proverbs has little to say about Jesus Christ. That supposition would be wrong for at least two reasons. First, Proverbs 8:22-31, deep in the book's splendid introduction, reveals Christ so directly that it was among the prophetic Hebrew Bible passages that the early church distinctly embraced. Revealing Jesus, the passage tells us that wisdom was with the Lord before his ancient deeds, at the very beginning, delighting not only in the Lord's presence but also in the Lord's creation, especially humankind. This and other passages in

Proverbs' introduction make clear that the book's sayings emanate as attributes of Christ's divinity. If, as 1 Corinthians 1:24 confirms, Christ is God's wisdom, then Proverbs in its every reference to wisdom describes none other than Jesus Christ. Every saying reflects the character of Christ. We ask today what Jesus would do, and in Proverbs we find the answers. God's wisdom, Christ, is from the Father, as the exact representation of the Father's being, Hebrews 1:1-3 tells us. God's wisdom is the pattern of both creation and its redemption, in and through Christ.

Application. Proverbs should be the easiest of Bible books to apply because of the direct and practical nature of its lessons, together with their simplicity and numerosity. Proverbs gives a ton of direct, simple advice. Yet doing what Proverbs exhorts is not easy. If it were, then we wouldn't need its lessons. Proverbs' sayings often cut against the ingrained selfishness and sin of the human condition, which is exactly their value. Listen to Proverbs' cautions, and then follow them. Turn, for instance, from the knee-jerk, emotional response that you wish to make to your neighbor's insult, and instead do as Proverbs 12:16 says, which is to overlook an insult. The Hebrew Bible is meditation literature, not meant for a once-over reading but instead meant to be read and re-read constantly, embraced, mulled, and incorporated into character to produce life action. Treat Proverbs as a dear friend from whom you benefit by constant listening. Do not let your relationship with Proverbs' wisdom, who is the Son of God, grow cold.

Memory Verses. 1:7: The fear of the Lord is the beginning of knowledge, but fools despise wisdom and instruction. 3:1-2: My son, do not forget my teaching, but keep my commands in your heart, for they will prolong your life many years and bring you peace and prosperity. 3:5-6: Trust in the Lord with all your heart and lean not on your own understanding; in all your ways submit to him, and he will make your paths straight. 4:7: Get wisdom. Though it cost all you have, get understanding. 8:22-23: "The Lord brought me forth as the first of his works, before his deeds of old; I was formed long ages ago, at the very beginning, when the world came to be." 10:12: Hatred stirs up conflict, but love covers over all wrongs. 12:1: Whoever loves discipline loves knowledge, but whoever hates correction is stupid. 13:24: Whoever spares the rod hates their children, but the one who loves their children is careful to discipline them. 15:1: A gentle answer turns away wrath, but a harsh word stirs up anger. 18:21: The tongue has the power of life and death, and those who love it will eat its fruit. 21:2: A person may think their own ways are right, but the Lord weighs the heart. 31:10: A wife of noble character who can find? She is worth far more than rubies.

Reading Guide

Imagery

The Bible's authors fill it with imagery, from Genesis's creation story at the beginning right through to Revelation at the Bible's end. Indeed, Genesis's creation narrative and Revelation's end-time visions are among the most imagery-laden texts in the whole of the Bible, although the writings, especially Psalms, and the prophetical books, are also heavy with evocative images. We read of waters, skies, gardens, plants, fruits, forests, and trees. We read of stones, boulders, rocks, hills, valleys, mounts, and mountains. The Bible gives us birds of the air, animals of the land, livestock of the pasture and pen, and creatures of the sea. Texts offer us villages, towns, and cities, and their walls, towers, squares, and streets. We also read of human imagery, whether kings, queens, princes, princesses, merchants, landowners, shepherds, or slaves. And the Bible offers divine imagery, too, of angels, cherubim, elohim, fantastic creatures, and beasts, dragons, and other evil spirits.

Readers can simply follow the Bible's narrative, enjoying the scenery along the way. The text alone communicates so much, without deep reflection on its imagery. Not all imagery is symbolic. Sometimes, a tree or mountain is simply a landmark, not a message. Yet the imagery is often there for a purpose. Sometimes, the narrative makes those purposes obvious. Jesus taught in parables and, at times, explained privately to his disciples the point of his parable's imagery. Other passages reveal directly the purpose of certain imagery. More often, the authors are not explicit in those purposes, either expecting their ancient audience to know or inviting curious audiences to investigate. Let the narrative and context suggest how an author may be using imagery. Don't let your imagination run wild, but if the Spirit nudges you to reflect, then do so consistent with the narrative's larger purposes.

Ecclesiastes

Now all has been heard; here is the conclusion of the matter: fear God and keep his commandments, for this is the duty of all mankind. 12:13.

Theme. Ecclesiastes' theme is vanity, a word that the book repeats frequently in final assessment of the various human striving that the book records. Translations give the vanity theme different twists, sometimes as *meaningless*, other times as *nonsense, futility*, or even *vapor*. All convey the sense of a chasing after the wind, fruitlessness, waste. Every life fills itself with ambitions and activities that in retrospect can look these ways, as having no value, utility, good, or sense. Why, Ecclesiastes asks, do we even try? Why do we even bother? Ecclesiastes so determinedly drives home its vanity point that the book takes on dark cast, as despairing or more despairing than any other Bible book, which clearly is its goal. Ecclesiastes wants the reader to despair of every worldly pursuit that the reader might believe of value. Ecclesiastes is adamant: anything of the world, no matter how rich, pleasurable, aesthetic, or sensual, has no ultimate value.

Author. Tradition, both Jewish and Christian, credits Solomon with writing Ecclesiastes, for which the book itself has internal evidence. The teacher calls himself the son of David and king in Jerusalem, who would have been Solomon. We also know from 1 Kings of Solomon's renowned wisdom. Ecclesiastes attributes its words to the *teacher* or *preacher*, a reference to the book's title, which means to call out an assembly. Some translations use the name Ecclesiastes as the translation for teacher wherever it appears within the book. English draws its words ecclesiastical and church from the same root. Solomon may thus have intended the book to be his capstone address, reflecting over the extraordinary achievements of his unprecedented life. Solomon would have written Ecclesiastes sometime before his 931 B.C. death, probably later in his life when his hundreds of wives, vast wealth, and kingdom strife may well have wearied him.

Context. Ecclesiastes indeed has that historical context of Israel having reached its political, military, and wealth peak, where it yet found things not so different at that peak as from the valleys. Solomon's reign began in glory with the building of the temple, God's filling the temple, and Solomon building an even more-extensive palace, his coffers filled with the gold of nations. At that peak, though, Solomon married his many foreign wives who turned his heart to foreign idols. He also allied Israel with foreign powers. Relying no longer on God but on the strategies and diplomacies of humankind, Solomon's rule quickly fell from grace, so utterly as to divide the kingdom and plant its seeds of destruction in exile. Vanity indeed. Solomon would have had the personal perspective to write from firsthand experience of the desultory effects of chasing after the wind. Ecclesiastes has the canonical context of following the three main wisdom books Job, Psalms, and Proverbs, not as an afterthought but as a warning. Accept and embrace Ecclesiastes' warning.

Structure. Ecclesiastes brief introduction, comprising its first eleven verses, firmly establishes what the book's remainder then proves: all human pursuits independent of God are meaningless. The balance of Ecclesiastes' first eleven chapters, the book devotes to proof in clear order. First, chasing after knowledge is meaningless, then pursuing pleasure is equally vain, then tireless work, then reputation and relationship, and finally wealth, all pointless vapor. Ecclesiastes uses the end of its eleventh chapter and its concluding chapter twelve not to further prove its desultory point but to draw conclusions from it. Ecclesiastes 12:1 finally makes that turn, beginning, "So, remember your Creator in the days of your youth," repeating at 12:6-7, "Remember your Creator before … the dust goes back into the ground—just as it was before, and the spirit goes back to God who gave it." Ecclesiastes 12:12 reiterates, "This is the conclusion of the matter. Everything has been heard. Fear God and keep his commandments. For mankind, this is everything." Walking with God is the sole meaningful human pursuit, better assumed early than late. Read Ecclesiastes first for its proof but then for its final lesson.

Key Events. Ecclesiastes' key events are the teacher's efforts at pursuing meaning, searching for a solution to his vanity problem. Aiding the teacher in that effort is the teacher's great power, position, and wealth. As the prior paragraph on the book's structure indicates, the teacher first pursues knowledge, then pleasure, then great projects, position, and wealth. For the bulk of Ecclesiastes, the book's only evident actions are the teacher's own striving. Key events, then, become his repeated frustrated, discouraged, even sullen responses to his efforts. As Ecclesiastes 9:2 summarizes, "Everything turns out the same for everyone." Yet Ecclesiastes does offer another key event, drawn out through the brief course of its chapter twelve, which is the teacher's turn from proving his point to drawing his great lesson from it. God's fear, which the reader should take to meant reverent obedience to him, is our one beneficial purpose. Reaching that conclusion is indeed one's key event, even if it takes a lifetime of other pursuits to learn it.

Key Locations. Ecclesiastes is not a book of specific geographic location, of which it mentions none. Presumably, Solomon wrote and collected most of his insights in and around Jerusalem, even in his palace, of which Ecclesiastes makes no mention. Instead, Ecclesiastes repeats twenty-seven to twenty-nine times (depending on translations) a key phrase *under the sun*, highlighting its one significant location. Interpreters draw different conclusions, but the Hebrew idiom can mean in the material, physical world, rather than in the spiritual world or heaven. Under the sun reflects human pursuit without spiritual dimension, earth bound and separated from God. In its repeated references to what happens under the sun, Ecclesiastes thus assesses a materialistic, naturalistic worldview, without God. When Ecclesiastes 1:9 asserts that nothing is new under the sun, the verse likely means that any human invention, of which we certainly see many, has no future and is instead lost without God. The earth, and human nature within it, will not change without the participation of God. God alone redeems, and Ecclesiastes makes its one significant location a way of confirming it.

Revelation of Christ. The prior paragraph shows that the naturalistic worldview of the frustrated teacher in Ecclesiastes serves like a photographic negative of the world without Christ. In that sense, Ecclesiastes is all about Christ, revealing Christ in the world by assessing the world without Christ. Life is not meaningless, not hopeless and futile, in the embrace of Christ, only without Christ, as Ecclesiastes portrays life under the sun. Yet Christ does appear in Ecclesiastes, which twenty-five times refers to wisdom, that which we have already seen is Christ. Indeed, some have read Ecclesiastes 9:14-15 to be a reference to Christ, when relating the story of a poor man who by his wisdom saved a city from a great siege against it. Christ, the wise poor man, saves against both the siege of death and judgment of God. He also elevates life from its naturalistic dust-to-dust cycle into an eternal divine relationship in paradise. Find Christ in Ecclesiastes. He's there.

Application. Ecclesiastes 3 is one of the Bible's best-known passages, reminding us that a time exists for everything. Striving without God produces disharmony, imbalance. Too much of anything, even things that are good in appropriate measure, can do much harm, whether too much work or too much pleasure. Ecclesiastes teaches balance, to discern God's time for each thing, even things that appear opposites. Ecclesiastes 4:9 also teaches that two are better than one, and three even better. We ought not live in isolation but instead join with others to pursue God together. Ecclesiastes ends with its best application, which is to stand always in awe of God. In all circumstances, have the disposition to obey God. Ecclesiastes teaches that direct pursuit of the good life does not produce that goal. Some things we can only achieve by pursuing other things. Pursue God, and he will give you the good life that you desire.

Memory Verses. *1:1: "Meaningless! Meaningless!" says the Teacher. "Utterly meaningless! Everything is meaningless." 2:17: So I hated life, because the work that is done under the sun was grievous to me. All of it is meaningless, a chasing after the wind. 2:24: A person can do nothing better than to eat and drink and find satisfaction in their own toil. 3:1: For everything there is an appointed time. There is an appropriate time for every activity under heaven.... 5:1: Guard your steps when you go to the house of God. Go near to listen rather than to offer the sacrifice of fools, who do not know that they do wrong. 6:12: For who knows what is good for a person in life, during the few and meaningless days they pass through like a shadow? 7:20: There is surely not a righteous man on earth who does good and does not sin. 7:29: "God created mankind upright, but they have gone in search of many schemes." 12:6-7: Remember him—before the silver cord is severed, and the golden bowl is broken; before the pitcher is shattered at the spring, and the wheel broken at the well, and the dust returns to the ground it came from, and the spirit returns to God who gave it. 12:11: Of making many books there is no end, and much study wearies the body. 12:13: Now all has been heard; here is the conclusion of the matter: Fear God and keep his commandments, for this is the duty of all mankind.*

Song of Songs

Let him lead me to the banquet hall, and let his banner over me be love. 2:4.

Theme. The theme of the Song of Songs is love. Other Bible books teach us several forms of love. Christ, for best instance, exhibited sacrificial love, in Greek term *agape*. David and Saul's son Jonathan shared brotherly love, in Greek term *philia*, not far from the love between parent and child in *filial* relationship, exhibited by Hannah and young Samuel. Many Bible figures show a caring love, in Greek *storge*, meaning empathy, perhaps best illustrated in Christ's parable of the Good Samaritan. Each of these forms of love finds frequent mention and natural place in the Bible, which readers rightly regard as a moral, indeed the supremely moral, book. The form of love, though, that the Song of Songs celebrates is *eros*, referring to sexual attraction specifically and intimate attraction, perhaps deep-heart attraction, more broadly. Yes, the Bible addresses sexual attraction in positive relational terms, not simply negative or procreative terms. Watch, though, how Song of Songs treats the subject of physical attraction, in celebration acknowledging risk, marked by constraint to proper bounds, and as allegory for something deeper and richer.

Author. Tradition and internal evidence, including several explicit references to the king, one of which gives his direct attribution, credit Solomon with writing the Song of Songs, which we also know as the Song of Solomon. Verse 1:1 is simply, "The Song of Songs, which is Solomon's." Crediting Solomon with a love song would make sense simply from the fact of his seven-hundred wives and three-hundred concubines. The song also devotes its whole to elevating the kingly male lover above all others, as Solomon in his power, influence, wealth, and sexual appeal or prowess stood above all Israel's kings. Solomon was clearly the song's male type, if not its self-aggrandizing, or perhaps only frank, author. If Solomon is indeed the author, then he may have written the song earlier in his 971 to 931 B.C. reign, when his ardor may have better matched the song's heights. Do old men write love songs? The song also mentions his harem of one-hundred-forty women, which would have been well before Solomon had amassed his harem of one thousand, mentioned 1 Kings 11:3. No other known author than Solomon appears to have had plausible reason to write the song nor to promote it into the Hebrew canon, although unknown authors would also have had good reason to include it.

Context. As to its canonical context, the Song of Songs is an appropriate last of the five wisdom books. What more, after such a moving expression of love, can one say about wisdom? The Song of Songs wraps the wisdom subject into a neat package, putting a most-attractive bow on it. The Song of Songs seems to say to the reader to take a deep breath, pause, and exhale, before reading on in the Hebrew Bible. The historical context for Song of Songs also bears consideration. Assuming Solomon's early authorship, the song would have arisen much like Israel's glory dawn. Solomon may have just built the temple or just completed his nearby palace. Perhaps the Queen of Sheba had just visited to celebrate Solomon and the Israelite nation's burgeoning status and influence. In that world context, every Israelite must have felt as if the nation indeed had no limit in the embracing arms of God. The Song of Songs would have perfectly recognized and amplified that national mood, also giving context to its extraordinary king Solomon's growing harem. Unbounded hope for a glorious future is a beautiful thing. Reading the Song of Songs in that canonical and historical context gives the song even greater burnish.

Structure. The Song of Songs has a natural structure for what it so effectively accomplishes. Its first part involves the lovers' courtship, its second part the lovers' wedding, and its third part the lovers' marriage. In both subtle and not-so-subtle hints, the first part focuses on the lovers' shared allure, how beautiful is the bride like a lily among thorns, and how fetching the kingly groom in his banquet hall bannered with love. The second part focuses on the wedding's glory, neither lover seeing any flaw in the other in their consummation. The third part focuses on the lovers' possession of one another, reflected in Song of Songs 6:3 that "I am my lover's and my lover is mine," and natural fears over that possession. The Song of Songs has another structure, though, that heightens its power. The lovers go through several cycles of approach, opportunity for embrace, and then distance with embrace unfulfilled or at least untold. The song is not exactly explicit, although coming close. The song focuses somewhat more on the relational rather than sensual aspects of intimate love. The song's format as a duet in which the lovers sing back and forth to one another, occasionally separated by an enthralled chorus, entirely fulfills its object. Read the Song of Songs appreciating how each of these structures serves the song's theme and purposes.

Key Events. The song's major events, just mentioned, are the lovers' courtship, wedding, and ensuing marriage. The wedding, celebrated from verse 3:6, is perhaps the song's main point. Its long description makes sure that the reader appreciates the value, or perhaps the glory, or maybe the pleasure, of marital bliss, consummation of which verses 5:1-6 mark. Immediately, the Song of Songs turns to a very different event, as the bride prepares for her groom but discovers that he has left her to be beaten by the city's watchmen. The song swiftly resumes its marriage celebration until, a chapter later in verses 6:11-12, another puzzling interlude (so titled) shifts one of the two to a scene "among the chariots of my willing people." The song's last chapter ends with the couple's embrace, the bride's utter confidence in her groom, a warning to keep sexual access like a well-guarded wall, and the bride's call for the groom to run away with her. While these events, other than the two interludes, make sense within the courtship narrative, they may also allegorize God's intimate, even jealous relationship with his people, not to mention Christ's relationship with his bride the church. The reader can find similar allegorical meaning for the book's two unusual interludes, whether allegory was the author's intent or not.

Key Locations. The song's lovers contemplate and pursue one another in and around several locations (whether real, imagined, or allegorical) common to the time, including vineyards, fields, pastures, wilderness, mountains, valleys, clefts, houses, markets, squares, streets, walls, fountains, and streams. The song's location imagery is powerful and varied. Yet frankly, the Song of Songs' key location is likely instead the marriage bed, both anticipated and consummated. Verse 1:16 records the bride delighting in her lover, adding that their bed is fresh. Verse 3:1 has the bride seeking her love all night long on her bed. As to external locations, the Song of Songs several times mentions the daughters of Jerusalem searching for the groom, finding the groom, and swearing not to arouse desire. These references are the clearest suggestion that the author set the song in and around the nation's capitol, the City of David and home of Solomon. These locations, both marriage bed and Jerusalem, lend further symbolic support for the song's allegorical description of God's relationship with his people and Christ's relationship with his church.

Revelation of Christ. Note the unusual form of Song of Songs' title. What does an author gain by repeating a word in such form? The Bible does so in a handful of other places, most notably with respect to Jesus Christ, referenced in Revelation 17:14 as the Lord of lords and King of kings. Similarly, some translations refer to the innermost place in the temple, where God dwelled and appeared, as the Holy of holies, seen for instance in Ezekiel 41:4, 21, 23. The connotation is simply that the person, place, or thing so described is the archetype, the original, the greater and greatest of that person, place, or thing. The Song of Songs is thus the archetypical song, the original and greatest love song one could sing, which all other such songs merely copy, or from which all such songs emanate. So, too, is Christ over all persons, the great I am, God's eternally created Son of Man, both progenitor and end. Christ is ruler and Lord but also wisdom and love, both eternal and incarnate. By pointing us to the greatest possible love, even intimate love, the Song of Songs points us to the King of kings. Let the reader decide whether the Song of Songs' courtship is allegory for Christ's relationship with his church. The song offers us one more glimpse of Christ when verse 8:6 says that love is as strong as death. Christ's love conquered our death.

Application. The Song of Songs supplies several significant applications. First, sexual difference and sexual union are God's design, the latter after appropriate courtship, ceremony, and marriage. Intimacy occurs between two opposites committed to serving as one another's essential other, just as God first formed Adam and Eve in his garden paradise. Second, the journey toward intimacy is a large part, perhaps even the primary part, of its pleasure. Surely, relationship matters above sensual satisfaction. Godly intimacy does not objectify the other but instead heightens the value of the person. The Song of Songs' lessons, though, don't stop with the persons involved in the intimate relationship. In verse 8:9, brothers commit to protect their little sister who may, they recognize, be her own protector or, conversely, be unwisely too willing to entertain suitors. We should not only conduct ourselves appropriately but also watch for how we can protect others who are not so wise, especially vulnerable family members. Sexual intimacy, we know, is a powerful dynamic. Yet like every good thing, it has its place. The more we keep it in its proper place, the more we can enjoy it. God first, without bounds. Let him direct our course in intimacy as elsewhere.

Memory Verses. *1:7: You whom my soul loves, tell me where you pasture your flock, where you rest your sheep at noon. 2:4: He has brought me to the reception hall, and his banner over me is love. 2:8:*

Listen! It's my lover! Look! Here he comes, leaping on the mountains, bounding over the hills. 2:15: Catch the foxes for us, the little foxes that ruin the vineyards, our vineyards that are in blossom. 3:1: All night long on my bed I sought the one my soul loves. 4:7: You are altogether beautiful, my darling. There is no flaw in you. 6:3: I am my lover's, and my lover is mine. 8:6: Place me like a seal over your heart, like a seal on your arm, because love is as strong as death. Its passion is as relentless as the grave.

Reading Guide

Symbols

Symbols play significant roles in many Bible's books and passages. Take a symbol to mean a person, thing, or event the text invokes, that the author intends to represent something not directly revealed in that text. For instance, a mountaintop can represent a place of access to or presence before God. Eight different Psalms and multiple passages in Isaiah and other prophetic books refer to God's holy mountain or the mountain of the Lord. Moses met God on Mount Sinai, God dwelled in Jerusalem's temple built on a mount, and God transfigured Jesus on a mountain. Thus, when foreign nations and rebellious Israelites worship idols on high places, meaning mountaintops, the symbolism may especially be to reject God to his face. Many passages supply the symbol, and then supply its explanation, while other passages leave the reader to infer.

Not every mountain in the Bible, though, is a symbol. A key to grasping more of what the Bible's authors intended is to distinguish symbols from mere imagery. Mountains are always an image, as would be a river or a tree. But only sometimes are mountains, rivers, and trees symbols, such as mountains for God's holy place, rivers for baptismal passage, and trees for connection to the source of life. Recognizing symbols is primarily intuitive, coming to some from years of reading literature, especially reading the Bible. One method, though, for recognizing whether an image is a symbol is to remove the image to see if the passage retains its full meaning, that meaning which the broader context suggests. If so, then you've only removed an image. If not, then the image has symbolism that contributes to or illustrates the passage's meaning. Ask whether the image is essential, and thus a symbol, or non-essential, and thus merely an image.

Major Prophets

The Hebrew canon follows the Torah, history books, and wisdom writings with many prophetical books, seventeen in all. With one exception, the canon names those prophetical books after their prophet authors, dividing the books into five major-prophet books and twelve books by minor prophets. The exception is the book Lamentations, authored by the major prophet Jeremiah, who also authored a book carrying his own name. The division of major and minor prophets has mostly to do with the books' length and order. The major-prophet books Isaiah, Jeremiah, and Ezekiel are by far the longer of all the prophetical books, although the other two major-prophet books Lamentations and Daniel are shorter, more like their minor-prophet siblings. Together, their greater length and primary position before the minor prophets give the major-prophet books more attention, while the longer books also cover more history, prophecy, and related topics, as the following sections on each book will show.

Prophecy plays an important, indeed critical, role in spiritual understanding. A secular view would define prophecy as prediction or foretelling and consign it to fortuity, probability, chance. Yet the natural world, not just the supernatural realm, is fraught with cause and effect. Secularists and materialists depend just as heavily, and at times far more heavily, on prediction than do persons holding spiritual, supernatural, and faith beliefs. The person of faith is often at odds with prevailing wisdom, meaning secular thought, as to the probable course of events including their origin and cause. That difference of faith reveals the distinction between prophecy and simple naturalistic or probabilistic prediction. A prophet discerns in advance the coming movements of God. Everyone else, bereft of such discernment, relies on God's natural laws to predict what's up and what's coming, as if God were not a participant outside of his own laws.

Thus, a profitable way to read prophecy is to distinguish human discernment, thought of today as scientific, materialistic, probabilistic, or naturalistic discernment, from spiritual discernment. Read the prophetic books for how different what the prophets say is from the prevailing wisdom, even when that prevailing wisdom's source is within the religious hierarchy. Learn to identify godly prophecy. Then discern with the Spirit's guidance who your prophet is in your own life today. Still your mind of the routine and false fears, anxieties, and confidences of your own secular mind, in favor of the prophet's discernment of the will and movement of God. Reading the prophetical books has enormous value to the reader today when embraced in that fashion. Yes, the prophets' foretelling, especially of the crucified and risen Christ, were the most-amazing supernatural insights, confirming the divinity and eternity of the foretold events. But don't treat prophecy merely as confirming history. Prophecy lives today.

Isaiah

> Therefore, the Lord himself will give you a sign: the virgin will conceive and give birth to a son and will call him Immanuel. 7:14.

Theme. Isaiah's theme is salvation. The prophets carry a deserved reputation for condemnation of the Israelites' idolatry and other sins of their people and leaders. Isaiah's voice joins that judgment-of-God chorus. Yet Isaiah does more than simply condemn sin and idolatry, forecasting the judgment of God. Isaiah further prophecies the coming of the nation's deliverer, the Messiah. Jews treasured Isaiah's book not for its midnight but for its dawn. Isaiah's theme is not merely judgment, a theme it would share with the other prophetical books. Rather, its theme surpasses judgment to point the reader to judgment's other side. Something or someone must exist beyond judgment. Isaiah tells us what or rather who. Beyond judgment, salvation comes from the hand and in the person of the incarnate Lord. Through Isaiah, Israel anticipates its Messiah. Through Isaiah, Christians see certain prophecy of the gospel's very good news. As Isaiah 12:2 assures, "Behold, God is my salvation; I will trust and not be afraid."

Author. Few doubt that the book Isaiah records prophecies and experiences of the prophet Isaiah, just as tradition firmly credits Isaiah as the book's author. While much of modern scholarship divides the book into three sections, each written or compiled by different authors, that work, sound, helpful, Spirit-guided and informed or not, does not alter that the book represents itself to be the words and experiences of Isaiah. We know from the book itself that Isaiah's wife was also a prophetess and the mother of his two sons. We also know that Isaiah prophesied during the reigns of four kings Uzziah (referred to in 2 Kings 15 as Azariah), Jotham, Ahaz, and (most notably for Isaiah's recorded influence on the king) Hezekiah. Isaiah may have died under and by the brutal hand of a fifth king Manasseh. Isaiah prophesied during the Israelites' long decline, between about 739 and 681 B.C., when Israel's idolatry and Judah's injustices showed that the people had wandered far from God's desire for them.

Context. The condition of Israel generally and Judah more specifically, during Isaiah's life, is the prophetic book's most-significant context. The kingdom had divided nearly two-hundred years before Isaiah began to prophesy. Assyria then conquered the northern kingdom Israel halfway into Isaiah's prophetic term, exiling survivors to that nation. Judah would not follow Israel into exile for another hundred years after Isaiah's prophetic term, but Judah was still in steep decline during his prophesying. The first king under whom Isaiah prophesied, Uzziah (Azariah), reigned fifty-two years doing right under the Lord but without removing the high places where Judah's people sacrificed to other gods. Consequentially, the Lord made a leper of Uzziah who had to live in a separate house until his death. The next king Jotham followed a similar course, although without the resulting leprosy, reigning sixteen years. Then came the awful king Ahaz who burned his son to death in offering, 2 Kings 16:3 tells us, according to the other nations' despicable practices. The good king Hezekiah, though, reigning twenty-nine years in Jerusalem, is the one with whom readers most-closely associate Isaiah. Hezekiah heeded Isaiah, removing Judah's high places and destroying idols to other gods. Hezekiah survived Assyrian siege under Isaiah's reassurance and in prayer to God. He also survived deadly illness in prayer and prophecy, though he failed to raise a godly successor to the throne, leaving Judah to his evil son Manasseh. Isaiah's reader quickly discovers the complex and at times dire political, military, and spiritual milieu in which Isaiah prophesied.

Structure. Isaiah's sixty-six chapters make it such a long book as to be challenging to recognize its structure. The book's complexity increases given that Isaiah prophesied over such a long period, under several different kings facing differing circumstances. The book is also not necessarily chronological. Rather, Isaiah's organization, itself not entirely consistent throughout the book, is first to present Judah's problem that it was pursuing and trusting the wrong things including unfaithful leaders, other gods, other alliances, and themselves. Isaiah 29:13 summarizes its first part with God's observation that the people talk a good line but have hearts far from him. Isaiah's second part introduces the solution, which is to trust God who, verse 40:18 assures the reader, has no comparison. Those who trust God will, verse 40:31 assures, renew their strength. Isaiah's third part sharpens the solution's focus on the Lord Jesus Christ. Christ is the anticipated Messiah (9:6-7), a servant (42:1), pierced for our sins (53:5), one with us in person (7:14), making intercession while bearing our sins (53:12), and carrying the Lord's Spirit to preach this good news (61:1). Isaiah thus lays out before the perceptive reader the full gospel, although in prophetic anticipation.

Key Events. Isaiah is such a long book, filled with so many dramatic prophesies foretelling or connected to so many seminal events, that a brief summary is hard to share. Isaiah begins with prophesies of warning, proclamation, the glory of the Lord's coming, and the Lord's judgment on Jerusalem. Only then, in the book's sixth chapter, do we read of the Lord's call of Isaiah as prophet to the Lord's coming. Chapter nine famously prophesies again of the coming Immanuel, God with us, as does chapter eleven a third time. Chapter thirteen begins a series of prophecies against Judah's enemies, right up to Isaiah's prophecy in chapter twenty-one of the fall of Babylon, followed by a similar prophecy as to Judah's fall. Chapter twenty-four records Isaiah's spectacular prophecy of God judging the earth. But the Lord will soon deliver Israel, Isaiah continues, and a righteous king reigns on the earth. Chapters thirty-seven to thirty-nine record Isaiah's prophecies to king Hezekiah. Chapter forty-two records Isaiah's first servant song, describing the coming Messiah's humility, amplified with a similar song in chapter forty-nine, a third such song in the next chapter, and fourth and fifth songs in later chapters. Chapter fifty-three foresees the Messiah's crushing, the punishment that brought us peace. Chapter sixty prophecies the new day's dawn in glory. The extraordinary book ends with Zion's blessing. Read Isaiah in the Spirit to see the glory of the Lord.

Key Locations. While the book's salvation message means everything to the individual, Isaiah prophesied primarily to nations, where the subject includes geographic location. The locations his prophesies addressed, mostly condemned, ranged as far as Egypt and Cush east of Sinai's faraway Red Sea, to Babylon far to the west and Assyria to the north, not to mention nearby Moab and other tormentors of Israel and Judah. Isaiah's main target, though, was Israel, indeed his home Judah and its capitol Jerusalem, where Isaiah was so prominent as to have palace access. When Assyria's Sennacherib threatened to besiege Jerusalem, Hezekiah sought Isaiah's counsel. Isaiah shared the Lord's word that the Lord's angel would defend Jerusalem, as the angel did by striking dead one-hundred-eighty-five-thousand Assyrians. Isaiah also initially prophesied Hezekiah's death but, when Hezekiah prayed, returned with the Lord's word that the Lord had relented. Isaiah is thus a book of great regional and internal Israelite history. Its main contribution, though, will forever remain its prophecy to the human heart, not any city, nation, or region.

Revelation of Christ. No prophetical book, indeed no other book of the Hebrew Bible, is as clear, compelling, comprehensive, detailed, and extraordinary as Isaiah in its revelation of the coming Messiah, the Lord Jesus Christ. Isaiah prophesied to every stage of Jesus's life, from the announcement of his coming (40:3-5) to details of his birth (7:14), good-news ministry (61:1), crucifixion death (52:13-53:12), and anticipated return (60:2-3), among many other such references. Those references the Jews knew so well and so fully embraced that Jesus employed Isaiah's prophecies in revealing his identity, nature, and purposes. Isaiah left no doubt for the Christian that when prophesying Israel's salvation, and the broader salvation the coming Messiah would bring to the Gentiles, Isaiah was foretelling the very Jesus Christ of Nazareth who came, served, died on the cross, and rose from the grave to restore to God's intimacy all who look to him. Isaiah's prophecies assured the world of its Savior Jesus Christ.

Application. Isaiah's great application will indeed always be to know and embrace the long-foretold, prophecy-fulfilling world Savior. Isaiah shared the gospel many hundreds of years before Jesus fulfilled the prophecy. The book's application then is to seek salvation in none other than the Lord Jesus. Isaiah also serves a dire warning against idolatry in all national forms, especially as to power, violence, and unholy alliance. Those warnings, though, also have individual application. Another application that Isaiah shares is to know the Lord in the humble person whom he is. When Isaiah's prophesies remind us of Jesus as the suffering servant, taking on the world's sins out of love, seeking world redemption, we turn again to the good news for which our hearts long and our mouths have confessed. Readers, do as Isaiah did, which is to tell of the good news of Jesus Christ. Let you, too, be Jesus's herald.

Memory Verses. 7:14: Therefore, the Lord himself will give you a sign: The virgin will conceive and give birth to a son, and will call him Immanuel. 9:6: For to us a child is born, to us a son is given, and the government will be on his shoulders. And he will be called Wonderful Counselor, Mighty God, Everlasting Father, Prince of Peace. 32:8: [T]he noble man plans noble deeds, and by noble deeds he stands. 35:8: A highway will be there, a road that will be called the holy way. 40:31: But those who hope in the LORD will renew their strength. They will soar on wings like eagles; they will run and not grow weary, they will walk and not be faint. *42:3: A bent reed he will not break, and a dimly burning wick he will not snuff out. 45:15: Indeed, you are a God who hides himself. You are the God of Israel, the Savior. 53:2-3: When we saw him, nothing about his appearance made us desire him. He was despised and rejected by men, a man who knew grief, who was well acquainted with suffering. 53:5: He was crushed for the guilt our sins deserved. The punishment that brought us peace was upon him, and by his wounds we are healed. 55:8: For my thoughts are not your thoughts, neither are your ways my ways," declares the Lord. 60:1: Arise, shine, for your light has come, and the glory of the Lord is dawning upon you. 61:1: The Spirit of the Sovereign Lord is on me, because the Lord has anointed me to proclaim good news to the poor. 64:6: All of us have become like one who is unclean, and all our righteous acts are like filthy rags.*

Jeremiah

"For I know the plans I have for you," declares the Lord, "plans to prosper you and not to harm you, plans to give you hope and a future." 29:11.

Theme. Jeremiah's theme is exile. The exile that the prophet Jeremiah prophesied and experienced, and that marks the theme of his book, was Judah's national exile. Yet readers should identify the book not only with its theme of national exile but also with individual exile, personal banishment from the presence of God. The nation Israel's course reflects the course and character not only of its leaders, its kings, but also the character and commitment of its people. A nation does not move, does not set or change course, without its people. Judah's exile was not due simply to the failure of its kings but also to the idolatrous pursuits of its people. And then, Judah's exile was not simply something with which the nation had to deal but also something intensely personal. Imagine banishment from your home to a foreign location. Worse, imagine banishment from God's presence, his favor, his approval. Jeremiah is largely, although not entirely, a book of judgment and despair, the cause and character of which is exile.

Author. Jeremiah began prophesying in 627 B.C. at about age twenty and continued doing so for forty years. During that remarkable span, Judah suffered frequent attack and finally, in 586 B.C., exile to Babylon, after a group of Jerusalem's Jews had already fled to Egypt. Jeremiah wrote his book during an extraordinarily difficult time. Jeremiah's father was a priest from the small town Anathoth in Judah. Jeremiah, too, would have been a priest except that history, including his own lengthy book, makes no record of his service. Jeremiah may instead have pursued his prophesy ministry outside of priestly service. Prophets may always be outsiders of a sort, but Jeremiah's small-town upbringing, youth when starting his ministry, and lack of priestly position may all have contributed to the openly emotional and deeply personal nature of Jeremiah's accounts. These factors may also have aided Jeremiah's survival even while he prophesied against the Jewish leaders' actions.

Judah's kings, priests, administrators, and military leaders certainly came to know of Jeremiah's prophesies, with which at times they felt compelled to directly deal. Yet somehow, Jeremiah managed to escape execution to prophesy again. Jewish leaders seemed to regard him as more of an irritant than threat, while Jeremiah also found sympathies among lesser officials.

Context. Judah's course may have been set well before Jeremiah began to prophesy against it. Assyria had already taken Israel into exile and would besiege Jerusalem, though unsuccessfully after the Lord's extraordinary rescue. But Judah's national mood remained a fatal mix of spiritual corruption, leadership arrogance, and military ignorance. Jeremiah prophesied in the worst possible of political contexts, to a once-glorious nation about to suffer its deserved defeat through a series of awful twists, turns, and fatal stumbles. As to the book's canonical context, Jeremiah is the second prophetical book after the spectacular Isaiah, which fills with prophecies of the coming Messiah, giving Jeremiah a difficult role to fill. The book must somehow lead the reader on in the biblical narrative, when the narrative seems just to have reached its greatest height. And so indeed, Jeremiah supplies the great prophetic letdown, a long book of prophesy weeping over Judah's unnecessary but, in its obstinacy, nonetheless-sure demise. Jeremiah more than fulfills its difficult role. Read Jeremiah as representing the depths to which a nation and its people can fall.

Structure. Jeremiah has a two-part structure, the first thirty-eight chapters before Jerusalem's fall and the rest of the book after its fall. Certain verses serve as signposts within each of the two parts. Jeremiah 1:5 begins with God's declaration, "Before I formed you in the womb, I knew you; before you were born, I set you apart," references surely to Jeremiah, who answers that he is too young to speak, but perhaps also to Judah and to us. God then sends Jeremiah to say exactly what God directs. In Jeremiah 18, another signpost, God describes Israel as clay in God the potter's hand. God does with Israel and with us as he wants. In Jeremiah 29:11, God declares that he indeed has plans for Israel, as for us, not to harm but to prosper, in hope and for a future. God is not a destroyer but a creator, not an enemy but an ally and friend. Jeremiah 23:29 serves as another signpost, God declaring that his word is like fire, like a hammer that breaks rock. Neither Israel nor the individual stands against God's design. Jeremiah's second part, beginning at chapter thirty-nine, first describes Jerusalem's fall, then prophecies against surrounding gloating nations, and finally describes Jerusalem's ruins.

Jeremiah fulfills its promise as a thorough description of life without God, which is life headed for exile.

Key Events. Jeremiah brims with interesting events, some personal to the prophet and others of national concern, many involving symbolic items that the Lord directs Jeremiah to use to illustrate his prophesies. The book begins with Jeremiah's call and first vision, Jeremiah quickly seeing that God has forsaken Israel including Judah, which Jeremiah's prophecy calls treacherous. The Lord is bringing judgment, in siege form, to a people who practice a useless false religion, sin begetting punishment. Chapter eleven describes how Judah has broken covenant with God. Chapter thirteen has Jeremiah hide a new linen belt in a rock crevice, ruined and useless like Judah, facing drought, famine, and sword as its day of disaster approaches. Chapter nineteen has God directing Jeremiah to break a clay jar to show how God will smash Judah. The temple's priest in charge had Jeremiah beaten and put in stocks for these prophecies. Yet Jeremiah continued, in chapter twenty-four using a basket of rotten figs to represent Judah's heedless king Zedekiah, from whom Judah would suffer seventy years of captivity in Babylon. Zedekiah imprisoned Jeremiah, who nonetheless bought a field to prove God's promise of the exiles' return. Chapter thirty-six shows king Jehoiakim burning Jeremiah's prophetic scrolls. Officials also threw Jeremiah into a muddy cistern to silence his prophesies. Jeremiah was in prison when Babylonian troops conquered Jerusalem, but the Babylonian commander freed Jeremiah. Against his desire, Jeremiah accompanied Jews fleeing to Egypt, where he prophesied their destruction. Jeremiah likely died there, some believe at the hands of the Jews whom his prophesies had so exasperated.

Key Locations. As the prior paragraph shows, events of the book Jeremiah swirl in and around Jerusalem, where Jeremiah made many of his prophesies. As Judah's capitol, administrative center, and military command post, and the location of both the temple and king's palace, Jerusalem was emblematic of the heart and condition of the nation Israel and its chosen Israelites. Jeremiah's prophesies against Jerusalem were not prophesies against the place as much against its occupant leaders and represented people. Jerusalem generally and its temple specifically were to be God's home on earth among his chosen people. Yet the priests who served at the temple and the people who occupied Jerusalem and its environs were so corrupt that God had to cleanse the place, in effect, to start over. Jeremiah is a book about the spiritual condition, not the physical structures, of Jerusalem, but God had to allow destruction of

Jerusalem society, including its physical walls and temple, to accomplish his goal of renewing the people on their return from exile. Jeremiah documents Jerusalem's spiritual condition through its repeatedly foolish, arrogant, and fatal political moves.

Revelation of Christ. In the middle of its declarations and records of national misery, Jeremiah 23 makes a sharp about-turn to record a most-remarkable prophesy of Christ. Israel's shepherds have destroyed and scattered their sheep, the chapter begins, but the Lord will raise up David's righteous Branch, a wise King whom Israel will call the Lord our Righteous Savior. God himself, the chapter further foresees, will gather his flock from all countries to which they have dispersed, to bring them back to their pasture, to bear fruit under shepherds who will tend them. Jeremiah thus supplies salvific hope during times of great despair, even while the people weep and wail in misery. The prophet Jeremiah, though, is himself a type of Christ, weeping over Jerusalem's demise that Jeremiah prophesied, just as Christ so lamented and prophesied. The pattern of Jeremiah's prophesy and lament, and Jerusalem's destruction, is the pattern that Christ fulfilled. Indeed, Jeremiah's call, suffering, prophesy of demise, and yet good-news declaration prefigured the pattern for Christ's own ultimate ministry. In these declarations and patterns, Jeremiah reveals Christ as surely as any other Bible book.

Application. Jeremiah may look to be a despairing book, but in fact it proves both God's enormous patience with us and his extraordinary grace for us, both qualities of God on which we should rely from the evidence of this extraordinary book. God let Jerusalem stand for nearly a millennium before allowing its demise, showing his unprecedented patience. How many times did Jerusalem's leaders fail, and its people fail with them, but God persisted? How corrupt was Jerusalem at times, and its people with it, but God persisted? God is patient with us, too, though we fail repeatedly and sordidly, like Jerusalem. Trust him, Jeremiah tells us. Listen to him, Jeremiah repeats, so that we avoid Jerusalem's disaster. Yet we, like Jerusalem, have also fallen to temptation, forsaken God, turning our backs rather than our faces to him, and fallen further into desperate exile. To inform our personal exile, though, Jeremiah prophesied Israel's return from exile and its full hope in the coming Lord and Savior. We are in a far better position than were Jerusalem's exiles because we have seen Jeremiah's savior prophesy fulfilled in the Lord Jesus. We have more reason to hope than did the falling Jerusalem. We have only to hold fast to the risen Lord Jesus.

Memory Verses. *1:5: "Before I formed you in the womb I knew you, before you were born I set you apart...." 6:16: "Stand at the crossroads and look; ask for the ancient paths, ask where the good way is, and walk in it, and you will find rest for your souls." 10:8: They are all senseless and foolish; they are taught by worthless wooden idols. 12:5: "If you have raced with men on foot and they have worn you out, how can you compete with horses? 17:5: "Cursed are those who trust in mortals, who depend on flesh for their strength and whose hearts turn away from the Lord." 17:9: The heart is deceitful above all things and beyond cure. Who can understand it? 29:11: "For I know the plans I have for you," declares the Lord, "plans to prosper you and not to harm you, plans to give you hope and a future." 29:13: "You will seek me and find me when you seek me with all your heart." 31:3: "I have loved you with an everlasting love; I have drawn you with unfailing kindness." 31:33: "I will put my law in their minds and write it on their hearts. I will be their God, and they will be my people." 33:3: "Call to me and I will answer you and tell you great and unsearchable things you do not know."*

Reading Guide

Numbers

Numbers unquestionably signify things in the Bible. Not all numbers do so. The Bible includes many numbers that are incidental to the narrative, perhaps other than to show the general size of the numbered thing. Some passages, for instance, document the amount the Israelites contributed to building the temple or celebrating events. Those numbers may have no significance other than their large quantity. Likewise, when Moses counts the fleeing Israelites, David counts troops, or a history book or book of prophecy numbers the men in each tribe, the specific figures, running sometimes into the hundreds of thousands, may only be significant for their large or relative size. Read those numbers with interest. They tell us things like the leadership and supply challenge in the case of the fleeing Israelites, military might in the number of troops, or commitment of the people in their large contributions.

Yet other numbers, the Bible explicitly states, signify certain things. God created the world in seven days, resting on the seventh day. He accordingly instituted a seventh-day, or sabbath, rest. Bible passages may thus take the number seven to signify completion and the seventh day to signify rest in God's provision. Passages even use multiples of seven in their format or within their narrative, suggesting the author's effort to highlight God's created order and his direction toward ultimate rest in his presence. Likewise, the number forty can signify a time of testing, whether for Noah waiting forty days for the floods to stop, Moses meeting God for forty days on the mountaintop, the Israelites wandering forty years in the wilderness, or Jesus fasting for forty days. Don't take every number or even every possible pattern to signify meaning or relationship. But be willing with numbers to consider their context and investigate their significance when the Spirit so informs you.

Lamentations

Yet this I call to mind and therefore I have hope: Because of the Lord's great love we are not consumed, for his compassions never fail. They are new every morning; great is your faithfulness. 3:21-23.

Theme. The theme of Lamentations is weeping, and not just any few tears but instead bitter weeping over an event of great loss. The book's original Hebrew one-word title could better bear the translation *alas* as in the regretful exclamation *how could it be?!* Later translators substituted the title Lamentations to capture that deep sense of regret. To lament is to wish that things were not so, that one could go back and do it differently with opposite result. The book bears exactly that theme of wishing that Israel had listened to its prophets and turned from idolatry in time so that its gracious God would save it once again. Thundering prophecies of condemnation are fine, even necessary, but what of the emotion that must follow when the prophecies do no good? Lamentations satisfies that need to mourn, and not just to mourn inexplicable loss in the way that Job despaired over his blameless downfall, but instead to mourn one's own awful character.

Author. Lamentations does not identify its author, but tradition, internal evidence, and early attribution credit the prophet Jeremiah, giving Jeremiah two prophetic books in succession. Lamentations draws from Jerusalem's conquering and exile, both of which Jeremiah prophesied and experienced, giving him time and place to write Lamentations. The book's weeping is consistent with the emotion that Jeremiah expressed in the prophetic book of his name. The Septuagint, which was the first Greek translation of the Hebrew Bible, added an attribution to Jeremiah, as did the early church father Jerome. Jeremiah or its other author, if one doesn't credit Jeremiah, likely wrote the book very shortly after Jerusalem's 586 B.C. fall, given the detail of its record and the raw emotion with which the book fills. Read Lamentations for its remarkable record frankly and emotionally acknowledging the disaster of sin.

Context. The Hebrew Bible gives Lamentations its perfect place, following Isaiah's soaring warning and Jeremiah's dismal prophesy so awfully fulfilled. Lamentations lets the reader recover emotionally, and not in abstraction but instead in appropriate mourning. One must mourn tragic events, to avoid numb emotions. Lamentations supplies that emotional interlude, documenting and encouraging frank weeping. Israel's historical context of course supported lament, as the prior two paragraphs remind. The siege and conquering of Jerusalem were especially traumatic in that Judah's Babylonian attackers initially appeared merciful, until Judah's king Zedekiah revolted, leading to Babylon's successful year-and-a-half siege. Zedekiah fled, but Babylonian soldiers pursued, captured, and blinded him, dragging him off to Babylon, while destroying Jerusalem's temple. Babylonian officials then appointed an interim governor, allowing some citizens including Jeremiah to remain. But certain Jews nonetheless revolted, ambushing and killing the interim leader before fleeing to Egypt with Jeremiah as their prisoner. Babylon then killed or removed all remaining officials, leaving only the poorest laborers to tend fields and vineyards. Jeremiah had plenty of reason to lament.

Structure. Lamentations has the structure of five poems, each a chapter long. The first poem is the voice of the city announcing that Jerusalem has fallen, leaving its streets deserted. The Lord brought Jerusalem grief because of its many sins. The second poem is the voice of the Lord, expressing his anger, fulfilling his decrees. The third poem is the voice of the prophet, in which Jeremiah shares his deep grief. He also urges that the people examine their way and return to the Lord. The fourth poem is the voice of possessions, describing how the gold has lost its luster under God's punishment of Jerusalem's sins. The fifth and final poem is the voice of captives, those headed for exile, in which Jeremiah prays that God remember and restore them. The book's successive poems form a helpful structure for the book's deep lament.

Key Events. The single key event to which Lamentations refers is the destruction of Jerusalem whose inhabitants the Lord has sent into exile. Lamentations does not so much describe events as describe consequences, awful consequences deserved of the corrupt. Thus, royalty lie in ash heaps (4:5), the skin of princes shrivel on their bones (4:8), women cook their own children (4:10), Israel has lost its inheritance to strangers (5:2), and slaves rule Israel (5:8), while others violate Israel's women (5:11) and hang Israel's princes by their hands (5:12). The reader shudders, suspecting that the horrible images that Lamentations conjures are not allegorical but real. Know that Jeremiah had cause to lament.

Key Locations. Lamentations' single location is Jerusalem, mentioned expressly seven times in the book and clearly both the figurative and actual setting for the whole lament. The book at times personifies Jerusalem, so that, verse 1:8 tells the reader, "she herself groans and turns away" from her shameful state. Jerusalem's young women bow their heads to the ground, verse 2:10 shares, while children and infants faint in Jerusalem's streets, the next verse adds. Verse 2:13 calls Jerusalem *daughter*, noting that her wound is as deep as the sea. Verse 2:15 repeats that all who see Daughter Jerusalem's shame scoff and shake their heads. Enemies and foes entered Jerusalem's vaunted gates, verses 4:12-13 tell us, because of the sins of her prophets and iniquities of her priests who shed the blood of the righteous. Those prophets and priests, the next verse tells us, now grope blind and bloodied through Jerusalem's streets. The reader need keep in mind, though, that Jerusalem also represents a figurative location, perhaps the corrupt human heart that should be God's dwelling place but that instead fills itself with sin. Read Lamentations for the reality of Jerusalem's fall, but also read it for the reality of the heart's equally awful sin.

Revelation of Christ. Buried within Lamentations' weeping, at another one of its many nadirs, the author gives the reader the same salvation hope that we find in every other Bible book. After acknowledging how downcast the soul is in exile, Lamentations 3:21-26 begins by expressing that the Lord's love, his compassion for us, keeps us from utter destruction. These compassions of his, the passage continues, never fail but are instead new every morning. The passage then gives the reader the reason: God's faithfulness to us and to his love mission is great. The Lord, the passage concludes, saves those who hope in him and wait quietly for him. Jesus Christ came because God loved the world and so that we might hope in Jesus and, by doing so, never perish. Lamentations witnesses to the hope that Jesus fulfilled in crucifixion and resurrection.

Application. Lamentations offers the reader a most-significant and most-valuable application, by forcing the reader to consider, brick by brick, the horror of Jerusalem's destruction, after the prior prophetic books Isaiah and Jeremiah lay the cause for that destruction squarely on Jerusalem's idolatry, as does Lamentations. We, too, must look on the degradation that our sin has caused in our lives and relationships, especially our relationship with God. We, too, must consider directly how awful God perceives sin to be and how awful his judgment of it must be. We, too, should weep over our sins as we confess them and repent of them. Only then can we embrace Jesus's sacrifice and salvation. Salvation must begin with confession, before mercy may follow. Lamentations is a book of weeping confession from which we can learn the cost of our sin, Jesus's very death, and the great love of God that brought both his sacrifice and resurrection. Love has power over death, even when death is due sentence.

Memory Verses. 1:1: How deserted lies the city, once so full of people! How like a widow is she, who once was great among the nations! She who was queen among the provinces has now become a slave. 1:9: Her fall was astounding; there was none to comfort her. "Look, Lord, on my affliction, for the enemy has triumphed." 3:4: He has made my skin and my flesh grow old and has broken my bones. 3:6: He has made me dwell in darkness like those long dead. 3:21-23: Yet this I call to mind and therefore I have hope: Because of the Lord's great love we are not consumed, for his compassions never fail. They are new every morning; great is your faithfulness. 4:5: Those who once ate delicacies are destitute in the streets. Those nurtured in purple now lie on ash heaps.

Ezekiel

The Spirit lifted me up and brought me to the exiles in Babylonia in the vision given by the Spirit of God. Then the vision I had seen went up from me, and I told the exiles everything the Lord had shown me. 11:24-25.

Theme. The theme of Ezekiel is glory. Glory can be a difficult word to the modern secular mind, bereft as that mind is of awe for any superior being. But glory in modern terms might mean something like extraordinary, stunning, spectacular significance, subordinating the one who observes. Glory doesn't merely impress with aesthetic beauty or exciting display. Glory impresses, but glory also subordinates the one who encounters it, while elevating what the one who encounters its glory observes. Glory is more about the relative relationship of the observer and the observed. To see God's glory is to see God elevated toward the position he occupies, which in God's unique case is so far above and outside of his creation, including the observer, that only some of his glory can we even observe. Ezekiel gives hints, symbols, and suggestions of God's glory, which no printed text on a page could in any sense adequately represent.

Author. The priest and prophet Ezekiel wrote the prophetical book carrying his name. Ezekiel's status as a member of the priesthood is significant to his text in that he focuses on the temple and its worship forms. Ezekiel gives us an insider's view, a leader's and intimate participant's view, of worship. Ezekiel shared his prophecies from exile in Tel-Abib, a village about one-hundred miles to Babylon's south, where Judah's conquerors moved as many as ten-thousand Jews in 597 B.C., including Judah's last king Jehoiachin, 2 Kings 24:8-14 tells us. Ezekiel's book tells us that he began prophesying five years into exile, perhaps at age thirty, and continued prophesying for another twenty-two years. That Ezekiel prophesied from exile and across the duration of the exile's first half is significant to the message that his book imparts, in ways the following paragraph explores.

Context. A priest like Ezekiel prophesying to an exiled people like Judah, early in their exile, must communicate two messages. Five years into exile, lament may be largely over. The period of mourning has eased if not passed. The exiles, though, must still understand why they are where they are, in a strange village along a strange river in a strange land. Ezekiel had a lot to accomplish in informing, educating, and reminding the exiles of why God had allowed their downfall. Bitterness was not an option. The exiles had to understand that God doesn't punish for punishment's sake alone but instead for the good of the one punished, to prepare the heart to restore to good standing. After hundreds of years of extended grace, God found it wise and necessary to allow the exile. For the exile to accomplish its beneficial purpose, Ezekiel's explanatory message had to reach the exiles' hearts. The other message that Ezekiel had to communicate was one of hope. Exiles, though, need a lot of hope, not just mild reassurance. Hence, Ezekiel devotes the last third of his book to perspectives on the exile's restoration including dramatic visions of our holy God. One vision of God may be enough to survive decades of exile.

Structure. Ezekiel devotes the first three chapters of his book to his commissioning, perhaps to convince the reader either of his authority or at least the veracity of his message, which may have been a helpful beginning for a young prophet carrying a hard message to exiles in a foreign land. The book's opening vision of God's glory is itself a fully adequate demonstration of the authenticity of Ezekiel's call. The rest of the book's first half Ezekiel devotes to God's judgment on Judah, the difficult explanatory part of his message. Ezekiel then makes an important turn, redirecting his prophecies of judgment from the Jews in exile to the surrounding Gentile nations. How comforting that turn, filling the next quarter of Ezekiel's book in chapters twenty-five to thirty-two, must have been. Ezekiel devotes the last quarter of his book to God's restoration of his people, including Ezekiel's extraordinary glimpses of the glory of our stunningly spectacular God. Reading Ezekiel within this context and following this structure helps the reader digest its difficult but ultimately hugely uplifting message.

Key Events. The book's first event, Ezekiel's stunning call, begins with his first extraordinary vision of God's glory, including frighteningly complex figures whirring below a vault, where sat on a splendid throne a glowing-fire man surrounded by brilliant light. That figure, with the Spirit's help, ordains Ezekiel to address the exiles. He is to eat a scroll and then stand as watchman. The book then describes Jerusalem's siege and Israel's doom, in the context of Israel's idolatry in and around the temple. Incredibly, Ezekiel spends more than a year laying on his side, bound, to illustrate captivity. God's glory departs from the temple, Babylon carries Judah into exile as its sword of judgment, and the book condemns each responsible constituency from Israel's princes to its kings, priests, and citizens. Ezekiel uses eagles, vines, cooking pots, and other symbols to communicate his hard message. Ezekiel's prophecies continue against Israel's neighbors Ammon, Moab, Edom, Philistia, Tyre, Egypt, and Lebanon. The book's final part, foreseeing Israel's restoration, begins with Ezekiel's renewed call, followed by his visions of the Lord as shepherd and an assurance of Israel's hope. Ezekiel then shares his extraordinary vision of the valley of dry bones, followed by the Lord's great victory over the nations and the restoration of the temple, which Ezekiel details to great degree. God's glory then returns, in spectacular vision, to the temple, certainly the key event in all of Ezekiel. That event leads next to the restoration of the great altar and the priesthood until, at book's end, God has restored Israel, leading Ezekiel on a visionary tour of the restored lands. The book's concluding prophecies must have been deeply heartening to the exiles, as they can be to readers perceiving their own exile.

Key Locations. The prior paragraphs indicate the geographic setting for Ezekiel's book. Ezekiel received his initial vision, the vision itself makes clear, while in exile at the Babylonian village Tel-Abib along the Kebar (or Chebar) River. Ezekiel's Tel-Abib residence, though clearly demarcating the physical exile of the Jewish community among whom he prophesied, did not limit the geography of his extraordinary visions. Ezekiel's visionary itinerary included Jerusalem especially, but also the lands of its surrounding enemies in Ammon to the northeast, Moab to the east, Edom to the southeast, Philistia to the west, Tyre to the northwest, Lebanon to the north, and Egypt farther to the southwest. The key location in Ezekiel, though, outside of the Babylonian location of exile, is none of those places but instead the temple. Ezekiel, remember, is about God's glory in restoration. For the Israelites hearing or reading Ezekiel's prophesy, the temple was the location of God's presence. When the Israelites thought about their return to God, to God's favor, they likely thought about the temple's restoration, where their representative priests met God. God's glory filling the temple is the key event in Ezekiel, marking its key location. Humbling to think, then, that we are today God's temple.

Revelation of Christ. Ezekiel's book contains more symbolism than any other Bible book outside of its concluding book Revelation. While reading symbols can easily lead to error or misinterpretation, many well-versed readers interpret the winged, human-form, four-faced creatures in Ezekiel's first vision to represent the Lord Jesus Christ. Jesus is Judah's brave lion, one of the four faces, and Israel's strong ox, another face, and soaring eagle, another face, and finally its divine man, the last of the four faces. Jesus is also the figure of a man sitting on God's throne in the same opening vision. Much later in Ezekiel's book, Jesus is the one who opened the graves, giving life to Israel's valley of dry bones, as Ezekiel 37 describes, so that God could put his Spirit in them. Ezekiel thus prophesies the position, form, attributes, power, and glory of Jesus, as the way, truth, and life, bringing resurrection and restoration. Read Ezekiel's symbolism for its messianic vision, as every other Bible book reads.

Application. We each face and experience our own exile, from which each of us must hope for restoration to God's presence. Exile is not a physical event so much as a spiritual condition. God is present in all geographic places, just not in hearts filled with sin. We know our sinful condition, especially when its consequences lead us to mental, physical, social, and material losses, diseases, discomforts, and degradations. In those times that we sense our distance from God, we need to acknowledge our responsibility for that distance, accept our accountability to him, and yet see the hope for restoration. Confession and humility form the path back to him, along which he draws us out of our exile. God does not desire our exile but our proximity. He is ready to restore us when we are ready for him. Our restoration is through the forgiveness God himself offers in his sacrificed and resurrected Son Jesus Christ. Ezekiel is a strong witness not just to exile but to restoration to God's glory.

Memory Verses. 1:28: Like the appearance of a rainbow in the clouds on a rainy day, so was the radiance around him. This was the appearance of the likeness of the glory of the Lord. 18:20: The one who sins is the one who will die. The child will not share the guilt of the parent, nor will the parent share the guilt of the child. The righteousness of the righteous will be credited to them, and the wickedness of the wicked will be charged against them. 33:11: "I take no pleasure in the death of the wicked, but rather that they turn from their ways and live. Turn! Turn from your evil ways!" 36:26: "I will give you a new heart and put a new spirit in you; I will remove from you your heart of stone and give you a heart of flesh." 37:1: The hand of the Lord was on me, and he brought me out by the Spirit of the Lord and set me in the middle of a valley; it was full of bones.

Daniel

"My God sent his angel, and he shut the mouths of the lions." 6:22.

Theme. Daniel's theme is ability. That theme of being able, capable, effective, productive, enough, bears two connotations. The first is that God is able. God can do whatever he desires for us, which is always for our good. God has the authority, position, and power to provide for every one of our needs. He lacks no ability. Yet the theme's second connotation is also important: God makes us able. As co-rulers of creation with God, so appointed by God to work his garden to fruitfulness, we have God-given ability. The quality of that ability is also significant to us. We are not just able to barely survive. Rather, God has given us both the desire and means to flourish and to draw others with us into flourishing. Daniel did not live a subsistence life in exile. Daniel lived a good life in exile and promoted a good life for others in exile. God is able, and God shares his ability with those who desire to co-rule, to partner with him. Sovereignty is a related critical aspect of God's ability. God chooses to do precisely as he alone desires. No one controls God. The book Daniel shows how God exercises his authority utterly on his own terms, independent of earthly powers and figures.

Author. Daniel is the author of the prophetical book carrying his name. The Babylonians exiled Daniel and his three friends Shadrach, Meshach, and Abednego in the first 605 B.C. wave of three waves of Judah's deportations, the latter two occurring in 597 and 586 B.C. Daniel and his friends were among the more-fortunate deportees, young nobles selected for training in the capitol Babylon to aid its empire. Daniel remained in Babylon for the entire seventy years of Judah's captivity there, even after other exiles returned to Jerusalem. In his book, Daniel records events covering the span of his exile, from his first experiences impressing the Babylonian officials and leaders, to his miraculous rescue by God late in his life. Daniel did in fact impress the highest Babylonian officials, ascending to one of the three administrative positions directly below the Babylonian king. Daniel's access to and influence over the Babylonian leaders is further evidence of his high character and godly spirit. Daniel is one of very few biblical figures to have an entirely favorable portrait, another reason why readers like the book Daniel.

Context. The prior paragraphs outline the historical and spiritual contexts for Daniel's remarkable book, a popular book among both new and experienced readers. The historical context is that both the northern kingdom Israel and southern kingdom Judah were in exile when Daniel wrote his book, meaning that he prophesied and led for the exiles' survival and hope for restoration. The spiritual context involved reminders of the reason for exile, exile's goal, and God's ability, indeed his desire, to restore from exile. The canonical context for Daniel's book, written from exile, is that it follows another book from exile, Ezekiel. Isaiah, Jeremiah, and Lamentations address the decline toward, cause for, and event of exile. By contrast, Ezekiel and Daniel give the reader the exiles' perspective or, more to the point, a message for those of us in exile. Daniel is also the last of the books of the major prophets, firmly establishing the prophet's position and prophetic structure. Prophecy has a role, not simply to predict, but instead to point people back to God.

Structure. Daniel's prophetic book has a two-part structure helpful to its encouragement and vision goals. That structure begins, in the book's first six chapters, with a historical account of the exiles' survival in their challenging foreign land. The exiles must first impress the Babylonian leadership with their reliability and then navigate Babylonian culture in their daily lives. Those two objectives serve one another. Daniel's first six chapters record how he and the other exiles managed to accomplish both objectives, his record itself an encouragement to other exiles. The second part of Daniel's book records four visions of the near and long-term future. An exiled people must have a vision if they are to remain a people in exile rather than let their captors subsume their identity and thereby extinguish the people. Daniel's prophetic visions lift the exiled Israelites so far above their difficult circumstances as to help them carry on even in the absence of evidence for hope of restoration. The symbolic nature of Daniel's visions enabled the exiles to interpret them as they needed and wished, and as Daniel intended, without offending their captors. The long view of Daniel's vision reminded the Israelites that they kept an eternal promise, one that no circumstance, not even exile, could breach. The book effectively mixes detailed personal history with compelling prophetic vision, adding significantly to the book's power and impact.

Key Events. Daniel's book, as short as it is, fills with memorable events, which may be a large part of the reason for its popularity. The book begins with the arrival of Daniel and his three friends in Babylon, their training adjusted peculiarly to their Hebrew custom, and their swift elevation in service to the king who, the text tells us, found them ten times better than the kingdom's own officials. Daniel, through God, then interprets king Nebuchadnezzar's dream, when none of the king's own officials could, giving Daniel a high place in the king's court. Chapter three turns the narrative to Daniel's friends, who refuse to bow to worship the king's golden image, in consequence of which the king has them thrown in a raging furnace. The friends, though, come out of the furnace unscathed, without even smell of smoke, aided by a mysterious fourth figure, causing the king to honor God while elevating and protecting Daniel's three friends. Nebuchadnezzar then has another dream, which Daniel once again correctly interprets. A successor king Belshazzar fares less well when he calls Daniel to interpret mysterious writing on a great banquet's wall, in God's judgment of the arrogant Belshazzar. Darius the Mede succeeds Belshazzar, just as Daniel had foreseen, but Darius's officials trick Darius into throwing Daniel into a lion's den for refusing to honor a decree. God closes the lions' mouths, though, so that Darius can remove Daniel to cast his enemy officials into the lions' mouths. The rest of Daniel's book concludes with his four visions of beasts, a goat, sevens, and Israel's future in the end times. Daniel is indeed a fast-moving, powerful, and remarkable read.

Key Locations. Babylon, where the entirety of the book's narrative unfolds other than its first few sentences mentioning the exile, is Daniel's geographic and spiritual focus. Babylon was a polytheistic society, worshipping many gods including its kings, who borrowed an aspect of divinity or claimed divinity's approval. Babylonians would expect to bow not just in obeisance to kings but also in their worship. One sees throughout the book how Babylonia's polytheism challenged Daniel and his Hebrew friends, who to honor God could not worship other Babylonian deities, certainly not Babylon's king. They could and did serve honorably, in obedience to kingly authority, but they could not admit and must instead deny that anyone or anything other than God could be their deity. God protected Daniel and his friends in miraculous fashion, even as God's Spirit informed Daniel and his friends in how to serve the Babylonians while reducing and resolving the cultural and spiritual conflicts without dishonoring God. Faithful readers today can certainly learn lessons from Daniel in how to be respected and effective in secular positions while holding fast to one's faith.

Revelation of Christ. Daniel wrote his book in ways that his Jewish audience, specifically those Jews in exile, would especially understand and appreciate. All Bible books anticipate Christ, but Daniel may be somewhat less messianic in its details and perspective. Modern readers see Christ in specific references within Daniel, like Daniel's description of the mysterious fourth figure in the furnace, looking "like a son of the gods," as the amazed Nebuchadnezzar exclaimed, recorded in Daniel 3:25. It would not be wrong to do so, whether Daniel intended the figure's participation in saving his friends to witness to the coming Messiah or not. Daniel 7:13-14's vision of a "son of man" approaching the Ancient of Days to receive all glory, authority, and power, for all nations and people to worship, is a far clearer messianic depiction. Daniel 7:27 similarly prophesies the Most High reigning over an everlasting kingdom, while worshiped and obeyed by all rulers, again a messianic reference. And Daniel 12:2 prophesies multitudes rising from death to eternal life in the end times, again a clear messianic vision. Daniel anticipates Christ in broad strokes whether also in minor points or not. Daniel is not merely a book of moral lessons. It also carries and conveys Christ's spiritual life.

Application. Daniel's clear application has to do with how to live godly in a materialistic, political, and polytheistic world. Daniel's preference not to train on the king's food is prime example. Daniel's reluctance may not have had to do with food as much as with reliance. Daniel and his friends would grow healthy, fit, and wise not by dining from the king's table but from facing and honoring God. Daniel also teaches, though, to give one's best in service to others, even when the service does not relate directly to spiritual matters. God receives honor when the nation, state, or community rises under the service of godly leaders and citizens, even when they are subordinates or in the minority. Daniel several times shows directly, how the natural witness of the lives of Daniel and his friends made non-believing kings and officials respect if not honor and glorify God. Daniel also teaches that while navigating secular politics adroitly, a believer must not engage in practices that suggest the believer's sacrifice of belief. Do as the world demands of you, unless and until the world demands what God prohibits. Then, honor God at all cost, and he will save you against the world's threats. God can draw us out of every situation smelling like a rose, even when our circumstances look like fiery furnaces. Daniel is a most-remarkable book from which to draw most-timely lessons.

Memory Verses. *2:44: [T]he God of heaven will set up a kingdom that will never be destroyed, nor will it be left to another people. It will crush all those kingdoms and bring them to an end, but it will itself endure forever. 4:5: I had a dream that made me afraid. As I was lying in bed, the images and visions that passed through my mind terrified me. 7:9: As I looked, thrones were set in place, and the Ancient of Days took his seat. His clothing was as white as snow; the hair of his head was white like wool. His throne was flaming with fire, and its wheels were all ablaze. 7:13: "In my vision at night I looked, and there before me was one like a son of man, coming with the clouds of heaven. He approached the Ancient of Days and was led into his presence." 12:2: Multitudes who sleep in the dust of the earth will awake: some to everlasting life, others to shame and everlasting contempt. 12:3: Those who are wise will shine like the brightness of the heavens, and those who lead many to righteousness, like the stars for ever and ever.*

Minor Prophets

The minor prophets offer twelve books, from Hosea to Malachi, the last book of the Hebrew Bible, after which God's story begins again with the four New Testament books of the gospel. A challenge to reading and appreciating the minor prophets is their relative obscurity. Jonah is easily the best known of the twelve minor prophets, memorable to all of us for the book's account of the prophet's survival in the belly of a great fish. Many who have never read the Bible or even been to church will have heard that beginning to Jonah's story, although they wouldn't know its context or conclusion, both equally fascinating. None of the other minor prophets come close to reaching the secular public's consciousness. Only avid Bible readers and committed students of the Bible know well the other books, although the books describe, refer to, and elaborate on some of the same fascinating and important historical figures and events as the other prophetical books by the major prophets, while disclosing new events, insights, and figures. Like Jonah, the other minor prophets are themselves remarkable figures. The books also include popular verses well worth committing to memory. Read the minor prophets with the same excitement and using the same commitment as any other part of the Bible. They, too, are God's gift of his holy word.

Hosea

"Go, marry a promiscuous woman and have children with her, for like an adulterous wife this land is guilty of unfaithfulness to the Lord." 1:2.

Theme. Hosea's theme is faithlessness. The faithlessness that the book illustrates so poignantly is, of course, our own, or in the historical context, Israel's faithlessness. Our holy, righteous God stands in utter contrast, always faithful. Hosea's book explores, in a remarkably personal context, the bitterness of faithlessness, how God must have felt when the Israelites lusted after other gods and how God must feel when we reject his love to devote ourselves to our own lusts. The book makes an extraordinary contribution to the canon in that respect. Our first concern should be with how God feels about our heart and the conduct that flows from it. Hosea shows how Israel made God's heart their last concern or no concern at all. Hosea's enormously valuable contribution to the reader, then, is to give the reader the clearest of pictures for how our faithlessness wounds God. If we cannot remember the principles, if we cannot follow the rules, then at least we should know and value the heart of God.

Author. Hosea is clearly the author of his book, given its extraordinarily personal account. From references in the book, especially his prophecies about king Jeroboam II, while Hosea's wife was bearing Hosea children, Hosea may have lived under Jeroboam II in the northern kingdom Israel rather than southern kingdom Judah. Hosea 1:1 also lists four southern-kingdom kings Uzziah, Jotham, Ahaz, and Hezekiah who ruled during Hosea's prophesies, giving firm indication that Hosea lived around 755 to 715 B.C., when the major prophet Isaiah was also prophesying. The way that God wove Hosea's personal and family life into his prophesy thus offers another, much-humbler perspective on the period already introduced by Isaiah's soaring prophesies.

Context. As the first book by a minor prophet, after the major prophets created the road map for the reader, Hosea has a challenge to meet. That challenge is to prepare the reader to cover the same ground

140

again but while discovering new details. The reader already knows from Isaiah that late in the period when Hosea ministered, Israel fell to the Assyrians while Judah persisted toward its later exile. Assyria began its attack in 733 B.C., about in the middle of Hosea's ministry, succeeding in Israel's destruction and exile in 722 B.C., nearer Hosea's last prophesies. The reader simply gets to marvel at Hosea's unique prophetic approach, commanded from God, to that ground Isaiah already covered.

Structure. Hosea's staggering approach, revealed promptly in the book's second verse, is for the prophet, at God's command, to marry an adulterous wife, whose relationship with the prophet would then symbolize Israel's idolatrous relationship to God. Hosea obeys, where others would surely not. Hosea's wife Gomer then represents Israel in its faithlessness toward God. When in the book's first chapters Gomer indeed leaves Hosea to live and dally with other men, Hosea must then take Gomer back, again to symbolize God's forgiving, pursuing response to Israel's faithlessness. After that rocky start, the book's second part emphasizes the faithless one's need for repentance and return, while a third part emphasizes the continuing need to acknowledge and know the Lord. God has Hosea name his children to send prophetic messages to the disobedient northern-kingdom king, further drawing Hosea's family into the narrative. Hosea's structure, to set the narrative within Hosea's own family, makes the book an enthralling read.

Key Events. The book's first key event, setting the book's whole tone, is Hosea's marriage to the faithless Gomer, followed in quick succession by the birth and naming of their three children, each name to shame the disobedient northern king Jeroboam II. The last two names stood for *not loved* and *not my people*. The book's second chapter contains Hosea's prophecy comparing his faithless wife to faithless Israel but also foreseeing their restoration in forgiveness. Indeed, the next chapter records God commanding Hosea to take back his now-prostitute wife, which Hosea did by purchasing her freedom. The book's next chapter records Hosea's prophecy against the besieged Israel, about to fall to the Assyrians, followed by chapters recording further prophesies of judgment on unrepentant Israel. Israel, chapter eight records, had sown the wind and would now reap the whirlwind, chapters nine and ten recording Hosea's prophecy of that punishment. Chapters ten and eleven contrast God's love for Israel with Israel's sin, while concluding chapters thirteen and fourteen contrast the Lord's anger toward Israel with Israel's need to repent, thus pursuing the book's theme of faithlessness to its logical end.

Key Locations. As the prior paragraphs indicate, the book's key location is the northern kingdom Israel, where Hosea likely lived. That northern kingdom is certainly the primary target of his prophecies and the geographic focus of the book. Its attacker Assyria, which would prevail to carry off the Israelites into exile, came from the north. Israel led a similar trend already well established in the southern kingdom Judah, that would eventually lead to Judah's own exile. Hosea's message was not limited to the northern kingdom Israel. And of course, the book has even broader application to other nations, indeed to individuals including us. Hosea does refer interestingly to locales within Israel. God, for one instance, has Hosea name his first son Jezreel to remind the disobedient northern king Jeroboam II of the horrific massacre his ancestor Jehu committed at the city of that name. Geography teaches lessons in Hosea, as it does in other Bible books.

Revelation of Christ. A first revelation of Christ in Hosea is that Matthew 2:15 quotes Hosea 11:1 that God would call his Son out of Egypt. More to the point, Jesus quoted Hosea 6:6 twice, to two different audiences, recorded at Matthew 9:13 and 12:7. Each time, Jesus connected Hosea's verse "I desire mercy, not sacrifice," with himself and his good-news, forgiveness mission. The apostles Paul in Romans 9:25-26 and Peter in 1 Peter 2:10 each quoted Hosea 1:10 and 2:23 to confirm that God intended to save not just Jews but also Gentiles, with whom Paul and Peter shared the gospel. Hosea thus reveals our Lord Jesus Christ, right at the core of his saving mission. What, after all, did the prophet Hosea do toward his own wife, other than reflect Christ's desire, that first of his Father, to rescue the sinner by Christ's own sacrifice, rather than rest on the sacrifices of the innocent? Hosea makes a powerful witness to Jesus Christ.

Application. The unique power of Hosea's witness is in how God made his prophetic message personal to Hosea, as personal as a wayward wife and odd prophetic names for their children. The book thus shows how these prophesies of the decline and fall of kingdoms apply equally to our personal lives and family relationships. Do we display Gomer's faithlessness, ignoring God's steadfast love and generous provision? Moreover, can we display God's attributes, especially his mercy and persistence with us, reflected in the forgiving Hosea? Hosea challenges readers to both return to faith fully repentant of sin and to show God's forgiveness to take back a wayward family member or friend. Close, even intimate, relationship is possible, even after the worst sins.

Memory Verses. *1:7: "I will save them—not by bow, sword or battle, or by horses and horsemen, but by the Lord their God." 1:10: "In the place where it was said to them, 'You are not my people,' they will be called 'children of the living God.'" 2:23: "I will show my love to the one I called 'Not my loved one.' I will say to those called 'Not my people,' 'You are my people'; and they will say, 'You are my God.'" 4:6: My people are destroyed from lack of knowledge. 6:1: "Come, let us return to the LORD. He has torn us to pieces but he will heal us; he has injured us but he will bind up our wounds." 6:6: "For I desire mercy, not sacrifice, and acknowledgment of God rather than burnt offerings." 11:1: "When Israel was a child, I loved him, and out of Egypt I called my son."*

Joel

Alas for that day! For the day of the Lord is near; it will
come like destruction from the Almighty. 1:15.

Theme. Joel's theme is destruction. No other book focuses so
acutely, with such compelling imagery, on such a short period, reflecting
such intensity of God's judgment. Several other Bible books include or
refer to Joel's theme and imagery, but none with such brevity and focus.
God judges sin. When God does so, the consequences of his judgment
aren't pretty. Joel's intent is to impress its reader with the fury and
awfulness of falling under God's sin-condemning judgment. Joel wants
the reader to rend the reader's heart in repentance of sin, lest the reader
fall under God's awful judgment.

Author. The book opens with an attribution to Joel, the son of
Pethuel. That brief detail is all that history reveals of the book's author.
Joel wrote the book, but scholars can only conjecture as to where or
when. The book does not refer to persons or events that give clear clues
for the book's time or place, not, for instance, to any of Israel's or
Judah's kings. Some scholars draw that omission to suggest that Joel
may have written when the priest Jehoida ruled for the child king Joash,
perhaps around 835 B.C., which would have made Joel a contemporary
of the prophet Elisha. Any such date, though, is unreliable. The book
does address the southern kingdom Judah, focusing further on Zion,
referring to Jerusalem, and temple worship. The possibility thus exists
that Joel lived in or near Jerusalem, even having some role in or
relationship to its temple.

Context. The prior paragraph shows the difficulty readers have in
drawing from the book's uncertain historical context. However, Joel does
use an awful plague of locusts to illustrate God's judgment. Judah was
familiar with periodic devastating locust plagues. The book uses that
naturalistic context and its economic devastation and social impact to
great effect in convincing the reader, even the modern reader less
familiar with such plagues, to take most seriously God's coming
judgment. Joel also occupies an unusual position in the Hebrew canon in

144

that it is the first book in the canon's order (not its chronology but its compiled order) to introduce the day of the Lord, which is an end-times period of God judging the people, whether for their faith or instead for their rebellion. Joel thus makes a considerable contribution, despite its brevity and its position among the minor prophets.

Structure. Joel structures his brief narrative, just three chapters comprising his whole book, around the illustrating locust plague. His first chapter describes the plague in which locusts invade in vast number and destroy everything in their path, devastating the people's economy and society. The chapter concludes aptly, calling the people to repent. Chapter two likewise depicts a vicious army invading and destroying Judah, once again leading Joel to call for the people's repentance, this time God promising to restore the people if they do so. Joel ends his book with a vision of the great day of the Lord, when all people must gather in the Valley of Decision, where God will bless the faithful and condemn the rebellious.

Key Events. As the prior paragraph suggests, Joel's first key event is the locust invasion, also referred to as a mighty army, invading and destroying the land. Joel then takes up a lament that further depicts the extent of the destruction. Joel 2:1 then resets the invasion to a future day of the Lord, of which Zion's trumpets should warn. Joel depicts the Lord at the head of the invasion, this time one of ultimate judgment. The people must rend their hearts, in answer of which God will relent in his judgment. God can then pour out his Spirit on all people, saving all who call on his name. The nations, though, who do not call on his name, God will judge and condemn, even as he blesses his own people. Joel's events thus signal and illustrate the coming judgment.

Key Locations. Zion, referring to Judah's capitol Jerusalem, which Joel also names while describing it as God's holy hill, is the book's key geographic location. Jerusalem also represents Israel and God's chosen people. Joel's prophetic condemnations late in his book reach Tyre, Sidon, Philistia, Egypt, and Edom, also likely representative of other nations that oppose Israel and whose idolatrous people do not honor the Lord. Joel 3:6 mentions specifically that Tyre, Sidon, and Philistia sold Judah's people to the Greeks far away, in response to which God will sell their children to Judah who will resell them to the far-away Sabeans. Joel thus uses nations and places to support his prophesies of God's coming judgment and punishment.

Revelation of Christ. As brief as Joel's narrative is, Joel clearly prophesies, early and late in chapter two and into chapter three, of the Lord's coming day in judgment, what Christians also know as the return of Christ. Joel depicts God's chosen people as purified, saved, and restored through great suffering, as Christ suffered and offers his cross to those who follow him. Joel 2:32 also ties the people's redemption to their calling on the name of the Lord, as we must confess Christ openly, believing of his resurrection, for our salvation. Joel in the same verse proclaims that everyone who calls on the Lord's name receives the Lord's salvation, as Christians look to Jesus for salvation. Joel further prophesies God pouring out his Spirit on all people, as Jesus sent the Father's Spirit at Pentecost, following his ascension. For anyone doubting these parallels from Joel's prophesies to Jesus, Acts 2:16-21 records Peter quoting those very verses from Joel to explain what the people had just witnessed at Pentecost. The book Joel is thus a remarkable witness to our Lord and Savior Jesus Christ, a wonderful jewel hidden among the minor prophets.

Application. What does one do with an ancient prophecy of awful judgment in the end times, for those who rebel? End-times imagery can be a powerful reminder, more so than mere moral lessons or guiding principles. Ecclesiastes 12:13, among other verses, tells us that our whole duty is to fear God and keep his commands. End-times reminders, with their vivid, even horrific, imagery, can help to instill that sense of other-worldly awe we must have for our wholly other God. Taking Joel even just a little seriously in his warnings may do far greater good for us than reading many books of self-help principles. Joel's reminder of the salvation we have from judgment and death, in the person and work of Jesus Christ, should indeed be our constant companion.

Memory Verses. *2:1: Let all who live in the land tremble, for the day of the LORD is coming. It is close at hand.... 2:12: "Even now," declares the LORD, "return to me with all your heart, with fasting and weeping and mourning." 2:13: Rend your heart and not your garments. Return to the LORD your God, for he is gracious and compassionate, slow to anger and abounding in love, and he relents from sending calamity. 2:28: "And afterward, I will pour out my Spirit on all people. Your sons and daughters will prophesy, your old men will dream dreams, your young men will see visions." 2:32: And everyone who calls on the name of the LORD will be saved; for on Mount Zion and in Jerusalem there will be deliverance, as the Lord has said, even among the survivors whom the Lord calls.*

Amos

Away with the noise of your songs! I will not listen to the music of your harps. But let justice roll on like a river, righteousness like a never-failing stream! 5:23.

Theme. The theme of Amos is justice. Yes, justice includes the treatment one receives from a court, whether in criminal conviction and sentence, or in adjusting rights between disputing private parties. We tend to associate the justice that a judge offers in court with the justice that we expect from God. God, like the judge in court, acts with superior authority, neutrally, independent of the claims and causes before him. Yet the justice to which Amos gives greater attention is the justice between fellow humans in their daily interactions outside of court. Justice isn't solely a matter of a superior authority settling relative rights. Justice is instead a daily issue of how we treat our family members, neighbors, co-workers, employer and employees, and especially those in and outside of our communities who have little or no power to protect their interests nor to serve or provide for themselves. Amos is a tremendous reminder of the significance of justice to the heart, character, and spirit within us and how God will indeed judge.

Author. Amos wrote his book from a perspective unique among known Hebrew Bible book authors, most of whom were kings, priests, prophets, or officials, or held other high and influential position. Amos makes clear in his book, beginning with his introduction, that he was instead a simple shepherd, from a family of shepherds, and, he reveals later in verse 7:14, a caretaker of sycamore-fig trees. His low, outsider status within society's power structure made his prophetic critique of Israel's many daily injustices especially nettlesome for the oppressors. Amos resided in Tekoa, about ten miles south of Jerusalem, and thus in Judah, although he prophesied against the northern kingdom Israel, making his outside status and pointed criticisms even more irksome. Amos wrote sometime between 767 and 753 B.C., during the overlapping reigns of Judah's king Uzziah and Israel's king Jeroboam II.

Context. Arrogance, material prosperity, and spiritual poverty marked Jeroboam II's reign in northern Israel, toward which Amos directed his condemning prophesies. Israel was prospering economically, through its many alliances, but that prosperity was drawing the Israelites away from God, while increasing rather than decreasing injustices within its society. The people had not kept up but had instead abandoned their religious devotions that would have tempered their greed and arrogance, preserved their conscience, and led to better treatment of the poor and neighbor. In targeting Israel, Amos had fertile ground for his justice critique.

Structure. Amos has a three-part structure beginning with prophecies against Israel for its having rejected the Lord and letting the false gods of its neighbors lead it astray. God, Amos 2:13 warns, would crush Israel. Chapters three through six then offer a series of sermons first as to idolatrous Israel, then against its immoral and prideful people, then against its complacent leaders who oppress the poor, and finally against Israel's religious practices and its need to seek good and return to God to live. The book's last part offers visions of judgment, that God sets up a plumb line against which to measure his people, and that Israel is headed for exile, although in the end God in his mercy will restore. Amos thus offers his unique critique of justice within a more-traditional prophetic form.

Key Events. Amos first prophesies against Israel's idolatrous neighbors, necessary to his next prophesy against Israel. The neighboring nations' idols had drawn away Israel in its enriching commerce with those neighbors. To prove his prophesy, Amos calls witnesses against Israel, mimicking courtroom form. Amos then summarizes that Israel has left its God, for which it should lament and of which it should repent in return to God. Amos then warns the complacent, showing how the Lord abhors Israel's pride. God's judgment, Amos continues, will bring locusts and a plumb line. Amos' prophesy must have had effect, because Bethel's priest ordered Amos out of Israel and warned Israel's king Jeroboam II. Amos simply redoubled his criticism, ending his book first with a prophecy of Israel's destruction and then restoration.

Key Locations. The northern kingdom Israel is the key location for the book's prophecies, although Amos also warns its neighbors Aram, Ammon, Edom, Philistia, Tyre, and Moab. Although Amos was from south of Jerusalem, in Judah's northern region, Amos must have traveled north of Jerusalem into Israel to give his prophesies, given that the priest of Bethel, at the time just to the north of the border between Judah and

Israel, ordered Amos out of Israel. Israel would indeed soon go into exile in Assyria, to Israel's north.

Revelation of Christ. The New Testament book of Acts makes two references to Amos, first from the martyr Stephen quoting a prophesy against Israel and later from James quoting a prophesy of the Gentiles, meaning all people, turning to the Lord. Amos' prophesies of Israel's exile and restoration indeed extended to the redemption of all people, reflecting Christ's great commission of his disciples to go to all nations. On the practical side, Amos' concern for justice for the poor anticipated Christ's great concern. Christ's ministry bent toward the powerless and lost, the sinner needing his pursuit and salvation rather than those who found no need. Amos 5:18-20 also referred to the end-times day of the Lord, a frequent New Testament theme. Amos reveals the heart and return of Christ.

Application. For Christians, Amos is a call to action. Prayer, worship, and meditation must inspire, invoke, include, and incorporate service, especially to the poor. Amos 5:21-24 roars that God would do away with our religious celebrations and songs to see his justice roll on a like a river. We cannot take pleasure in corporate worship at the expense of our commitment to one another in heartfelt and earnest service. We worship in order to care, to form the heart and inspire to serve. We must look at how we treat our neighbors in their need to see the condition of our own heart before God. Amos has a strong justice message for followers of Christ today. Needs can be both material and spiritual. We cannot ignore one expecting to satisfy the other.

Memory Verses. *3:3: Do two walk together unless they have agreed to do so? 3:7: Surely the Sovereign Lord does nothing without revealing his plan to his servants the prophets. 5:23-24: "Away with the noise of your songs! I will not listen to the music of your harps. But let justice roll on like a river, righteousness like a never-failing stream!" 8:11: "The days are coming," declares the Sovereign Lord, "when I will send a famine through the land – not a famine of food or a thirst for water, but a famine of hearing the words of the Lord."*

Reading Guide

Parables

Parables play an important role in the Bible. Readers associate parables with Jesus's ministry, as indeed he taught about God's kingdom using parables and at times explained those parables to his disciples. Other books beyond the gospel books, though, also employ parables, generally shorter in length than Jesus's parables but still parables in form. Indeed, Jesus sometimes borrowed his parable's form from parables or allegory already in the Hebrew Bible. A parable is a story or similar construct meant to reveal a truth indirectly, one that the reader or hearer must draw. A very short parable, so short as to be less a truth-laden tale and more like an evocative phrase or sentence, would work more like allegory. The words describe one thing while suggesting something deeper, carrying more significance, instructing the one who is willing to learn.

Jesus intimated that he used parables to attract hearers who had the heart to learn from him. Let those who have ears hear. He also intimated that he used parables to repel those who did not have that heart. Some persons are ever hearing, never understanding. Jesus also appears to have used parables to buy his ministry time, so that hearers antagonistic to his cause had only indirect evidence to use against him. His parables permitted him to teach about his coming kingdom without suffering prompt arrest for blasphemy. Arrest and execution would come later, after Jesus had taught, trained, and prepared his disciples and other hearers, often through parables. As with symbols, a key to not reading the wrong things or too much into a parable is to first recognize the context. What was the preacher or prophet trying to communicate to what audience? Then, let persons and things within the parable represent the few persons or constituencies, whether God, religious leaders, believers, or non-believers, whom the parable modeled.

Obadiah

"The day of the Lord is near for all nations. As you have done, it will be done to you; your deeds will return upon your own head." 15.

Theme. Obadiah's theme is indifference, a specific kind of indifference. We can certainly be indifferent to many things, perhaps to the ways of the world and the frivolous things that the world values. But the indifference that Obadiah condemns is indifference to God's things, especially God's people. We cannot *stand aloof*, as Obadiah puts it, while others harm God's people and carry off their wealth. Indifference is fine when its subject is the distracting or useless thing. Indifference is fatal when its subject is the essential concerns of God.

Author. History tells us nothing of Obadiah, the author of this shortest book of the Hebrew Bible. Twelve other Hebrew Bible figures bear that name, meaning *worshipper of Yahweh*, but no evidence suggests their connection to this book. The book's twenty-one total verses leave only bare inferences, at best, of where and when Obadiah might have lived. Obadiah's prophetic target Edom was to Judah's south, in what is now southwestern Jordan. Obadiah's prophetic concern was Jerusalem and Edom's treatment of Jews fleeing from Judah. Those clues may suggest that Obadiah wrote from Judah, even Jerusalem. Edom's participation in the attacks of stronger Philistines on Judah may indicate the book's date as early as 840 B.C., in which case the book would be the earliest of the minor prophets.

Context. Obadiah's target Edom was too weak to carry out its own military conquest of Judah, even to attack Jerusalem in Judah's north. That weakness makes Edom a peculiar target for Obadiah's condemnations except in one respect: Edom could stand by, watch stronger nations plunder Jerusalem, and then harass and raid Jews as they fled Judah. This context, national and military more than historical and spiritual, is critical to appreciating Obadiah's prophecy against indifference. Sometimes, the greater sin is in standing by among the hecklers while others carry out the unrighteous attack.

Structure. Obadiah uses his spare twenty-one verses well, still offering clear structure. Obadiah first supplies the character evidence against Edom, that its people are prideful, arrogant, and violent toward their brothers, thinking that they soar while God prepares to bring them down. Obadiah's second part makes the charge that Edom has been indifferent to its neighbor Judah's suffering, looking down on Judah while becoming one of Judah's oppressors. Obadiah's third part is to reach God's verdict against Edom and to pass sentence. Edom would become stubble, never to rise again, just as the day of the Lord is near for all nations, over whom God will stand in judgment.

Key Events. The single key event in Obadiah's brief prophesy is the Lord's word to Edom. Obadiah's prophecy embeds within that word several past and future events. The nations rose against Judah in battle. Small and weak Edom, in her pride, had allied with those nations against Judah, expecting that it would soar, when instead God would turn those nations against Edom. Edom had stood aside when those nations attacked Judah, gloating over Judah's misfortune, and becoming like her attackers. Edom had stood by the crossroads to cut down the fleeing Jews, the result of which would be that God would destroy Edom. Edom, history confirms, disappeared from earth's face, never heard from again.

Key Locations. As the prior paragraph indicates, Obadiah's prophetic target Edom was to Judah's south, below the Dead Sea, in what is now southwestern Jordan. Edom would have stood in the path of Jews fleeing south and west, around the Dead Sea's southern end, to avoid the strong Philistines attacking from the west and violent Assyrians, Moabites, and others attacking from the north and northeast. Edom may not have initiated wars against Judah, but it gladly accepted the role of beneficiary from those wars, raiding the fleeing Jews of any treasures they might have tried to carry with them. These location considerations are significant to appreciating Obadiah's unusual but valuable warning against indifference.

Revelation of Christ. As short of a book as Obadiah is, and as much as it focuses on condemnation of the foreign nation Edom, it conceals its messianic message more than other books. But the message is there. Obadiah refers to Judah at times as Jacob and to Edom at times as Esau, invoking the Jacob/Esau brother relationship. Jacob, the deceiver and younger, was nonetheless God's chosen in grace. Esau, the older and a man of appetite, was rejected but saved through the grace God showed Jacob. And so, Jesus, Judah's king, saves the non-Jews, the Gentiles, represented by Edom. Obadiah hints at a remnant of Edom surviving, especially when connected with the prior book Amos. We, too, are Judah's beneficiaries, saved by their Christ Jesus's grace.

Application. Obadiah's lesson to us is indeed a valuable one. We find easier standing by out of the fray, not getting involved, than to stand alongside and stand up for the oppressed. *None of my business,* we want to say, so that we can continue to enjoy our comforts and pursue our pleasures. Yet Obadiah teaches us that in doing so, we join the oppressors. One cannot be indifferent to injustice without reaping its undue benefits. We must stand for the oppressed, especially for the people of God when under attack from their oppressors.

Memory Verses. 3: *"The pride of your heart has deceived you, you who live in the clefts of the rocks and make your home on the heights, you who say to yourself, 'Who can bring me down to the ground?'"* 11: *"On the day you stood aloof while strangers carried off his wealth and foreigners entered his gates and cast lots for Jerusalem, you were like one of them."* 12: *"You should not gloat over your brother in the day of his misfortune...."* 15: *"The day of the Lord is near for all nations. As you have done, it will be done to you; your deeds will return upon your own head."* 21: *"Deliverers will go up on Mount Zion to govern the mountains of Esau. And the kingdom will be the Lord's."*

Jonah

"In my distress I called to the Lord, and he answered me. From deep in the realm of the dead I called for help, and you listened to my cry." 2:2.

Theme. Jonah is a powerful book of God's grace. Readers typically associate Jonah with its account of his sojourn in the belly of a great fish. What a fish has to do with grace is not so obvious. Yet while God showed grace to Jonah in using the fish to deliver him from his fatal flight, Jonah's book is more about the grace God showed a violent foreign nation Assyria. God sent Jonah to Assyria's capitol Nineveh to preach its destruction unless it repented. Remarkably, Nineveh did so, which Jonah least expected. When God relented in the face of Nineveh's repentance, and did not bring about its destruction, God showed the violent foreign Nineveh extraordinary grace, which Jonah did not fully appreciate. The book thus stands testament to God's love for all, not just his chosen people, whom Jonah represented. The book is a precious demonstration of God's great grace.

Author. Although Jonah's book gives a third-person account and does not directly indicate its authorship, the personal nature of the account suggests that Jonah was either the book's author or at least the one who initially recorded or shared the account for a later compiler. The book tells us that Jonah was from Gath-Hepher, which was near Jesus's hometown Nazareth in what Jews later identified as the Galilee region, in the northern kingdom Israel. Most prophets were instead from the southern kingdom Judah, making Jonah an especially interesting figure. Jonah served as Israel's prophet during the reign of the northern king Jeroboam II between 793 and 753 B.C.

Context. During Jeroboam II's reign, the northern kingdom Israel was at a peak of its political and military power, and regional influence, allying and trading peacefully with its surrounding traditional enemies. Those alliances, though, contributed to Israel's spiritual depravity during Jeroboam II's reign. Israel was strong in the world's eyes but weak in God's eyes. God, though, had Amos and others prophesy to Jeroboam II.

Jonah would instead prophesy to the Assyrians, a violent people to Israel's north who were especially known for their cruelty to captives. Hence, Jonah's initial flight from God's commission and the need for his rescue and reversal in the fish's belly. Hence, also, Jonah's lack of appreciation for God's having spared the cruel and violent, but in this rare instance repentant, Ninevites. Historical, political, military, and cultural context thus means much to Jonah's message.

Structure. Jonah's four-chapter book has a clear chronological and narrative structure. Chapter one records God's commission of Jonah and Jonah's hazardous flight, ending up in the belly of the fish. Chapter two records Jonah's fervent prayer from the fish's belly for God's help, and God's command that the fish vomit Jonah onto land. Chapter three records Jonah's obedient journey into the violent metropolis Nineveh, where he preached the city's overthrow in forty days, leading the Ninevites and their king to believe God and repent in sackcloth and fasting. Chapter four shows Jonah's anger when God relents, and God's grace toward Jonah despite his anger. Jonah's book moves swiftly in short chapters, bringing the reader quickly to its point: God gives grace even to those whom his people might not desire he show such grace.

Key Events. The book opens quickly with God's call to Jonah to go to Nineveh and Jonah's rebellious flight aboard a ship headed in the opposite direction. God sends a tempest at the ship, causing its crew to throw Jonah overboard to appease God. God, though, sent a huge fish to swallow and hold Jonah for three days. As the prior paragraph indicates, Jonah prayed from inside the fish, in answer to which God had the fish save Jonah by depositing him on land. Jonah proceeded dutifully to Ninevite with God's message of destruction, upon which the Ninevites repented. Jonah prayed petulantly to the Lord that the Lord should have destroyed Nineveh and so should now kill Jonah. Jonah sat outside the city, likely sulking, but God made a plant grow to shade Jonah's burning head. Jonah appreciated the comfort, but when God made the plant die, Jonah again wished that he were dead. The extraordinary little book ends with God pointing out Jonah's greater concern for the shade plant than for the hundred-twenty-thousand residents of Nineveh.

Key Locations. For such a short book, Jonah has several key locations. Jonah likely began his reluctant journey from within Israel, but rather than heading north to Nineveh as the Lord called him, Jonah headed as far west across the sea as he could likely imagine, toward Tarshish in Spain. The ship carrying Jonah west is among the little book's key locations, where the crew and Jonah debate their best course.

The huge fish's belly is another critical location, from which Jonah pleads his fervent prayer. God's fish brought Jonah back to the shore, sending him on to the book's principal location Nineveh, Assyria's capitol well to Israel's north. The book makes clear Nineveh's great size, taking three days to traverse. Jonah had a great work ahead of him, to spur Nineveh's repentance. The book's last key location lies outside Nineveh, where Jonah sat in the scorching sun, playing out his sulking exchange with his God of grace.

Revelation of Christ. Jonah contains remarkable revelations of our Lord Jesus Christ, to which Jesus himself referred. Matthew 12:39-41 records Jesus's prophecy that he would be three days and nights in the earth's heart, just as Jonah was three days and nights in the belly of a fish. As Hebrews 2:17 confirms, Jesus would experience everything humans experience, including death. Jonah's fervent prayer from within the fish reads not like the rebellious, reluctant, and sulking prophet whom Jonah was but instead like a prayer Christ could have prayed. That prayer, in another remarkable witness to Christ, ends with Jonah's confession that salvation comes from the Lord. Though Jonah was reluctant and even regretful in witness to Nineveh, the effect of his prophecy foreshadowed Christ's own salvation to the Gentiles, even to violent sinners like the people of Nineveh. Being a book of grace, Jonah is also clearly a book of salvation, whether of the Jew Jonah or the Gentile city Nineveh. Jonah's book reflects Christ, from beginning call to go to the Gentiles, to ending grace.

Application. Jonah is also a thoroughly modern book in reflecting the reluctance, rebelliousness, and sulking of called witnesses. How often do we hesitate, turn the other way, and even run away from our call? And when God does compel us to witness to his Son's extraordinary grace, how often do we sulk at our call's inconvenience and the mercy God shows to undeserving sinners? Jonah clearly warns us to answer the call to witness. The book also clearly warns us to press forward without the necessity of God's compelling. And the book ends with the best of reminders not to sulk in carrying out God's mission. Jonah well reflects the modern witness's mind, one against which the Spirit properly warns us. Answer the call, and don't complain.

Memory Verses. 1:17: Now the Lord provided a huge fish to swallow Jonah, and Jonah was in the belly of the fish three days and three nights. 2:1: "In my distress I called to the Lord, and he answered me." 2:3: "You hurled me into the depths, into the very heart of the seas, and the currents swirled about me; all your waves and breakers swept

*over me." 2:6: "[Y]ou, Lord my God, brought my life up from the pits."
2:8: "Those who cling to worthless idols turn away from God's love for
them." 2:9: "Salvation comes from the Lord." 4:4: "Is it right for you to
be angry?"*

Micah

What does the Lord require of you? To act justly and to
love mercy and to walk humbly with your God. 6:8.

Theme. Micah's theme is judgment. Micah's book shows the reader
two paths, one toward evil and the other toward good, while also
assuring that repentance and reliance on the coming Savior lead to
restoration and participation in God's glorious kingdom. At the center of
Micah's book, after condemnations of the idolatrous but before
invitations to salvation, Micah presents a courtroom scene with the
people on trial. Micah's theme treats fully, judgment's tension between
justice for wrongs and mercy for repentance, with the ultimate invitation
of salvation. Micah thus provides the full context for God's judgment,
including his holy and righteous nature, but also his intense love for
humankind, the great offer from which is his Son Jesus. Micah is a most-
remarkable book from the Hebrew canon.

Author. Micah, the author of the book by his name, was from the
agricultural town Moresheth Gath, southwest of Jerusalem near Judah's
border with Philistia. Micah's humble station well outside Jerusalem's
power structure gave him an affinity for the poor and outcast, sharpening
his prophesies against rulers in Israel and Judah who did not hear and
follow the Lord in his demands for justice. Micah prophesied during the
reigns of Judah's alternately good-and-evil kings Jotham, Ahaz, and
Hezekiah, while Israel to Judah's north was under the reigns of evil kings
leading to Israel's exile in 722 B.C. Micah was thus a contemporary of
Isaiah and Hosea, like those prophets predicting Israel's demise in a
larger context of coming restoration.

Context. Israel was indeed decaying under its leaders' corruption
during Micah's prophesies. Its first tribes fell to its Assyrian attackers led
by king Pul in 740 B.C. and its final tribes in 722 B.C. to Assyrians
under Shalmaneser V. Micah prophesied before, during, and after Israel's
fall, predicting it, witnessing it, and speaking to the Israelites in exile.
Micah also prophesied against his own kingdom Judah, whose good
kings Jotham and Hezekiah discouraged Judah from Israel's idolatry but

whose evil king Ahaz did not. In either case, Micah had fertile ground in prophesying judgment against those rulers who abandoned the Lord's commandments to oppress their own people and worship foreign gods.

Structure. Micah's book begins in its first two chapters with prophesies of a day of judgment. Israel had abandoned the Lord and, in doing so, turned its people toward cheating and mistreating one another. Micah's middle three chapters make an unexpected turn, though, to Judah's coming day of triumph. The Messiah would come to teach the people his ways and lead the people to glory. Micah's book ends with two chapters describing Israel's day in court on trial before God who makes his case against his own people. God, though, is merciful, desiring to pardon all who repent of their sin and return humbly to him, their Savior.

Key Events. Micah first prophesies that the Lord was coming to make a rubble heap of Samaria, Israel's capitol, as indeed Israel would soon fall. Micah's prophesy also gives the reason, that Israel's people had plotted evil against one another, stealing one another's fields and houses, while following false prophets. Micah's prophesies rebuked the leaders of Israel and Judah who had led their people into hating good and loving evil, despising justice and distorting all right. Micah then foresaw the last days establishing the Lord's temple, to which many nations will come in peace. Out of Bethlehem would arise Israel's ruler of ancient origins, who would shepherd his flock in the Lord God's majesty, reaching to the earth's ends. Micah returned briefly to the judgment of Israel before ending with Israel's rise in praise. Micah's narrative thus mixes alternately condemning and soaring prophesies in extremes that warn and delight the reader.

Key Locations. Micah's prophecies focus internally toward both the northern kingdom Israel and southern kingdom Judah. Micah often mentions Israel's capitol Samaria and Judah's capitol Jerusalem in those prophecies, highlighting the leaders' roles in the kingdoms' rise and fall. Micah prophesies both Israel's exile to Assyria, occurring later during Micah's ministry, and Judah's exile to Babylon, not to occur until generations later, giving the book its important regional context. Micah also refers to nations outside Israel and Judah coming together in extraordinary peace and God's praise, giving the book a much-broader world view. For a humble prophet residing far from the Jews' power center, Micah lifts his prophesies to an elevated national and world view.

Revelation of Christ. Micah's book supplies one of the Hebrew Bible's most stirring revelations of Christ's reign in the last days. Micah's chapter four records Micah's last-days prophesy, how many nations would come to the Lord's mountain temple where the Lord would judge many people, settling disputes and restoring peace. The Lord would gather the lame and exiles as his people. Remarkably, the Spirit also reveals to Micah a prophesy of Jesus's Bethlehem birthplace. That prophesy, recorded in Micah 5:2, would seven-hundred years later lead Magi from the East to travel hundreds of miles to pay homage to the child Jesus, as Matthew 2:5-6 records. Micah is one of the first books to which Bible readers point for its revelation of the coming Christ.

Application. Micah, much like Amos, reminds the reader of the need to do justice to one's fellow. Micah speaks to us just as he did to ancient Israelites, when he condemns dishonest merchants, robbers and thieves, people who mistreat vulnerable women and children, and rulers who live in luxury off the oppression of their people. We must deal honestly and fairly in transactions with others. We must especially not take advantage of the vulnerable, instead protecting them against all such wrongs. We must also lead as servants rather than oppressive rulers, while holding our own rulers accountable to do likewise. Each lesson that Micah holds for his contemporaries applies equally in modern setting. The evils that Micah saw among his leaders and people are evils to which we succumb today.

Memory Verses. *2:7: "Do not my words do good to the one whose ways are upright?" 2:13: "The One who breaks open the way will go up before them; they will break through the gate and go out. Their King will pass through before them, the Lord at their head." 4:3: They will beat their swords into plowshares and their spears into pruning hooks. Nation will not take up sword against nation, nor will they train for war anymore. 5:2: "But you, Bethlehem Ephrathah, though you are small among the clans of Judah, out of you will come for me one who will be ruler over Israel, whose origins are from of old, from ancient times." 5:4: He will stand and shepherd his flock in the strength of the Lord, in the majesty of the name of the Lord his God. And they will live securely, for then his greatness will reach to the ends of the earth. 7:18: Who is a God like you, who pardons sin and forgives the transgression of the remnant of his inheritance? You do not stay angry forever but delight to show mercy.*

Nahum

The Lord is good, a refuge in times of trouble. 1:7.

Theme. The theme of Nahum is refuge. We see in the world around us, and too often within ourselves, the chaos of a creation without God. The degradation that Nahum witnessed around him spurred his prophecies of destruction, but that degradation also inspired his prophecies that our wholly good God would protect during that chaos. God is a God of order, safety, and protection. He is shelter in a storm and sanctuary against oppression. God is hope in our darkest hour for a coming dawn. Nahum's inspired mission was to convey that hope to his readers, against a very dark and threatening storm.

Author. Nahum means comfort, the perfect name for a book about God as refuge. The first verse of Nahum's three-chapter book describes him as the Elkoshite, suggesting a residence in a town the location of which history does not confirm. A town of a similar name Elcesi was in the agricultural region of southwestern Judah, not far from the prophet Micah's home. Whether that location was Nahum's residence or not, his prophecies clearly displayed a fear of the violent Assyrians' great power, constantly threatening Judah to Assyria's south. Nahum thus identifies as Judean, in the concern of his prophecies. Nahum's prophecy most likely dates to between 663 and 654 B.C., based on its mention of the fall of Thebes without mentioning Thebes subsequent reconstruction, during a period that Assyria was a growing threat to Judah.

Context. If one accepts the dating the prior paragraph suggests, then Nahum would have been prophesying during the reign of Manasseh, among the most evil of Judah's kings, until his humbling near the end of his reign. These days were Judah's darkest and most idolatrous, when the people were furthest from God, up until Judah's later exile. For God to call Nahum to stand tall with prophesies that both told the truth of Judah's fallen condition while also comforting its faithful remnant shows the depth of God's love, mercy, and grace. Nahum's historical and spiritual context emphasizes its message of humankind's darkness pierced by God's judgment and light.

161

Structure. Nahum's book has a two-part structure. Its first chapter depicts God as Nineveh's supreme judge, in which he simultaneously shows that he is a stronghold and refuge for those who trust and obey him. Nahum's last two chapters depict Nineveh destroyed in God's righteous judgment. Nineveh's destruction would have been a substantial comfort to the people of Judah, thus making the book's last part work well with its first part, in which God had promised to be his people's refuge.

Key Events. Nahum begins his book with a section on the Lord's righteous anger against Nineveh, focusing on the Lord's good qualities. The Lord is slow to anger but sure to act, avenging wrongs with his unmatched, earth-trembling power. Yet, the book's first chapter continues, the Lord is also good, caring for those who trust in him during troubles. Indeed, that first chapter ends with an invitation for Judah to look at the one on the mountains who brings good news of peace and protection against the wicked Assyrian invaders. Nahum then prophesies the stumble and fall of the Assyrian's best troops, the Lord destroying the violent and feared Nineveh. The book ends with clapping at the fatal wound the Lord has inflicted on Nineveh.

Key Locations. As the prior paragraphs indicate, Nahum's book recognizes the great tension between the warring Assyrians, also called Ninevites after the Assyrian capitol Nineveh, to the north and the weaker Judah fearing their attack. Judah's northern neighbor Israel had already long ago fallen to the Ninevites. The book draws out that tension in Nahum's prophesies of the greater power of God to do as he wished with the feared Ninevites. In the course of prophesying Nineveh's downfall, and to prove the Lord's greater strength, Nahum also mentions the destruction of Thebes on the Nile, deep in Egypt, taken captive despite Egypt's power and its alliance with Put and Libya. As is so often the case in the Bible, geography illustrates Nahum's theme of God's power, judgment, and refuge.

Revelation of Christ. As a book of judgment, Nahum reflects that Christ is judge before whom all knees will bow at the last day. Yet as a book of refuge, Nahum reflects that Christ is also our refuge, our protector against the forces of evil and our Savior from God's own wrath in judgment. Christ defeated forever the forces of darkness, over whom we now have Christ's power. As Nahum preached God's power to judge the evil of the Ninevites, Nahum also preached Christ's defeat of the evil one. With each invocation of God against the murderous enemy Nineveh, Nahum invoked the resurrection's power over death, in the salvation of

Jesus Christ. Nahum is not explicit about these revelations, except in verse 1:15 when he heralds the feet of the one *who brings good news* of peace. We have that good news in the gospel of Jesus Christ.

Application. Nahum is a cautionary book in the same manner as other books of the minor prophets, especially Amos and Micah. If not guarding our hearts, we could identify as readily with Nineveh, for all its wealth, confidence, and military power, as with the weaker but righteous Judeans. We may find ourselves enjoying God's prosperity, stronger and richer than our neighbors. But God wants our hearts in full devotion. The moment that we begin to become self-assured, using God's abundant provision to accumulate power to wield against others in what we perceive to be our own best interests, we risk losing God's favor. God wants us dependent on him, not on the blessings he bestows on us. At the same time, Nahum offers refuge for us in our darkest times, when others or circumstances oppress us. God is our refuge and our strength, both lessons Nahum offers us, whether we are up or down, rich or poor, in or out of power.

Memory Verses. 1:3: The Lord is slow to anger but great in power; the Lord will not leave the guilty unpunished. 1:7: The Lord is good, a refuge in times of trouble. He cares for those who trust in him.... 1:15: Look, there on the mountains, the feet of one who brings good news, who proclaims peace! 3:1: Woe to the city of blood, full of lies, full of plunder, never without victims!

Habakkuk

"See, the enemy is puffed up; his desires are not upright—but the righteous person will live by his faithfulness...." 2:4.

Theme. Habakkuk's theme is faithfulness. We wait for God to act, and then we wait some more. We wonder when, even whether, God will do as he has promised, as his attributes and intentions require. We have heard of God and believe that we know him. We want to trust him, but still we must wait because he has not yet acted. Habakkuk shows that this waiting on God, imploring and expecting him to act as we trust that he will, is faith. Faith, Hebrews 11:1 tells us, is confidence in the things of God that we have not yet seen but for which we hope. Habakkuk's extraordinary little book shows faith in both discussion and in action.

Author. Habakkuk tells us in his first verse and again later in his book that he is a prophet, which is about all that we know of him. Not all Bible prophets claim to be so. Some, we know, were priests, another a shepherd, and many we simply do not know. When Habakkuk calls himself *the prophet*, though, a reader could fairly infer that he came from Judah's school of prophets, trained, appointed, and compensated to prophesy, as the Bible's history books show those schools to have existed during the reign of Israel's kings. Habakkuk ends his book saying that he wrote it for the choir director, on his stringed instruments, perhaps indicating that he was also a priest involved in the temple service. The extraordinary nature of his brief prophecy supports both inferences. Habakkuk's prophesy of an impending Babylonian invasion, three of which occurred between 605 and 586 B.C., the last leading to Judah's exile, may indicate a date just before that period.

Context. History doesn't confirm the above inferences about Habakkuk and the dating of his book, but those inferences help the reader make sense of the book. If the dating is correct, that Habakkuk wrote just before the first Babylonian invasion of Judah, then he wrote during Jehoiakim's 609-to-586-B.C. reign, during Judah's nadir. Habakkuk's prophesies support that Judah had reached a historic low point, one to which the evil king Jehoiakim had finally brought the nation. The attacking Babylonians had no regard for God, trusting only in their own conquering powers, abetted they believed by other gods. Yet Judah's ruler Jehoiakim and many of its people were so corrupt and idolatrous that Habakkuk could simultaneously complain justly about his own people's corruption. Corruption was everywhere, both inside and surrounding Judah. This context informed, inspired, and inflamed Habakkuk's discourse.

Structure. Habakkuk is a remarkable book, unusual among even the prophets, in that he recorded his two extended complaints to God, and God answers those complaints. Habakkuk's complaints had to do with God not acting to end the awful corruption within Judah, nor to remove the threat of the corrupt Babylonians. God's two answers in effect told Habakkuk to be patient because God was preparing to address his complaints. Habakkuk had to be patient, as indeed he was. His book ends with his prayer to God, acknowledging God's holy and righteous attributes, trusting that God would act in due course and time. Habakkuk rejoiced in joyful faith, even though still waiting on God.

Key Events. Habakkuk's book does not record specific events, other than the dialogue between Habakkuk and God. The book's first chapter opens with Habakkuk's brief complaint that he had been crying for help, without God listening, leaving Habakkuk surrounded by corruption and injustice. God answers that he would indeed be acting while Habakkuk still lived, using the Babylonians to end Judah's corruption, even though the Babylonians were themselves corrupt, believing only in their own strength. Habakkuk understandably wonders back to God whether using the corrupt Babylonians to destroy other nations including Judah is such a good idea. God responds to write it down, that he would indeed destroy the Babylonians, too, in due time. God's response is fully effective, for Habakkuk then prays in an awe-stricken, eloquent testament to the power and sovereignty of God.

Key Locations. Habakkuk only clearly identifies the threatening nation Babylonia, not even his own likely home Judah, which he leaves the reader to infer. Babylon soon became Judah's conqueror, carrying its people into exile to settle in its lands between the rivers far to the east. Babylon, though, later fell to the Medes and Persia, ending in destruction, as God had promised Habakkuk. Habakkuk also incidentally mentions that God is the Holy One from Mount Paran, which is likely a reference to Mount Sinai in the south of that peninsula. Habakkuk's geographic concern, though, was that the Babylonians were attacking his people, about to carry them off in exile.

Revelation of Christ. Habakkuk ends his prayer, in verses 16-19, first saying that he would take joy in the *God of his salvation*, finding his strength in God his Lord. He then sees that God has made his feet like those of a deer so that God can make him tread high places. In Habakkuk's darkest moment, Habakkuk thus saw his salvation in Jesus Christ, the strength of God. Habakkuk saw Jesus lifting him to God's mountain, his paradise garden, the home Jesus had made for him and everyone else who looks to Jesus. The whole of Habakkuk's book, expressing to God his fear of death and frustration over corruption, but then hearing and trusting in God's answer, ending with a vision of God transforming him to bound like a deer up God's mountain, is one integrated salvific vision. One cannot miss Christ in Habakkuk.

Application. How many times have you felt like Habakkuk, complaining once again to a belated Lord? The lesson of Habakkuk is a highly practical one for all of us who wonder when God will answer our prayers. God answers in due time. He simply asks that we wait to behold his glory in action. Patience is a hard thing, and yet patience is evidence of our faith. One cannot have faith without having patience, Habakkuk seems to teach us. Habakkuk showed that faith; look at the glory it produced. Trust God, even when you don't see him yet acting. If we have no trust, no patience, no willingness to wait, then we cannot claim faith. Show God your faith by imploring him in prayer but being patient for his answer.

Memory Verses. 1:2: *How long, Lord, must I call for help, but you do not listen? 1:5: "Look at the nations and watch—and be utterly amazed. For I am going to do something in your days that you would not believe, even if you were told." 1:12: Lord, are you not from everlasting? My God, my Holy One, you will never die. 2:3: "Though it linger, wait for it; it will certainly come and will not delay." 2:14: "For the earth will be filled with the knowledge of the glory of the Lord as the waters cover the sea." 2:18: ""Of what value is an idol carved by a craftsman? Or an image that teaches lies? For the one who makes it trusts in his own creation; he makes idols that cannot speak." 3:13: You came out to deliver your people, to save your anointed one. 3:19: "The Sovereign Lord is my strength; he makes my feet like the feet of a deer, he enables me to tread on the heights."*

Reading Guide

Rereading

What does one do after having read the Bible cover to cover? Read it again. Many Bible readers have not read the Bible cover to cover, start to finish. They prefer instead to read their favorite books or have just never read the Bible as they would other books, beginning at the beginning and ending at the end. Because the Bible is God's integrated account of his history and intention through the Lord Jesus Christ, the Bible can work for readers in that piecemeal or partial fashion. One may get all one needs, or most of what one needs, from a single Bible book or a few books, knowing that the books refer to, quote, incorporate, reflect, and build on one another. Yet still, one wonders, what does one do after having read the Bible cover to cover other than start reading the Bible once again?

Rereading is a valuable activity. The more one reads a text, the more one recalls of it and the more one can see in it. Each reading reinforces prior readings, while inspiring new reflections. So, certainly, keep reading the Bible after having read it. Start again, either at the beginning or with a book or passage to which the Spirit guides you, alone or interacting with others. Some have read the Bible dozens of times, cover to cover, still discovering meanings that had always been there but they had never noticed. Indeed, for many of us, the more we read the Bible, the more we realize how little we know of its treasures. And the more we read the Bible, the more we wish to interact with its text. The Bible is God's living word. Reading the Bible is fine, but applying its words is better. To apply God's word, study, surmise, hypothesize, and reflect, until you can carry out and live out what it says.

Zephaniah

The great day of the Lord is near—near and coming quickly. 1:14.

Theme. Zephaniah's theme is coming, as in, something is sure to happen. We anticipate things, many things, some good, some bad. Anticipating, waiting, expecting—it's all part of life. The kind of coming, though, that Zephaniah makes his theme is the coming of the Lord, that day of the Lord's return. God is preparing now to return soon. The day approaches. Do not question it. God is not delaying unduly. He has his reasons for his timing. But he is coming. Expect it. Anticipate it. Prepare for it. And live for it.

Author. Zephaniah is unusual in beginning his book by elaborating his royal lineage back to Judah's good king Hezekiah. Zephaniah was not a king, although his lineage suggests that he could have been. Instead, Zephaniah was a prophet in Jerusalem, familiar with the temple's religious services, and so likely an insider, closely connected with the religious and royal authorities. Zephaniah's breaking prophetic form, to trace his lineage back to a famously good king of Judah, suggests Zephaniah's interest in impressing his readers with his insider status. Zephaniah tells us that he prophesied during Josiah's reign, which was between 640 and 609 B.C. Details within the book, like the predicted fall of Nineveh and frequent references to the Law, when the Book of the Law remained lost until later in Josiah's reign, suggests a date later in that reign.

Context. Josiah's reign was a time of much-needed reform within Judah. Zephaniah would have grown up during the reigns of the evil Manasseh and his equally evil son Amon, each of whom led Judah in shocking idolatry including child sacrifice. Josiah instituted reforms, but Judah's stain remained. The Judaeans not only had their high places for idolatrous worship but were also bringing those practices into God's temple. Just four short years after Josiah's reign ended, Babylon would attack, beginning the first of Judah's three successive defeats and three waves into exile. So, Zephaniah was preaching during an only temporary reform, as if too little, too late, in the face of the impending exile that Zephaniah prophesied. Zephaniah's insider status would have made his prophesies more shocking than they otherwise would have been, if they had come from an outsider like the shepherd prophet Amos.

Structure. Zephaniah's brief, three-chapter book has a clear and helpful, two-part structure. Zephaniah's two-part structure begins with prophesies of God's impending judgment, compelling Judah to repent and reform. Zephaniah's prophesies call these coming judgments *the day of the Lord*, a phrase and concept that Zephaniah invokes more than any other book in the Hebrew Bible. Zephaniah's second part foresees God preserving a faithful remnant, those who have trusted in the Lord and will sing and shout for joy. The Lord will purify and save, rather than judge, punish, and condemn, that remnant.

Key Events. Zephaniah begins his book with a prophesy of the Lord sweeping away everything on the earth, all humankind including Judah and its capitol Jerusalem filled with its idolatrous images. Zephaniah prophesies the specific punishment of Judah's rulers, merchants, complacent, and rich. In that day, God will consume all people on earth for their wickedness. Chapter two gives the reader a brief interlude, encouraging Judah to gather and humble itself before the Lord, before Zephaniah returns to condemnations of Judah's surrounding enemies, each for God to destroy. Zephaniah's final chapter returns to Jerusalem's future, in which the prophesy sees its future, too, destroyed for wickedness, although here the book ends with the restoration of Israel's righteous remnant, those whom God purifies when having called on the name of the Lord.

Key Locations. Zephaniah focuses his prophecies on Judah and its capitol Jerusalem, where plenty of evidence remained of the evil, idolatrous practices that Manasseh and his son Amon had elevated. Zephaniah's prophecies, though, cast a wider net in condemning Judah's warring neighbors Philistia, Moab, and Ammon, and near neighbors Cush and Assyria, and an even wider net in condemning the whole world. Zephaniah in his geographical references displays his insider, Jerusalem-centered perspective, but one that is quite conscious of the condition of surrounding nations and of the world, too.

Revelation of Christ. Zephaniah 3:14-15 is a wonderful revelation of the Lord Jesus Christ. Believers, the passage exclaims, will rejoice with all their hearts that the Lord, the King of Israel, has taken away our punishment. The King is with us so that we never again fear any harm.

Verse seventeen continues that the Lord our God, who is with us, is the Mighty Warrior to save, desiring to delight over us with his love. Jesus is our warrior whose mission among us, completed on the cross, is to save. Zephaniah turned the hearts of his hearers to Jesus, mighty to save.

Application. Readers may find it easy to agree with Zephaniah, as he points his finger at the hypocrisy of religious leaders and worshippers whose lives fill with sin and idolatry. Pointing fingers at others, though, is never the core lesson of application to draw. We must instead remove the plank from our own eye before pointing out the speck in the eye of others, the smaller defect of others. Zephaniah encourages us to examine our own worship, our own spirituality and religious practices. We must remove any idolatry, those things that honor only ourselves, our own strengths and accomplishments, or perhaps our own idolatrous creations, while dishonoring God. Purify yourself, purify yourself. Remove all idolatry. Seek humble reform before the Lord.

Memory Verses. 1:7: *Be silent before the Sovereign Lord, for the day of the Lord is near. 1:14: The great day of the Lord is near—near and coming quickly. 2:3: Seek the Lord, all you humble of the land, you who do what he commands. 3:5: Morning by morning he dispenses his justice, and every new day he does not fail.... 3:12: But I will leave within you the meek and humble. The remnant of Israel will trust in the name of the Lord. 3:15: The Lord has taken away your punishment, he has turned back your enemy. 3:17: "The Lord your God is with you, the Mighty Warrior who saves. He will take great delight in you; in his love he will no longer rebuke you but will rejoice over you with singing."*

Haggai

Now this is what the Lord Almighty says: "Give careful thought to your ways." 1:5.

Theme. The theme of Haggai is priorities. We are all busy with our own things. What time, though, do we give to the things of God? Have we ordered our priorities as God would have us do? God takes a back seat to no one. We cannot serve ourselves first and serve God only as an afterthought, and yet call ourselves obedient to God. God rightly demands devotion. Unless we afford God his due priority, we cannot rightly call ourselves devoted. To follow the Lord is to obey, while to obey is to put his desires above our own whenever they conflict. That knowledge, that awareness, means discerning and prioritizing, Haggai's clear theme.

Author. Haggai's first verse identifies him as a prophet to Judah, eighteen years after its return from Babylonian exile in 538 B.C. Haggai tells us that he prophesied during the second year of the Persian king Darius's reign, firmly dating the book to 520 B.C. Haggai's prophesy thus dates late in the Hebrew canon, after the books Ezra and Nehemiah had already documented the exiles' return and efforts at rebuilding. Haggai also tells us that he prophesied to Judah's governor Zerubbabel and high priest Joshua, suggesting that Haggai may have had a trusted place of access to Judah's leaders. A reference in Haggai 2:3 suggests that Haggai may have seen the glorious old temple before its destruction, in which case Haggai would have been seventy years or older, making him a senior prophet calling Judah to both look back and forward.

Context. The returning Israelites faced external opposition rebuilding Jerusalem's walls, gates, and towers, and reconstructing the temple. Surrounding powers would not have wanted Judah to rise again and so surely harassed the rebuilders while invoking other greater powers, including the Persian rulers, against them. Haggai's account shows that the opposition may have had its intended effect, at least in that the temple remained a relative ruin nearly two decades after the exiles' return. Haggai's account also shows, though, that the returnees had managed to rebuild their houses into states of relative luxury, suggesting that the returnees also faced internal challenges prioritizing God. They were not honoring God but instead prioritizing their own comfort. This context showed that Haggai had solid grounds on which to both chastise and encourage, correct and reassure, as Haggai did so eloquently.

Structure. Haggai structures his brief, two-chapter book into four messages. His first message is for Judah to examine its ways, reorient to God, reprioritize its commitments, and rebuild God's house. Haggai then saw that his challenge could discourage the Israelites, and so his second message was one of encouragement. Haggai's third message was one of God's reward and his final message that God had chosen them. These successive prophecies well served and soon accomplished Haggai's prophetic purposes.

Key Events. A first key event informing Haggai's prophesy is that the exiles had already returned to Jerusalem and made some effort, opposed and incomplete, at rebuilding. Haggai begins by recording that the Israelites were saying that the time had not yet come to rebuild the temple, to which Haggai records God responding that the time had indeed come. Haggai also records the response of the governor, high priest, and people, who began to work on the temple. Haggai then answered the Lord's call to tell the working people that the Lord's new house would be glorious. God would fill his new house with glory. God then had Haggai prophesy blessings to the working people, after reminding them that he had already punished them in destruction of the old temple. Haggai ends his book prophesying that God would shatter foreign powers to once again make Judah his chosen. A final key event, just outside Haggai's text but well known to history, is that the Israelites soon succeeded in rebuilding the temple, which would stand until Jesus's coming but not long after.

Key Locations. Jerusalem is the focus of Haggai's book, where Haggai found the returned Israelites living in their paneled houses but God's temple a ruin. Consequently, the people were eating and drinking, but never having their fill. Haggai then turns the narrative to the temple in Jerusalem, suggesting that Haggai had seen the former temple's glory. God, though, would make his new temple more glorious than the former temple, and a place of peace. Haggai does refer to God's overthrow of the powers of the foreign kingdoms, without specifying those kingdoms, leaving the reader to infer either Judah's traditional surrounding enemies or perhaps a much broader reference to all world powers.

Revelation of Christ. Although his focus is on the rebuilding of Jerusalem's temple, a feat the exhorted Israelites soon accomplished, Haggai simultaneously reveals Christ in extraordinary fashion. The temple that the Israelites built would not last, although Haggai's prophesy says nothing about its subsequent destruction. That clue turns us again to Christ, whom we know from Christ's own words and ministry is God's indestructible temple. Haggai refers at least as much, and in his prophetic sense surely far more, to Christ as he does to Jerusalem's literal temple. Christ is the temple who brings eternal peace. Christ was the one who on the cross forever shattered all worldly powers. Though powerful for its moment in Judah's history, Haggai is far more powerful for its eternal witness to Christ.

Application. Haggai's revelation reminds us to build on Christ. We, too, must examine our ways when we devote ourselves to improving our paneled houses. We must instead devote ourselves to Christ, to letting him build his temple within us. His kingdom is near, indeed within us. We must become his partners in building that kingdom. The temple he desires is not one of stone and wood but within our hearts. Joining Christ in his kingdom work requires examining our ways, prioritizing our time and labor, accepting his encouragement and blessing, and recognizing how he has chosen us out of the world. Haggai's message is as modern as it is ancient, a practical message for the follower of Christ today.

Memory Verses. *1:3: "Is it a time for you yourselves to be living in your paneled houses, while this house remains a ruin?" 1:5-6: "Give careful thought to your ways. You have planted much but harvested little." 1:7-8: "Give careful thought to your ways. Go up into the mountains and bring down timber and build my house, so that I may take pleasure in it and be honored," says the Lord. 2:4-5: "Be strong, all you people of the land," declares the Lord, "and work. For I am with you," declares the Lord Almighty. "This is what I covenanted with you when you came out of Egypt. And my Spirit remains among you. Do not fear." 2:9: "'The glory of this present house will be greater than the glory of the former house," says the Lord Almighty. "And in this place, I will grant peace," declares the Lord Almighty. 2:19: "From this day on, I will bless you."*

Zechariah

"Not by might nor by power, but by my Spirit," says the Lord Almighty. 4:6.

Theme. Zechariah's theme is deliverance. Everyone at some point in life looks for relief from circumstances that seem intractable. Sometimes, the route out of hardship doesn't seem possible to navigate. Deliverance suggests a miracle, a sudden, unforeseen opening that only God could provide. Deliverance is divine, transformative. To deliver is not only to remove from one undesired circumstance but also to bring to another desired circumstance. To deliver suggests something permanent, as if one will never go back to the former degraded state. These implications are Zechariah's deeply heartening theme.

Author. Zechariah's name indicates that Yahweh remembers, which is fully appropriate to Zechariah's deliverance theme. Zechariah was the young grandson of an elderly priest who brought Zechariah back with him from Babylon to Jerusalem in 538 B.C. Of priest lineage, Zechariah likely would have been both prophet and priest, as his knowledge of and interest in worship practices indicates, although the returnees had not yet rebuilt the temple when Zechariah began his prophetic ministry.

Context. The above dating indicates that Zechariah, when mature enough to prophesy in 520 B.C. (as his book firmly indicates the date), was the elderly Haggai's young contemporary. The returned exiles had not yet rebuilt the temple but were, as Haggai notes, living in their relatively luxurious paneled houses. One can almost imagine Haggai bringing his harder message to the returnees that they needed to reprioritize their commitments, while Zechariah brought his more-positive message of the returnees' coming deliverance. Zechariah's later prophesies may have been as late as the Persian king Xerxes' 485-to-465-B.C. reign, during which the Jew Esther became his queen, making Zechariah a very late book in the Hebrew Bible.

Structure. The structure of Zechariah's book is to begin with eight visions, continue with four messages, and end with two oracles. Each of the eight successive visions, spread across the book's first six chapters, offer distinct symbolic images. Zechariah is a highly symbolic text. Together, his eight visions speak of judgment and restoration, and removal of evil from the earth. Zechariah's four messages in chapters seven and eight demand that the Israelites act with justice and in mercy, in consequence of which the Lord will bless. Zechariah's concluding two oracles see the first and second coming of the Messiah Jesus Christ. Zechariah is thus a remarkable book fully worthy of his day and our own day.

Key Events. Zechariah's first vision is of a rider, the angel of the Lord on a red horse, who will return to Jerusalem to rebuild his house. The second vision is of four horns, indicating the nations that scattered Judah and Israel. The third vision is of a man with a measuring line, a plumb line, heralding Jerusalem's restoration. The fourth vision is of new clothes for Judah's high priest, indicating God's forgiveness of Judah's sin. The fifth vision of a golden lampstand and two olive trees indicates the anointing of the Holy Spirit, lighting the leaders' way for God's people. The sixth vision of a flying book prophesies God's word moving across the world. The seventh vision of a woman in a basket sees God removing evil from Israel. The final vision of four chariots indicates heavenly spirits bringing God's judgment on the unrepentant. Zechariah's four messages of justice and mercy, over fasting, and God's blessing, follow. Chapters nine through fourteen to book's end then record the two grand oracles of the Messiah's first and final comings.

Key Locations. Jerusalem is Zechariah's geographic focus, understanding that Judah's capitol city represents so much more within the prophet's extraordinary visions. As the former and rebuilt temple's location, Jerusalem is not only Judah's capitol but also stands in symbolic place for God's presence, even his paradise garden and kingdom. Within Zechariah's heartening vision of Judah's deliverance with the Lord's return to Jerusalem, Zechariah prophesies the fall of its surrounding enemies Damascus, Tyre, Sidon, Gaza, Lebanon, and Philistia, and the far-away late-rising power Greece. Zechariah thus offers a similar geographic vision to prior prophets.

Revelation of Christ. Zechariah's prophesies, starting at verse 9:9, of two comings of Zion's king are among the Hebrew Bible's most evocative revelations of the Messiah Jesus Christ. Zechariah is a fully messianic book. The Lord, Zechariah 9:16 pointedly clarifies, will come to shepherd and save his flock. Zechariah 11:12 prophecies the thirty pieces of silver Jerusalem's priests paid for his life. Zechariah 12:10 then makes an extraordinary prophecy of Jerusalem looking on the one whom they have pierced, mourning bitterly at his passing, as Jerusalem pierced Jesus on his cross. On that day of the Lord's piercing, Zechariah continues at 13:1, a fountain will open to cleanse Jerusalem from impurity, as we know that Jesus's taking our sins to the cross cleanses us of our sins. God will have stricken the shepherd close to him, Zechariah 13:7 continues, scattering the sheep, as we know the Father allowed men to strike the Son Jesus, who after his resurrection and ascension sent the Spirit to accompany his followers across the earth. Zechariah 14 then prophesies the Lord's return, when the Lord will rule the whole earth, with his name the only name, as in the end Jesus alone will rule on the earth. Thank God that his Son Jesus fulfilled Zechariah's messianic prophecy.

Application. Zechariah's clear lesson is that we look to the Lord's coming, no matter our circumstance. We find depression quickly upon us, whether from the burden of our own sin, the sins of others, or a broken world. Yet we must not look to our circumstance, when God has given his Son so that we look instead to him. We, especially, more so than the ancient Judeans, should have that hope because Jesus has already fulfilled Zechariah's first vision of his coming. We then must look to his second coming, always preparing, always trusting, always looking up. Hold fast to Jesus, Zechariah offers. Hold fast to the Lord.

Memory Verses. 1:3: This is what the Lord Almighty says: "Return to me," declares the Lord Almighty, "and I will return to you," says the Lord Almighty. 4:6: "Not by might nor by power, but by my Spirit," says the Lord Almighty. 9:9: See, your king comes to you, righteous and having salvation, lowly and riding on a donkey, on a colt, the foal of a donkey. 9:16: The Lord their God will save his people on that day as a shepherd saves his flock. 10:4: "Shepherd the flock marked for slaughter." 11:12: I told them, "If you think it best, give me my pay; but if not, keep it." So, they paid me thirty pieces of silver. 12:10: They will look on me, the one they have pierced, and they will mourn for him as one mourns for an only child and grieve bitterly for him as one grieves for a firstborn son. 13:7: "Awake, sword, against my shepherd, against the man who is close to me!" declares the Lord Almighty. "Strike the shepherd, and the sheep will be scattered...." 14:9: The Lord will be king over the whole earth. On that day there will be one Lord, and his name the only name.

Malachi

> But who can endure the day of his coming? Who can stand when he appears? For he will be like a refiner's fire or a launderer's soap. 3:2.

Theme. The theme of Malachi is refinement. God loves humankind but not its sin. We often look to our own judgment of what is good and evil, our own way to value and accomplish and acquire things, when we know that the Lord is the only way. With every turning away from God, we become less like him. He must turn us back to him, but we ignore his words and gracious way. And so, he at times refines us through hardship but at other times refines us by withdrawing into silence until we seek him once again. We call this difficult process *refinement,* and as hard as it is, we embrace and value it, knowing that God only disciplines and refines those whom he loves.

Author. The name Malachi in Hebrew means *messenger,* which is all that history tells us of the prophet, who included nothing further in his introduction other than that he was bringing the Lord's word to Israel. Hints within the book, though, give it a very late date, fitting to the last book of the Hebrew Bible. One such hint is Malachi's Persian word for Jerusalem's governor, indicating a date while Judah was under Persian rule between 538 and 333 B.C. Malachi's warning of the rebuilt temple's corruption might indicate a date well after the temple's 515 B.C. rebuild, perhaps well after Nehemiah left Jerusalem in 432 B.C.

Context. Accepting these dates, Malachi prophesied as much as or more than one-hundred years after Judah rebuilt the temple. Whatever Judah had learned from its destruction, exile, and return should still have been evident, as those lessons initially were evident in the holiness of the returned exiles when in their commitment, they bravely rebuilt the temple. But Malachi's prophesies show the sad result that the lesson hadn't remained. Judah had yet again lapsed into corruption in society and worship. God must thus share more of his ancient plan for humankind's redemption. Malachi must prophesy again of the coming

177

Messiah, before God falls silent for the last several hundred years leading to that glorious Bethlehem day.

Structure. Malachi's first part of his three-part structure briefly reminds the Israelites how God has loved them, only to have the Israelites ask how. Malachi's second part, continuing to the end of his second chapter, warns the Israelites how they have not listened to God. Their priests should have preserved the knowledge of God but instead have shown contempt for his name, and so the people have fallen into corruption, unwilling to listen. Malachi's third part, comprised of his third and fourth chapters, tells of the coming Messiah who will refine like fire and purify like soap, while offering hope for the coming ages.

Key Events. Malachi's first key event records the Israelites doubting God's love. God responds in anger, documenting how the Israelites have broken their covenant with him, defiling his altar with cheap sacrifices, while calling it a contemptible burden. God warns the priests how he will punish them, for they have let Judah's men marry foreign wives who led them to worship foreign gods. The Israelites pursue injustice, while robbing the Lord by withholding their tithes and calling futile the serving of God. Malachi ends with God's promise to save a remnant of Judah in covenant renewal. God will send a prophet, whom Malachi calls Elijah, to warn of the great and dreadful day of the Lord's coming.

Key Locations. Malachi places his prophesies in Jerusalem, centering his narrative around the temple, its altar, and its priests in their corrupt practices. The short, four-chapter book is not one of geography. Malachi makes no mention of surrounding enemies other than to condemn the priests' permitting marriage of foreign women and worship of corrupting foreign gods. Malachi is thus more a book of allegorical than of literal place. In practicing corrupt temple worship, Judah has corrupted its relationship with God.

Revelation of Christ. Malachi 1:2 begins with the Lord saying how he has loved us, echoing John 3:16, where Jesus says how God so loved the world as to give him, his only Son. Malachi 3:1 prophesies the Lord coming to his temple, which is the body of Christ, constituted of his followers. While God desires our obedience, our repentance itself does not save, though it prepares our hearts for the Lord Jesus who saves. Malachi 4:1-2 then reveals the salvation of the Lord, healing us like a warming sun of righteousness, while saving us from the fiery furnace for those who refuse to embrace the Lord. Malachi is a striking final revelation of the coming Lord Jesus, concluding the Hebrew Bible.

Application. Surely, Malachi's message to accept the Lord's refinement is one that we can embrace today. We are his treasured possession, needing to return to him. No life newly embracing Jesus as Savior remains the same. Instead, God's Spirit leads us in sanctification, increasing our love for and devotion to the Lord. Gradually, our hearts turn from the things we once worshipped to worship God only, and then to love our neighbors in reflection of the Lord's own saving love. Accept God's refining fire, to embrace your salvation in the Lord. Malachi also urges generous giving, offering the Lord's promise of blessings in return so abundant that we have no room for them.

Memory Verses. *1:2: "I have loved you," says the Lord. "But you ask, 'How have you loved us?'" 1:14: "...I am a great king," says the Lord Almighty, "and my name is to be feared among the nations." 2:5: ""My covenant was with him, a covenant of life and peace, and I gave them to him; this called for reverence and he revered me and stood in awe of my name. True instruction was in his mouth and nothing false was found on his lips. He walked with me in peace and uprightness and turned many from sin." 2:15: "Has not the one God made you? You belong to him in body and spirit. And what does the one God seek? Godly offspring." 3:1: "I will send my messenger, who will prepare the way before me. Then suddenly the Lord you are seeking will come to his temple; the messenger of the covenant, whom you desire, will come," says the Lord Almighty." 3:6: "I the Lord do not change." 3:7: "Return to me, and I will return to you," says the Lord Almighty. 3:10: "Bring the whole tithe into the storehouse, that there may be food in my house. Test me in this," says the Lord Almighty, "and see if I will not throw open the floodgates of heaven and pour out so much blessing that there will not be room enough to store it." 4:2: "But for you who revere my name, the sun of righteousness will rise with healing in its rays." 4:5: ""See, I will send the prophet Elijah to you before that great and dreadful day of the Lord comes. He will turn the hearts of the parents to their children, and the hearts of the children to their parents; or else I will come and strike the land with total destruction."*

Reading Guide

Digital

For some, whether to read the Bible in print format, as a physical book, or in digital format, from a smartphone or tablet, is a big debate. Proponents of physical books argue for the value of having pages to touch, turn, crease, highlight, annotate, and visually recall. Indeed, some studies show the greater value of print over digital for learning, memorizing, and remembering. Yet digital format can be extraordinarily convenient. We carry smartphones anyway, wherein resides our digital Bible. Digital format can be more readily searched and linked than physical books, although physical books have their own way of searching from tables and concordances, and newer physical books can even supply electronic hyperlinking. And so, the debate goes on, one that began with the print proponents in the lead but that is strongly trending toward digital, like the rest of the world.

We need not, though, decide on which side of the debate to stand. Print and digital are not in any way exclusive. Instead, they are alternatives or, better put, companions. Many of us hope never to give up our heavily marked and well-worn print Bible, carrying so many landmarks and memories. We continue to use those Bibles, or use newer print versions, for certain occasions, like services, sermons, and studies. At the same time, many of us find great convenience, access, and efficiency in using digital Bibles. To have a dozen or more translations at one's fingertips can make for more-frequent, more-timely, and more-powerful use of God's word, on any planned or unexpected occasion. So, print or digital, digital or print? In this case, you can have the best of both worlds.

The New Testament

The New Testament begins with four parallel books sharing the good news, or gospel, of our Lord and Savior Jesus Christ. The virgin Mary bore Jesus in Bethlehem, most likely between the years 4 and 6 A.D., that designation standing for Anno Domini or the year of our Lord. One might assume that Jesus's birth occurred in 0 or 1 A.D., but scholars today find errors in the calculations of the sixth-century monk Dionysius who first established the common B.C. (before Christ) and A.D. dating. In any case, the dating of the New Testament's first events around Jesus's birth means a four-hundred-year silence from the last Old Testament book Malachi.

The relationship of Old Testament, or Hebrew Bible, to New Testament is important to understand. The New Testament does not contradict the Old Testament but instead fulfills, builds from the foundation of, and carries forward the Old Testament to its prophesied conclusion. One must not read the New Testament as something apart from, reversing, denying, or otherwise challenging the Old Testament. To do so would be to read the New Testament wrongly, neither as Jesus instructed nor as God's Spirit guides us. Matthew 5:17-18 records Jesus saying that he came not to abolish but to fulfill the Old Testament in every little mark of its every letter. New and Old Testaments are God's integrated account of his love for humankind, so intense that he gave the life of his Son Jesus for us. Reading the Old Testament deepens our understanding of Jesus's New Testament words, actions, and intentions, the Lord having so often quoted, paraphrased, and referred to the Old Testament.

The New Testament includes twenty-seven books, following the Old Testament's thirty-nine. After the first four gospel books Matthew, Mark, Luke, and John, comes the book of Acts, a history of the gospel moving through the early church. The next twenty-one books are a series of letters by early church leaders or attributed to them, providing guidance on carrying out Jesus's good-news mission. Many of the letters are to specific churches, although often intended for sharing with other churches or in fact addressed to the church generally even though identified by a church or regional name. A few other letters are to individuals or named for their authors, still informing of Jesus's gospel mission. The New Testament ends with the extraordinary book Revelation, addressing many things but especially God's plan, recorded in spectacular vision, for the future. Read and relish the New Testament.

The Gospel

The word *gospel* is an old-English translation of the Greek word *euangelion* meaning the good news. Around the time of Christ, that Greek word had a special association with the accession of a new Roman emperor as the divine protector of the realm. That Greek word is also the root for the English word *evangelical*, generally meaning one committed to the good news of Jesus Christ as Savior of the world. The gospel thus refers to the uniquely good, profound, and extraordinary news of Jesus's salvation and all that salvation means, both heavenly paradise for the believer at death and kingdom flourishing for communities of believers on earth. Common usage also applies the word *gospel* to each of the first four New Testament books the Gospel of Matthew, Gospel of Mark, Gospel of Luke, and Gospel of John, witnessing to that good news, books that we know more simply as Matthew, Mark, Luke, and John. The book of Acts, a continuation of Luke's gospel, gives an account of the apostles carrying the gospel to the early church.

Readers may at first find curious that the New Testament has four parallel books, each of which records events across the course of Jesus's life. The books both overlap in their accounts and offer distinct events that the other gospel books do not include. They also occasionally differ in tiny, largely immaterial respects in some of their common accounts. While to some, those differences would appear to undermine the accuracy of the differing accounts, those who study and know how humans witness and record events tell us that minute differences make the accounts more credible, not less credible. Perfectly matched testimony among eyewitnesses means a manufactured and rehearsed account. Credible testimony will differ in small and largely immaterial details, given the witnesses' different perspectives and memories.

The New Testament's four gospel books serve other purposes beyond adding weight and credibility to the record of Jesus's words and life. Each book had a different author who wrote at a different time, drawing on different sources, for a different audience. The authors' multiple viewpoints, drawing on their different backgrounds, skills, and interests, add a richness to the whole record that a single author could not have matched. While readers may each find their favorite gospel book, no one who knows well the four-book gospel record would wish to do without any of the four books. Readers also draw more from one gospel book than another, at different times on different topics for different insights. Every famous ancient life should have multiple chroniclers, although few do. Experts who study and know these things regard the gospel record to be so reliable compared to other ancient chronicles of other famous lives, as to be beyond reasonable challenge.

But that argument for veracity is beside the basic point for followers of Jesus Christ. As the gospel books make clear, and following books and letters illustrate and emphasize, at some point we must each choose to believe or reject God's truth. Belief of anything, even whether the sun will rise in the morning, takes at least some degree of trust and faith. Rejection of God's truth doesn't make God any less a truthteller. Don't read the four gospel books for whether they correctly relate real events and true words of the world's Savior, God incarnate Jesus Christ. Believe that they do, as indeed they do. And then learn from them, as the Spirit will then guide you. Let those who have ears to listen hear and those who have eyes to see look.

Matthew

From that time on Jesus began to preach, "Repent, for the kingdom of heaven has come near." 4:17.

Theme. The theme of the Gospel of Matthew is God's kingdom. The gospel is Jesus's good news of salvation, taking the individual view of his mission on earth. Yet Jesus emphasized a communal, corporate aspect to his mission. He was bringing God's kingdom very near. Salvation is to a place, a kingdom. A king is necessary to a kingdom, which is simply a place under the authority of a king. The kingdom to which Jesus referred had to do with the extension of God's beloved rule into the human heart. Yes, salvation means everything for the individual. But consider the good news from God's perspective: Jesus, as God's King of kings, Savior of the world and ruler over all creation, is extending God's kingdom into the deepest reaches of the whole world. Matthew urged his Jewish audience to see the royalty and rulership of their Messiah King.

Author. Matthew, one of Jesus's twelve disciples who traveled with Jesus for his three-plus years of public ministry, wrote the gospel book bearing his name. A 140 A.D. writing from an early Christ-follower Papias indicates that Matthew first wrote his gospel in Hebrew for the Jews before translating it to Greek for a wider audience. The gospel books identify Matthew as a tax collector when Jesus called him to follow. Matthew promptly took Jesus to a banquet at Matthew's house, filled with partiers and other figures who, like the tax collector, the Jewish religious leaders would have disdained as sinful. Matthew, himself a Jew intimately familiar with Jewish ways from his tax-collector role, was thus able to write as a Jew and for the Jews but also as a religious outsider, from a commoner's perspective. Matthew probably wrote his book before the temple's 70 A.D. destruction, of which he makes no mention, and so as early as twenty-five to thirty-five years after Christ's resurrection.

Context. As the first New Testament book, Matthew has a critical role to both introduce the gospel while also connecting it to the Hebrew

Bible. Matthew's book, written by a Jew and for the Jews, perfectly fulfills that role, focusing as it does on those Hebrew scriptures to herald the Messiah's coming. The prophets' four-hundred-year silence made especially significant that scriptural foundation for Matthew's announcement of the King's coming. The political context was that Rome occupied Israel and the rest of the region, oppressing the Jews with heavy taxes while tolerating the Jews' religion. Rome's Caesar, after all, claimed his own divinity. Israel's religious leaders thus had an uneasy alliance with the Roman governors to preserve that accommodation, even as the hated Romans oppressed the Jewish people. Note that the political context for the four gospel books is thus quite different than any book of the Hebrew Bible. Times had changed.

Structure. Matthew has a four-part structure beginning with Jesus's arrival, necessary to show the Jewish reader his fulfillment of the long-awaited Messiah role. Matthew's first part includes elaborate detail about Mary's conception and maternity, and Jesus's birth, with references to the Hebrew scriptures Jesus fulfilled. As Matthew 1:23 announces, quoting Isaiah 7:14, "'The virgin will be with child and will give birth to a son, and they will call him Immanuel,' which means 'God with us.'" Matthew's second part from chapters eight to eighteen addresses Jesus's teaching and healing ministry, again with Hebrew scripture references to adorn the narrative. That second part has many events like the one that Matthew 8:3 records, "Jesus reached out his hand and touched the man," healing him instantly. The book's third part from chapters nineteen to twenty-seven address Jesus's suffering and death, again in fulfillment of Hebrew scriptures. The book's last part in chapter twenty-eight documents Jesus's resurrection and his commissioning the disciples to carry that good news to the earth's ends. Matthew 28:6 records an angel announcing to the women who first saw Jesus's empty tomb, "Do not be afraid, for I know that you are looking for Jesus, who was crucified. He is not here; he has risen, just as he said." Matthew's chronological structure makes for the greatest story, the most-compelling historical narrative, ever told.

Key Events. Matthew charts the full course of Jesus's life events beginning with Jesus's royal Jewish lineage, Mary's extraordinary virgin conception, her husband Joseph's acceptance, Jesus's Bethlehem birth fulfilling prophecy, the visit of the Magi, and the family's escape to Egypt to fulfill another prophecy on their return. The accounts continue with John's baptism of Jesus at which the Holy Spirit descends on him and God announces his sonship, followed by Jesus's wilderness testing.

Matthew then records Jesus's spectacular Sermon on the Mount, describing the kingdom's heart contours. Jesus heals many, forgives others, and sends out his disciples to do likewise, all during which he teaches through parables and events. Peter recognizes Jesus as the Christ, the Messiah. Tensions rise with the religious leaders, who plot Jesus's murder. Three disciples witness Jesus's mountain transfiguration as Jesus turns to Jerusalem, where after a triumphal entry and last supper, he suffers arrest, trial, flogging, crucifixion, and entombment. Women who followed Jesus discover his empty tomb, after which Jesus appears to the disciples and many others, then to give the disciples their great commission before ascending to heaven. Matthew illustrates this record, containing many more exquisite events, with frequent explicit references to the Hebrew scriptures.

Key Locations. Jesus's prophesied birthplace Bethlehem is the book's first key location. The visit of the Magi to Jerusalem, where they meet the corrupt Jewish king Herod before traveling on to Bethlehem, establishes early that Jewish religious and Roman political leaders have no interest in seeing a Messiah rise. Matthew mentions Jesus's upbringing in Nazareth, southwest of the Sea of Galilee in the north of Israel, fulfilling another prophecy. Jesus's Jordan River baptism is a next key location, just north of the Dead Sea, soon followed by his Sermon on the Mount well to the north, above the Sea of Galilee. Jesus traveled widely during his three-plus-year public ministry, between Jerusalem to the west of the head of the Dead Sea, and the region of Galilee in the north of Israel, and even farther north. Peter's declaration of Jesus as the Son of God, Matthew records occurring far to the north at the pagan site Caesarea Philippi. Jesus's transfiguration occurred on Mount Hermon, well north of the Sea of Galilee. Jesus made preaching circuits around his home region of Galilee earlier in his ministry, before spending more time in and around Jerusalem and nearby cities and towns like Bethany. Jesus was itinerant in his travels, adorning Israel's geography with the profound events of his earthly ministry.

Revelation of Christ. Matthew reveals Jesus as the Jews' long-awaited Messiah, their King of kings, fulfilling the Hebrew Bible's prophesies of the Lord's coming rescue and restoration. Matthew's Hebrew Bible quotations are so numerous, literally dozens, as not to easily summarize. Matthew drew from Genesis, Exodus, Leviticus, Deuteronomy, Psalms, Isaiah, Jeremiah, Daniel, Jonah, Micah, Hosea, Zechariah, and Malachi. Many times, when Matthew quotes the Old Testament, he does so while saying expressly that Jesus had just fulfilled

187

them. Matthew 16:16 records Peter's dramatic declaration that Jesus is indeed the Christ, Son of the living God, and Matthew 17:2 Jesus's amazing transfiguration. Matthew is, in other words, as direct in his intention to prove Jesus to be God's Son, the Savior of the world, as one could possibly be. His gospel would not have been subtle for a Jew reading it for insights into whom Jesus was or claimed to be.

Application. Matthew has two fundamental applications for followers of Jesus Christ today, as the gospel did then when Matthew was first announcing it. The first application is to accept his extraordinarily good news while standing in utter awe of it. Have you seen the empty tomb? Do you know that Jesus is with you? Has Jesus touched you yet? Make no mistake: the world changed forever when Jesus entered it. Humankind could no longer proceed as it had, once he completed his ministry. Everyone must now decide: do you wish to have eternal life in God's paradise kingdom? Jesus offers that kingdom life and access. The second application, though, is equally significant. We must accept Jesus's great commission to share the good news with others. The good news does not bear fruit by its hoarding. We show our heart for Jesus by sharing his profoundly generous offer.

Memory Verses. 5:7: *"Blessed are the merciful, for they will be shown mercy."* 5:14: *"You are the light of the world. A city on a hill cannot be hidden."* 5:17: *"Do not think that I have come to abolish the Law or the Prophets; I have not come to abolish them but to fulfill them."* 6:19: *"Do not store up for yourselves treasures on earth, where moth and rust destroy, and where thieves break in and steal."* 6:33: *"But seek first his kingdom and his righteousness, and all these things will be given to you as well."* 7:1: *"Do not judge, or you too will be judged."* 7:7: *"Ask and it will be given to you; seek and you will find; knock and the door will be opened to you."* 7:13: *"Enter through the narrow gate. For wide is the gate and broad is the road that leads to destruction, and many enter through it."* 7:21: *"Not everyone who says to me, 'Lord, Lord,' will enter the kingdom of heaven, but only those who do the will of my Father who is in heaven."* 11:28: *"Come to me, all you who are weary and burdened, and I will give you rest."* 22:37: *"Love the Lord your God with all your heart and with all your soul and with all your mind."* 28:18: *Then Jesus came to them and said, "All authority in heaven and on earth has been given to me."* 28:19: *"Therefore go and make disciples of all nations, baptizing them in the name of the Father and of the Son and of the Holy Spirit."*

Mark

"Anyone who wants to be first must be the very last, and the servant of all." 9:35.

Theme. The theme of the Gospel of Mark is servanthood, as in to serve others rather than demand service. While Matthew portrayed Jesus as the Jews' Messiah King, Mark's perspective on Jesus was that he is the Son of Man come to serve. As Mark 10:45 states, "The Son of Man did not come to be served, but to serve, and to give his life as a ransom for many." Mark portrays Jesus as the suffering servant, whose sacrifices served humankind. Mark's servant theme adds dimensions not usually associated with servants. Jesus stepped down from his throne, from his position of supreme authority, to serve. Jesus was born the King but made himself a servant. We do not usually think of servanthood as voluntary, when that sacrifice is exactly the essential choice that Jesus made. We also would not ordinarily think of service as including sacrifice of the servant's life. An unwilling, peasant servant's sacrifice would not have shown God's love. God must instead ask his own Son, the King of kings, to willingly serve to the point of death. Mark shares a profound theme.

Author. Mark, the author of the gospel bearing his name, was not one of Jesus's twelve disciples. He was, though, very close to the disciple Peter, who often visited Mark's mother's house, often enough that Acts 12:12-14 records a servant at the door recognizing Peter's voice outside. Some scholars believe that Jesus's last supper may even have occurred at that house. Mark appears from his account to have been with Jesus at Gethsemane after the last supper, when Jesus was arrested. Mark later traveled with the apostles Paul and Barnabas on mission trips, spreading the gospel and nurturing the churches. Paul mentions Mark, in one of Paul's last letters. Some scholars also attribute the apostle Peter's letters to Mark as Peter's scribe. Mark thus knew Jesus, witnessed key events of Jesus's life himself, and had intimate access to Jesus's disciples. Mark, like Matthew, probably wrote his gospel book before the temple's 70 A.D. destruction, of which he makes no mention. His account may have been the first of the four gospel books, perhaps written from Rome as early as fifteen to twenty years after Jesus's resurrection, as Peter related events to Mark before Peter's execution. Some credit the disciple Peter with substantial contributions to Mark's gospel book. Mark, also called John Mark in the book of Acts, traveled extensively with Peter as Peter carried out Jesus's great commission. Mark's gospel account treats in detail events that only Peter and the other inner-circle members John and his brother James would have witnessed. Whether Peter dictated the gospel to Mark, Peter may well have contributed to Mark's account over the course of the three-plus decades that Peter served as a witness after Christ's resurrection.

Context. Following Matthew in the New Testament, Mark need not take Matthew's Hebrew-scripture approach and in fact does not. Hints in Mark's use of terms, like interpreting Aramaic terms for his readers, indicate that Mark was not writing for a Jewish audience but instead a reader unfamiliar with, or perhaps not especially concerned with, Jewish culture and religious practices. If, as some suppose, he wrote in Rome, then his audience may have been Roman readers. Mark's shorter, action-packed book is thus quite different from Matthew's longer book filled with Hebrew scripture references. The historical and political contexts for Mark's book was, of course, the same as that for Matthew's book. They both wrote after a long prophetic silence, when the Jews may have especially wondered of their messianic expectations, and in the face of Roman occupation mitigated only somewhat by the Jews' suspect religious leaders.

Structure. Mark's first ten chapters show Jesus serving the people. Mark dispenses with any mention of Jesus's Jewish lineage, prophesied birth, presentation at Jerusalem's temple, and prophesied flight to Egypt. Mark simply begins with relatively brief accounts of Jesus's baptism, wilderness testing, and calling his disciples. By the first chapter's end, Jesus has already healed many, setting the servant pattern for the book's first half. The second part of Mark's book, from chapters eleven to sixteen, presents Jesus as preparing to suffer, announcing his coming sacrifice, and then suffering excruciatingly before dying for others. The earliest manuscripts of Mark's book end with the women at the tomb, learning from an angel that Jesus has risen. Later manuscripts include details of the resurrected Jesus appearing to the disciples and ascending. While Mark includes abundant detail, his book leaves the impression of an author wanting to relate as directly as possible the extraordinary events recently witnessed. One can image the blunt disciple Peter's voice behind Mark's account.

Key Events. Mark's key events begin with Jesus's baptism, the Spirit descending and the Father announcing Jesus as his Son. Mark's narrative moves quickly into Jesus healing many, while calling disciples including the tax-collector and later book-author Matthew (Mark calls him Levi). Mark notes the religious leaders accusing Jesus and his own family calling him insane. Mark records Jesus teaching in parables while challenging the religious leaders and law teachers. Mark also notes several of Jesus's miracles including calming the storm, raising a dead girl, and feeding thousands, not to mention Jesus's transfiguration, making it one of two books, along with Matthew, chronicling that event. Mark also records Jesus's triumphal entry into Jerusalem and clearing the temple courts of dishonest merchants. Mark's narrative of Jesus's last supper, Gethsemane prayer, arrest, trials, and crucifixion track Matthew's narrative. Mark's resurrection narrative is brief, ignoring its later addition. Mark moves the account swiftly, without embellishment.

Key Locations. Mark's narrative of Jesus's life events shows no concern with identifying Jesus's birthplace, hometown, and travels about Israel, as connected with Jewish prophecy. That omission may have been another indication that Mark was not writing for a Jewish audience familiar with the religious history and spiritual significance of Israel's many towns. Mark does show how Jesus recruited his disciples around Galilee including calling fishermen Simon and his brother Andrew off the sea. Much of Mark's action occurs around Galilee, its towns Capernaum and Bethsaida, Jesus's hometown Nazareth to the southwest, and even farther west to Tyre along the Great (Mediterranean) Sea. The action then moves south to Judea, at the Jordan River again, and then on to Bethphage and Bethany, on Jesus's way to Jerusalem, where the book's final events unfold. Mark's geographic treatment gives his book a more-practical, almost-ordinary setting, less political and religious in its tone than Matthew's prior book, except for those concluding events at Jerusalem.

Revelation of Christ. Mark's revelation of Christ is undoubtedly as God's suffering servant more so than Matthew's Messiah King. Mark depicts and emphasizes Christ as such, three times in his chapters eight, nine, and ten. Mark 8:34 records Jesus saying that his disciples must deny themselves and take up their cross to follow him. Mark's ninth chapter records Jesus predicting his suffering death and warning his disciples that they must be ready to gouge out their offending eyes and cut off their offending hands. Mark's passage beginning at verse 10:35, in which disciples ask to sit beside him in glory but Jesus responds that they must instead serve, further illustrates Mark's sacrificial, suffering focus. When Jesus continues at verse 10:44 that "whoever wants to be first must be slave of all," he makes a remarkable statement not only about his disciples' role but about his own intention and course. Even the Son of Man, Jesus continues at verse 10:45, also quoted above, "did not come to be served, but to serve, and to give his life as a ransom for many." Mark's revelation of Christ thus balances Matthew's revelation, identifying Jesus both as King of kings and yet servant of all. Readers need find no tension between the two depictions, only the profound nature of an incredibly loving but supremely powerful God.

Application. Jesus's disciples struggled with his servant message. They instead saw themselves as trusted officials of the Messiah King. They desired to rule, when Jesus was teaching them to serve. We struggle in the same way, seeing first and often only our own interests. In bringing to us Jesus's model and words, the Spirit helps us break our enslavement to our own pursuits and instead to see and serve the needs of others. We must serve, for only by serving can Christ set us free. We must serve, for only by our love will others see Christ in us. Understanding Mark's lesson is not especially hard. We see how others serve us and appreciate service's value. The question is whether we can break our old habits of thinking of ourselves first, to show greater love to our neighbor.

Memory Verses. 1:15: "The kingdom of God has come near. Repent and believe the good news!" 8:34: "Whoever wants to be my disciple must deny themselves and take up their cross and follow me." 8:36: "What good is it for you to gain the whole world, yet forfeit your soul?" 9:23: "Everything is possible for one who believes." 9:43: "If your hand causes you to stumble, cut it off. It is better for you to enter life maimed than with two hands to go into hell, where the fire never goes out." 10:45: "For even the Son of Man did not come to be served, but to serve, and to give his life as a ransom for many." 11:24: "Therefore I tell you, whatever you ask for in prayer, believe that you have received it, and it will be yours." 13:32: "But about that day or hour no one knows, not even the angels in heaven, nor the Son, but only the Father." 14:22: While they were eating, Jesus took bread, and when he had given thanks, he broke it and gave it to his disciples, saying, "Take it; this is my body." 16:15: "Go into all the world and preach the gospel to all creation."

16:16: "Whoever believes and is baptized will be saved, but whoever does not believe will be condemned."

Luke

Then Pilate announced to the chief priests and the crowd,
"I find no basis for a charge against this man." 23:4.

Theme. Luke's theme is perfection, that Christ came from God to become the perfect sacrifice of a sinless, ideal man. Luke records Jesus referring to himself twenty-two times as the Son of Man, a title the Hebrew Bible used to refer to the coming Messiah but that also had the connotation of the true or ideal human, God's own image for a humankind made to bear that image. As Adam was the broken man who sinned, separating humankind from God, so Christ is the ideal Son of Man who did not sin, and in sacrifice reunited God and humankind. As Luke 19:10 states, "The Son of Man came to seek and save what was lost." Luke depicts Jesus's humanity within his divinity, united, holy, ideal, and pure, with the purpose of remaking a corrupted humankind in his uncorrupted image. Luke is a book about Jesus's relationship with and ultimate love for people.

Author. Luke does not mention his name in the gospel book that tradition and other internal and external evidence firmly credits to him. The book is the first of two connected books by the physician author, the other the book of Acts. Luke wrote both books to a real or imagined benefactor Theophilus, as well-researched, precise, and factual accounts, as one might expect from a professional trained in observation. Introductions to both books so state, the introduction to Luke's gospel at verse 1:4 further stating Luke's purpose in writing, "so that you may know the certainty of the things you have been taught." Luke expected his readers to take a scientific, evidentiary, and logical, if not necessarily skeptical, view, those readers apparently having already been taught the gospel before Luke wrote. The apostle Paul in Colossians 4:14 names Luke among other Gentiles, and, in fact, Luke writes from a factual rather than Jewish religious perspective. Luke likely wrote his gospel book ahead of its second volume Acts, evidence from which suggests that the gospel book's date may have been around 60 A.D., about twenty-five years after Christ's resurrection.

Context. Luke's gospel book shares the prophetic, religious, and political context of the other gospel books. The Jews had not heard from God through their prophets for several-hundred years. They lived in desultory fashion under a despotic Roman occupation, with which their religious leaders maintained an uncomfortable and at times unholy alliance, seen in those leaders' manipulation of the Roman governor into crucifying Jesus. Yet Luke's interest in writing a factual account for his benefactor Theophilus gave him reason to record some different events and details from Matthew and Mark, to achieve his different purpose. Theophilus is Greek for *friend of God* or *loved of God*, suggesting that Luke was writing to a non-Jewish audience sympathetic to the Jews' holy God. Roman occupation was certainly a burden but also facilitated travel between Jerusalem and Rome, opening new avenues for the gospel's spread, in which Luke's travels and accounts, both here and the book of Acts, played significant roles.

Structure. Luke's three-part book begins with three chapters documenting how Jesus came to be the Son of Man. Luke's narrative includes abundant detail foretelling not only Jesus's birth but the earlier birth of his relative John the Baptist. Luke also records details of Jesus's birth, angelic attestation that Jesus is the Messiah, and presentation at the temple, not to mention Jesus's baptism and genealogy, making for a lengthy and convincing account. Luke's second part, formed of chapters four through nineteen, shows Jesus's compassion for the lost. Luke records teaching and healing events much like those of the other gospel books, although his focus tends to be on Jesus's interaction with outcasts and outsiders like the Roman centurion, widow whose son he raised, crippled woman and ten lepers whom he healed, little children who ran to him, and tax collector Zacchaeus who sought Jesus and believed. When Luke records that a woman anointed Jesus with perfume as he approached his crucifixion death, only Luke among the other gospel authors includes the detail of the woman's sinfulness. Luke seems a precise recorder, too, of parables like the three consecutive teachings of the lost sheep, lost coin, and lost son, again emphasizing Luke's theme of Jesus as the Son of Man seeking the lost. Luke's third and final part, comprised of chapters twenty through twenty-four, shows Jesus ultimately saving the lost, as he promised, in his crucifixion, resurrection, and ascension. Luke's account concludes with abundant post-resurrection detail, like Jesus's teaching two disciples on the road to Emmaus, ending with his ascension.

Key Events. Luke does not so much record seminal events, like Peter's declaration of Jesus as the Messiah and Jesus's mountain transfiguration, events that Matthew and Mark also document, as Luke records abundant detail of Jesus relating to the people he encountered. Luke's training as a physician may have made him take special interest in those relationships, how Jesus responded to disease and other need and people responded to Jesus's healing. One such profound event that Luke records, borne out of details that other gospel books overlooked or for their own reasons omitted, involved the criminals crucified next to Jesus. Matthew and Mark only record the criminals hurling insults at Jesus, crucified between them. But Luke 39:43 records that one criminal reached the point of defending Jesus, telling his fellow criminal that while they deserved to die, Jesus had done nothing wrong. That criminal then asked Jesus to remember him when Jesus came into his kingdom, to which Jesus replied that the criminal would that day join Jesus in paradise. Indeed, Luke's book communicates above all that Jesus came to save the lost.

Key Locations. While Matthew's book in places reads like a religious history of Israel's geography, and Mark's book focuses on Jesus's ministry in mostly out-of-the-way places, Luke takes his own meticulous approach. He details locations not so much by history or practicality as by the involved actors' status and relationship. Thus, Luke 2:1-5 records Joseph taking the pregnant Mary from their Nazareth home to Bethlehem to satisfy Caesar's census, Luke 2:8-9 angels appearing to shepherds in nearby fields, Luke 4:14 Jesus returning to Galilee in the Spirit's power, Luke 5:1 Jesus standing by the Sea of Galilee, Luke 5:27 Jesus meeting Matthew at his tax collector's booth, and Luke 14:1 Jesus's visit to the house of a prominent Pharisee. Luke fills his book with location details, not for the location's prominence but to prove the accuracy of his record. Hence, we see Luke's careful reconstruction of exactly what happened at the cross, including that Jesus promised salvation to a criminal about to die, who had just finished hurling insults at Jesus before his last-breath repentance. Luke convinces that Jesus came to save the lost.

Revelation of Christ. Luke's keen eye and ear for detail helped his gospel book capture another event that the other gospel books omit, an event that led to Jesus's defining statement recorded in Luke 19:10 that "[t]he Son of Man came to seek and save what was lost." That event, the wealthy chief tax collector Zacchaeus climbing a tree out of his intense desire to see and honor Christ, illustrates again Luke's sinless-Savior theme. Zacchaeus's extraordinary commitment to pay back four times anyone whom he had cheated produced Jesus's exclamation, recorded at Luke 9:9, that salvation had just come to Zacchaeus's house. Repeatedly, Luke shows that Jesus came to reach, attract, and save those sinners whom the religious authorities most regarded as beyond their own concern or reach. Indeed, Luke 14 records Jesus dining at the house of one of those religious leaders, teaching the prominent guests to seek the poor, crippled, blind, and lame. Luke alone of the gospel books records the parable that Jesus shared there of a great banquet to which the master invited the usual guests, all whom were too occupied with their own matters to come, and so the master sent his servant to invite in those same lost. Luke alone of the gospel books also records, at verse 4:18, Jesus's own quotation of Isaiah 61:1 that he carries the Lord's Spirit to proclaim good news to the poor, freedom for the prisoner and oppressed, and sight for the blind. The master Jesus's concern is clearly for his lost. Luke supplies a core revelation of the sinless Savior Jesus Christ.

Application. Luke teaches us that we cannot fall so far, cannot be so outcast, cannot be so poor or blind, that Jesus does not seek us out. We must know the heart of our Savior for us, in whatever weakened, broken, or corrupted condition we are. We must not see ourselves as outside of his love, when Luke shows that Jesus came to us precisely because he loves the lost. Luke also teaches that we must show the same regard for those around us who may be our own lost. We cannot look at others in any way other than Jesus sees them, which is as worthy of his love and capable of his salvation. We have that gospel message to share, clarified and put into the richest perspective by the keen observation of the physician Luke.

Memory Verses. 4:18: *"The Spirit of the Lord is on me, because he has anointed me to proclaim good news to the poor. He has sent me to proclaim freedom for the prisoners and recovery of sight for the blind, to set the oppressed free...."* 6:20: *"Blessed are you who are poor, for yours is the kingdom of God."* 6:27: *"I say: Love your enemies, do good to those who hate you...."* 6:38: *"Give, and it will be given to you. A good measure, pressed down, shaken together and running over, will be poured into your lap. For with the measure you use, it will be measured to you."* 9:23: *"Whoever wants to be my disciple must deny themselves and take up their cross daily and follow me."* 12:32: *"Do not be afraid, little flock, for your Father has been pleased to give you the kingdom."* 14:26: *"If anyone comes to me and does not hate father and mother, wife and children, brothers and sisters – yes, even life itself – such a person cannot be my disciple." 19:10: "For the Son of Man came to seek and to save what was lost." 23:34: "Father, forgive them, for they do not know what they are doing." 23:43: "Truly I tell you, today you will be with me in paradise."*

John

"For God so loved the world that he gave his one and only Son, that whoever believes in him shall not perish but have eternal life." 3:16.

Theme. The theme of John's gospel book is the word, or more specifically, Jesus as God's Word. John begins his gospel book at verse 1:1 with precisely that declaration, "In the beginning was the Word, and the Word was with God, and the Word was God," that Word become flesh in the incarnated Jesus. John 3:16 recites the single most-popular verse in the whole Bible that "God so loved the world that he gave his one and only Son, that whoever believes in him shall not perish but have eternal life." John 8:38 also records Jesus identifying himself as the *I am*, meaning God. John ends his book at verse 20:31 with the same declaration, that he had written his book "that you may believe that Jesus is the Messiah, the Son of God, and that by believing you may have life in his name." John was not presenting Jesus as Matthew's King of kings, nor as Mark's suffering servant, nor as Luke's sinless Son of Man, but, John 1:3-5 announces, as God, through whom all things were made, in whom is life, and whose life is the light of humankind, Jesus as the very Word of God.

Author. The disciple John wrote the gospel book bearing his name, internal and external evidence strongly supports. John 13:23 identifies its author as the disciple who laid his head on Jesus's breast at the last supper, whom Jesus loved. The book is clearly the work not just of an eyewitness to Jesus's life but likely one of Jesus's smallest inner circle, comprised only of Peter, James, and John. The book itself indicates that Peter is not its author, and James died too soon after Jesus's resurrection to have been the book's author. Christians as early as the second century unanimously credited John as author. The martyr Polycarp, who knew John, told another second-century Christian leader Irenaeus that John had written the book while at Ephesus. Multiple inferences date John as the latest of the four gospel books, likely written between 85 and 95 A.D., fifty or more years after Jesus's resurrection, and late in John's life.

Context. John's later authorship of his gospel book, while still an eyewitness account, may have helped John to deepen his understanding and sharpen his recollection of all that he observed. The earlier three gospel books readers know as *synoptic*, referring to their having made a summary of observed events. Unique among the four books, John's book is not synoptic. It reads instead like a richly developed thesis. Writing as late as he did, after Rome had destroyed Jerusalem's temple, John also had a different historical perspective than the other three gospel books. Jesus had prophesied the temple's destruction, referring to both the Jerusalem building his disciples had unthinkingly admired in his presence and to himself, especially when Jesus added that the temple would rise again in three days. John wrote after Rome had fulfilled both prophesies of destruction. John, in short, had a longer view than the other writers Matthew, Mark, and Luke. John's gospel book is no summary but the deepest of looks back to the beginning of time.

Structure. John's book follows a two-part structure. The first part, half of the book's chapters, from chapter one through eleven, proves that Jesus is the Son of God. John does so not only by Jesus's own declarations that he is the world's light (8:12), resurrection and life (11:25), and way, truth, and life (14:6), but also by recording seven different miracles. The most dramatic of those miracles, one that especially convinced the religious leaders that Jesus must die, was raising his friend Lazarus from the dead, a miracle that only the Son of God could perform. The second half of John's book, from chapter twelve through twenty-one, documents the final week of Jesus's life in and around Jerusalem. The other gospel books of course also addressed Jesus's triumphal entry and final week leading to his crucifixion and resurrection. John, though, devotes several chapters to Jesus's last words to his disciples, at the last supper. John's narrative gives readers an unprecedented glimpse into what walking with Jesus, and hearing his most-intimate thoughts, might have been like.

Key Events. John's eleventh chapter records a key event in his book, around which the book turns from proof that Jesus is the Son of God to the account of his final week leading to his death and resurrection. That event is the death of his friend Lazarus. John's narrative makes clear that Jesus delayed knowing that Lazarus would die and be entombed dead for several days, over which Jesus himself, he who loved Lazarus and his sisters, wept. Yet Jesus with a prayer and word called Lazarus back from the dead. Many in the crowd who witnessed the miracle believed that Jesus was the Son of God, a development that spurred the chief priest to prophesy, recorded in John 11:50, that Jesus must die for the people so that the whole nation need not perish. Jesus indeed came to show how much God loved the world, giving the world Jesus's death, so that all who believed Jesus was God's Son would not die.

Key Locations. The event just described, Jesus raising Lazarus, occurred at Bethany, a town about two miles from Jerusalem. Jesus stayed in Bethany with Lazarus and his sisters Mary and Martha on occasion. John's chapter twelve records that on one of those occasions, a dinner they hosted in Jesus's honor after he had raised Lazarus, Mary anointed Jesus's feet with expensive perfume and wiped his feet with her hair, an act that Jesus acknowledged was to prepare him for burial. John relates other intimate events in common setting, peculiar to his book, like Jesus's first miracle, turning water into wine at Cana at his mother's request. Mary did not want the bridegroom embarrassed for running out of wine, and so at her request, Jesus turned several huge vats of water into the best wine, to the banqueters' delight. These exquisite events at home settings echo the intimacy of Jesus's last supper with the disciples, itself in a home's upper room. John 20:11-18 offers the reader one last such intimate event at the book's most-significant location, the empty tomb. There, one of Jesus's followers Mary Magdalene met the risen Jesus, who asked why she was crying. Thinking that he was a gardener, Mary asked him where he had taken Jesus's body. When Jesus said her name "Mary," she exclaimed "Teacher" and moved to take hold of him. John knew how to relate intimate depictions of the Son of God.

Revelation of Christ. John's revelation of Christ as the Son of God reaches a remarkable conclusion, again one that only John among the four gospel books records. John 20:26-28 gives an account of the disciple Thomas, known popularly as *doubting* Thomas for his refusal to believe the eyewitness testimony of the other disciples that the crucified Jesus had risen. Jesus, though, returned to appear to Thomas, telling Thomas to put his finger in Jesus's pierced hands and his hand in Jesus's pierced side, and to stop doubting and believe. Thomas then exclaimed, "My Lord and my God," to which Jesus replied that Thomas had believed because he saw but that blessed are those who have not seen but still believe. John's book is not a synopsis, not a detailed record on which the author hopes that the reader will believe. John instead declares Christ's full divinity and shows why not just the eyewitness disciples but also all others should likewise believe.

Application. John's book offers doubting Thomas as a precious lesson for the modern reader. Thomas was a devoted follower of Christ, a disciple who gave up his family and work, and risked his life, to travel and minister with Christ. Few of us today have done as much as Thomas did to show devotion to Christ. Yet John shows Thomas still doubting until he saw and touched the risen Christ. Whether we give up much or give up little to follow Christ, we must believe that he rose from crucifixion's grave. Do not demand Jesus's appearance standing before you but instead believe on the testimony of those before whom he did. God so loved you that he gave Jesus for you, that you would believe in him and not perish but live eternally in his paradise.

Memory Verses. 1:1: In the beginning was the Word, and the Word was with God, and the Word was God. 1:12: Yet to all who did receive him, to those who believed in his name, he gave the right to become children of God.... 1:14: The Word became flesh and made his dwelling among us. We have seen his glory, the glory of the one and only Son, who came from the Father, full of grace and truth. 3:3: "Very truly I tell you, no one can see the kingdom of God without being born again." 3:5: "Very truly I tell you, no one can enter the kingdom of God without being born of water and the Spirit." 3:16: "For God so loved the world that he gave his one and only Son, that whoever believes in him shall not perish but have eternal life." 4:24: "God is spirit, and his worshipers must worship in the Spirit and in truth." 8:31-31: "If you hold to my teaching, you are really my disciples. Then you will know the truth, and the truth will set you free." 13:34: "A new command I give you: Love one another. As I have loved you, so you must love one another." 14:1: "Do not let your hearts be troubled. Trust in God; trust also in me." 14:6: "I am the way and the truth and the life. No one comes to the Father except through me." 14:26: "[T]he Advocate, the Holy Spirit, whom the Father will send in my name, will teach you all things and will remind you of everything I have said to you."

Reading Guide

Plans

Readers have options and plans available for how to approach reading the Bible. The Bible's length alone makes reading it a formidable challenge. Dividing that reading up into digestible bites is necessary for any reader. Many readers thus set an objective for each day leading to a goal to complete reading the whole Bible within a year, half year, two years, or longer or shorter period. Various readers will have read the Bible in thirty days, sixty days, ninety days, or, at the spectrum's other end, five or ten years. Whatever your capacity may be, daily reading plans can help. A one-year plan may have the reader completing an average of about four chapters a day. Four chapters is not a difficult read, although the discipline then becomes to keep reading day after day. Miss a day or two, or a week or two, and the reading challenge grows, discouraging the discipline.

Electronic reading plans that chart and display your progress, and remind you daily of your goal and progress, can help establish and maintain the necessary discipline. So, too, can sharing your reading goal with another person or group, creating a sense of accountability, achievement, and even excitement. Bible-reading plans don't even have to be from cover to cover. Some plans help the reader see how integrated the Bible's books are, by having the reader read a chapter a day from each of four different parts of the Bible. Those plans give the reader daily continuity within each of four different books, while helping the reader see the connections between and among books. Other plans turn the Bible's canon into a chronological order. Reading the Bible cover to cover at least once in a lifetime, and perhaps several times in a lifetime, seems wise, though, even if at other times you skip around or read only favorite parts. The thing to keep most in mind is that reading the Bible is both a command and privilege. Discipline and achievement aren't the reasons. The reason is God.

Acts

In this way the word of the Lord spread widely and grew
in power. 19:20.

Theme. The theme of the book of Acts is the gospel, more pointedly, the spread of the gospel. Good news, as the gospel means, travels quickly. We want to hear good news, and we like to share good news, too. The world has too much bad news in it. Give us a little good news, please. Indeed, give us a lot of good news, or better yet, some very, very good news. Good news carries power. It buoys hope, adds a pep to the step, and renews one's energy. Good news lifts burdens, causes a smile, even makes one more generous and caring for others. The book of Acts documents the swift spread of the very good news of Jesus Christ as Lord and Savior, after Jesus's resurrection. Acts 1:8 records the resurrected Jesus telling his disciples that they would receive power when the Holy Spirit came on them, which it did shortly after at Pentecost, and that they would then be Jesus's witnesses to the ends of the earth. The book of Acts shows that good-news prophesy carried out.

Author. The physician Luke wrote the book of Acts for his benefactor Theophilus, just as he wrote the gospel book carrying his name. Acts 1:1 refers to that former book and benefactor, and then promptly resumes the narrative of the resurrected Jesus addressing the disciples. The book quickly makes clear that it records the acts of the apostles as the Spirit guided them around the region, as far away as Rome. The book's chronological narrative ends with the apostle Paul under arrest again, awaiting his appeal to Caesar in Rome. Because the book does not mention Paul's death, which occurred somewhere between 64 and 68 A.D., nor Nero's persecution of Christians beginning in 64 A.D., Luke probably completed the book between 60 and 62 A.D., about twenty-five to thirty years after Jesus's resurrection.

Context. In recording the apostles' movement and challenges around the region, the book of Acts supplies some of its own political context. Rome still occupied Jerusalem and governed the entire region. Jews still lived and worshipped at the temple in Jerusalem, under religious leaders who maintained an uneasy alliance with the Roman governor and his occupying forces. The apostles, still gathering in Jerusalem to chart their missionary outreaches, had to beware of both the Romans and the Jewish religious leaders. As they traveled about the region, well north of Israel's borders, up into Asia Minor (modern-day Turkey), and west into Greece toward Rome, they had to beware of local rulers worshipping various deities, who were also under Roman authority, though more loosely governed than the Romans governed the troublesome Jerusalem. The Romans had not yet destroyed Jerusalem's temple in response to Jewish uprisings, by the time the book of Acts closes.

Structure. Though the book at times reads like a helter-skelter travelogue of the Great (Mediterranean) Sea's eastern perimeter, Acts has both two-part and three-part structures. Its two-part structure divides the narrative between the first twelve chapters focusing on the apostle Peter's ministry to the Jews and the rest of the book focusing on the apostle Paul's ministry to the Gentiles. Acts three-part structure has to do with the church's growing reach, never mind the gospel's Jewish or Gentile audience. Chapters one through seven show how the Spirit-guided apostles defended and established the church, centered in Jerusalem. Chapters eight through twelve show the church enlarged in reach and influence through Judea and Samaria. Chapters thirteen through twenty-eight show the church expanding all the way to Rome, figuratively to the ends of the known earth. That the Spirit could, in just twenty-five years, from a tiny band of eleven scared disciples, establish, enlarge, and expand the church to such an extent is a profound achievement, ministry that the Spirit continues today through the lives of well over a billion Christ followers.

Key Events. Following Acts 1:9-11's record of Jesus's ascension, Acts 2:1-13 records another key event, indeed the key event for the entire growth of the gospel through Christ's church, which was the Holy Spirit's descent at Pentecost. Jesus had told the disciples to wait for the Spirit's power, and indeed, immediately following the Spirit's descent, Peter preached to a great crowd, resulting in the baptism of about three thousand. The tiny band of disciples instantly had a substantial church. In following chapters, Acts records Peter's miracles, bravery, and preaching, and the administration of the Jerusalem church. Acts 7 records the Jewish leaders' resistance to the church, resulting in the martyring of Stephen, supported by a young Jew Saul, and dispersion of the church. Acts 9 records Saul's conversion in a dramatic encounter with Jesus.

Acts 10-11 describe Peter's encounter with the Gentile Cornelius, from which Peter helped open the church leadership to accepting Gentiles. Most of the rest of Acts centers on the travels of Saul, renamed Paul, and other apostles, north and then west toward Rome, on long missionary journeys. The narrative stops at points, indicating that the Spirit urged or prevented certain actions. The final narrative begins with Paul's arrest back in Rome, his trial before Roman governors, his appeal to Caesar in Rome, and his hazardous Great Sea crossing, finally reaching Rome, where the book ends with Paul awaiting his appeal hearing. Acts' exhausting itineraries, including shipwrecks, beatings, stoning, and floggings, accentuate the Spirit's power under which the apostles proceeded.

Key Locations. Acts has too many locations to list in this brief writing. Jerusalem, though, was certainly a key location where the Holy Spirit descended, Peter stood trial before the Sanhedrin, the Jews stoned Stephen after his Sanhedrin trial, and Peter made a miraculous prison escape. Roads supplied other key locations, as with Saul's dramatic encounter with Jesus on the road to Damascus, where Saul planned further Christian persecution, and Philip's evangelizing and baptizing the Ethiopian eunuch on the road to Gaza. Regions to the north and then west, beginning with Syria, Cilicia, Pamphylia, and Lycia, and then further west to Asia Minor, Macedonia, and Achaia, became increasingly critical locations as the gospel spread to growing churches there, toward and into Europe. Paul made four missionary journeys through those areas. Paul suffered shipwreck on Malta, a Great Sea island well off Italy's southern coast, where he performed miracle healings, before resuming his sea crossing to Rome. Excepting Rome, the great center of military and political power throughout the whole region, and Jerusalem, the many locations Acts names are less important for their history than as demonstration of the gospel's spread.

Revelation of Christ. Acts opens with Christ's promise of the Holy Spirit and his ascension, both profound revelations of Christ as the world's sinless Savior. Every subsequent act of the apostles, whether miracle healings, courageous preaching, or miraculous escapes, and especially every subsequent conversion of Jew or Gentile to belief in the risen Lord Jesus, reveal the Spirit's power in pursuit of the glory of Jesus Christ. Acts does not focus on Jesus, not his teachings, healings, nor nature. Rather, Acts displays the apostles doing as Jesus would have done, healing, raising the dead, preaching, teaching, braving hostile leaders and crowds, and preparing hearts to receive him. Acts need not show Jesus directly, whether through his own words and acts or through prophesies, types, and figures, because his followers now revealed Jesus, as the Spirit guided and empowered them.

Application. The compelling application of the book of Acts is to accept the Spirit's power and guidance, as the apostles accepted the Spirit, so that we, too, may care, love, serve, and witness bravely in the name of Christ. The apostles worried little over their hearers' reactions. Indeed, they appeared to expect violent opposition. Yet they persisted with excitement and joy, even singing from prison. We, too, should have such attitudes toward sharing the good news that we hold so dear ourselves. News is for sharing, not for concealing. Good news of Jesus's salvation especially warrants sharing, when we know that nothing has greater value than that which Jesus offers. Wherever you are, share Jesus. Wherever you go, share Jesus. And let the Spirit of Christ be your comfort, power, companion, and guide.

Memory Verses. 1:8: "But you will receive power when the Holy Spirit comes on you; and you will be my witnesses in Jerusalem, and in all Judea and Samaria, and to the ends of the earth." 2:1: When the day of Pentecost came, they were all together in one place. 2:4: All of them were filled with the Holy Spirit and began to speak in other tongues as the Spirit enabled them. 2:38: "Repent and be baptized, every one of you, in the name of Jesus Christ for the forgiveness of your sins. And you will receive the gift of the Holy Spirit." 2:42: They devoted themselves to the apostles' teaching and to fellowship, to the breaking of bread and to prayer. 4:12: "Salvation is found in no one else, for there is no other name given under heaven by which we must be saved." 17:30: "In the past God overlooked such ignorance, but now he commands all people everywhere to repent." 20:28: "Keep watch over yourselves and all the flock of which the Holy Spirit has made you overseers. Be shepherds of the church of God, which he bought with his own blood."

Letters

When God speaks through his word the Bible, readers don't hear mere whispers, hints, suggestions, myths, or comforts. The Bible, far and away the most-widely published book in history, instead tells God's story in unparalleled clarity, antiquity, scope, import, originality, and perspective. God's word is fully worthy of its inestimable author, with every verse perfectly crafted in its proper place. For all its perfection and unmatchable significance, though, the Bible does not tell its story easily. The Bible can put off even intrepid readers, when they do not read with the Spirit's discernment. Plenty of books, indeed rafts of exquisite commentaries, explain the Bible. Yet wouldn't reading the Bible itself be especially valuable, if authors writing under the Spirit's guidance had explained it to us?

The letters, or if you prefer *epistles*, give us that opportunity. The Bible's sixty-six books include history, law, teaching, genealogy, prophecy, wisdom writing, song, revelation, and, yes, letters. The Bible places the letters in a New Testament series, after the four gospel books and the history of the early church in Acts but before the concluding book Revelation. The letters play a critical role in confirming, clarifying, and encompassing the doctrine that the Bible's other books imply across complex histories, events, and prophecies. The epistles provide an invaluable confirmation of the gospel, an absolute treasure spelling out the gospel's concepts and meanings in plain language, while leaving no doubt as to the lessons to draw.

Without the epistles, a reader would have to infer the correct meaning of many widely varying Bible books recording or suggesting histories, trends, tendencies, patterns, peoples, conflicts, characters, and events. A reader would also have to wrestle applications and lessons from that meaning. The four gospel books and Acts of course provide the gospel foundation, but the letters clarify critical understandings, commitments, concepts, principles, and doctrine. If you want to think, walk, and talk Bible, having God's word dwell in you most richly, which is a profound desire, then read the letters.

The Bible organizes the twenty-one New Testament letters by their authors. The first thirteen letters claim Paul's authorship, with a fourteenth letter Hebrews having no identified author but placed next in order after the thirteen letters attributed to Paul. These fourteen examples, give or take Hebrews, traditionally comprise the Pauline letters, notwithstanding substantial question over the authorship of some of the letters. The next letter identifies itself as having James as its author, followed by two letters claiming Peter's authorship, three letters claiming John's authorship, and a final letter claiming Jude's authorship. Questions also exist over the authorship of some of these last seven letters.

Questions over authorship, as to letters claiming specific authors, in no sense imply that any anonymous authors meant to mislead readers as to attribution. To the contrary, devoted students, in the role of the attributed author's trusted scribe or memoirist, may have been the anonymous authors, in honorific attribution, following a convention common to ancient schools. Better for a student to credit the teacher than to claim credit alone. Thus, even if Paul did not write several of the letters claiming his authorship, then his attribution still bears authority in tracing to Paul the experience that formed the thought, all under the Holy Spirit's inspiration. Keep that reassurance in mind when considering the following discussion of individual authors.

Because the Bible's twenty-one New Testament letters generally take the form of correspondence, they do presume certain recipient audiences, from which we learn more about the letters and their intended meaning. Appropriate to the prevailing conventions for correspondence, the letters typically begin with a greeting that identifies the letter's author and recipients. A thanksgiving prayer typically follows. The letters then devote their main content to practical instruction in tenets of Christian faith, often addressing specific challenges that the letter's recipients face. The letters tend to include relatively specific counsel and direction on conduct, drawn from the more-general doctrinal presentation. The letters typically conclude with personal information about the author and acquaintances, greetings, and pleas.

One can group the letters according to audience and attributes, beyond grouping the letters according to their stated or presumed authors. For instance, four of the Pauline letters, including Ephesians, Philippians, Colossians, and Philemon, bear the mark of *captivity* letters, Paul having written from prison. Three other Pauline letters, including 1 Timothy, 2 Timothy, and Titus, we know as the *pastoral* letters because addressed to protégé pastors and carrying advice on how to guide the congregation. Aside from Hebrews, the other Pauline letters outside of the pastoral letters all had specific church communities as their audience. The last seven letters outside of the Pauline corpus, including James, 1 and 2 Peter, 1, 2, and 3 John, and Jude, we know as *catholic* or *universal* letters because not addressed to a specific church community. The universal letters have general application, although the letters addressed to church communities facing specific challenges also have universal value and appeal for the warnings that they hold. Read the letters under the Spirit's guidance. They hold riches untold.

Romans

> For in the gospel the righteousness of God is revealed—a righteousness that is by faith from first to last, just as it is written: "The righteous will live by faith." 1:17.

Theme. The theme of Paul's letter to the Romans is faith. Faith is a precious commodity, especially in a skeptical world filled with self-constructed and self-involved persons who see no superiority other than their own. Faith implies trusting something, specifically the good news of Jesus Christ, and someone, in salvation's instance God. God in Christ is not the world's message. Yet that good news of Jesus Christ is the world's only hope. The letter to the Romans spells out the roadmap to eternal life through faith in Christ Jesus.

Author. Romans attributes Paul as its author, about which scholars also show strong consensus. Scholars generally attribute the apostle Paul's birth to Jewish parents in A.D. 6 in Tarsus, in the east of modern-day Turkey. Paul, then known as Saul, was a Roman citizen from birth but spent his formative years in Jerusalem, studying the Jewish Torah under the prominent rabbinical scholar and Sanhedrin member Gamaliel. Paul was by his own claim a Pharisee's Pharisee, so strict of a Jewish religious adherent that he persecuted the new Christians in Jerusalem and throughout Judea. Poignantly, Paul was present and approving at the first recorded Christian martyr Stephen's stoning, as the book of Acts notes. Paul came to Christ around 33 A.D. in his dramatic encounter with the risen Lord on Paul's way to Damascus to persecute believers. Acts records that Paul completed that trip blind, receiving his sight and the Holy Spirit when meeting the visiting convert Ananias. Paul then spent three years in Arabia before returning to Damascus briefly to preach Jesus, until persecution caused him to flee to Jerusalem. Paul met with the apostles in Jerusalem before returning home to Tarsus and nearby Antioch, to preach for approximately the next decade from 36 A.D. to 46 A.D. Paul then spent another decade on three missionary journeys throughout the eastern Great (Mediterranean) Sea, from about 47 A.D. to 57 A.D., when he may have written about half of his letters. Paul spent much of his last seven years under arrest and imprisoned in Caesarea and Rome, guiding the churches and defending the faith. Paul may have written the other half of his letters during this period, before his death by execution in Rome around 64 to 68 A.D.

Audience. Consensus is that in Romans, Paul wrote between 56 and 58 A.D. to a church in Rome that no apostle had yet visited. Jewish converts at Pentecost may have migrated to Rome ahead of any apostle, witnessing to new Gentile converts, establishing the church there. The letter appears to address both Jewish and Gentile believers. Despite that Paul expresses his deep love for the church's members, Paul was likely writing to believers whom he did not know, intending instead to introduce himself while also confirming with passion their remarkable and growing faith. Paul planned to visit the church but wanted in advance to confirm the gospel message that he would bring. Paul may have written Romans from Corinth while preparing to visit Jerusalem to deliver a collection, before heading to Rome and then on to Spain, having finished his work in the Eastern Mediterranean.

Structure. Although Romans includes greetings appropriate for a letter, the heart of Romans is a long, bold statement of faith and argument for the faith, more so than correspondence addressed to a specific audience. Romans first declares the gospel's facts before confirming the reader's desperate need to receive salvation. Romans then presents the gospel as available to all, God having extended his grace to all, and anyone by faith alone able to accept God's grace. Romans next describes the freedom that salvation brings, before confirming God's plan for Christ's body to unite Jews with Gentiles. Romans then describes the service that follows submission to Christ, each believer having one's own spiritual gifts, exercised in unity to build one another up in faith. Romans ends with Paul describing his personal plans while extending further greetings.

Application. The clear truths that Romans boldly expresses hold endless encouragement for readers at any point in their growing faith. As Romans 10:17 asserts, "Faith comes from hearing the message, and the message is heard through the word about Christ." Listen to God's word about Christ. Dwell in the word. Accept and believe God's word. Romans presents the gospel as clearly and forthrightly as any other Bible book or letter, and with greater detail and comprehensiveness than most. For those reasons, many favor Romans as a first read for new Bible readers, even while it remains a stalwart for Bible veterans. Some evangelists use the so-called Roman Road through the letter to lead explorers to Christ: we all have sinned (3:23); the wage of sin is death, but God's gift is eternal life through Christ (6:23); for while we were sinners, Christ died for us, out of God's love for us (5:8); if your mouth confesses Jesus Christ as Lord, and your heart believes God raised him from the dead, then you will be saved (10:9); no condemnation exists for those who are in Christ Jesus (8:1); and nothing can separate us from God's love in Christ (8:38-39). Embrace the gospel fully, first in confession, then in belief.

Memory Verses. *1:17: For in the gospel the righteousness of God is revealed—a righteousness that is by faith from first to last, just as it is written: "The righteous will live by faith." 3:22: This righteousness is given through faith in Jesus Christ to all who believe. 3:23: For all have sinned and fall short of the glory of God. 5:8: But God demonstrates his own love for us in this: While we were still sinners, Christ died for us. 6:23: For the wages of sin is death, but the gift of God is eternal life in Christ Jesus our Lord. 8:1: Therefore, there is now no condemnation for those who are in Christ Jesus. 8:28: And we know that in all things God works for the good of those who love him, who have been called according to his purpose. 10:9: If you declare with your mouth, "Jesus is Lord," and believe in your heart that God raised him from the dead, you will be saved. 10:17: [F]aith comes from hearing the message, and the message is heard through the word about Christ. 12:1: Therefore, I urge you, brothers and sisters, in view of God's mercy, to offer your bodies as a living sacrifice, holy and pleasing to God – this is true worship. 12:2: Do not conform to the pattern of this world, but be transformed by the renewing of your mind. Then you will be able to test and approve what God's will is – his good, pleasing and perfect will.*

1 Corinthians

Do you not know that in a race all the runners run, but only one gets the prize? Run in such a way as to get the prize. 9:24.

Theme. The theme of 1 Corinthians is striving. Christ strove mightily to complete his salvation mission and reach us. His offer is a gift, meaning wholly unearned. Yet in receiving Christ's gift, we accept certain holy responsibilities and develop certain righteous desires. Sometimes, those things require striving. We must, at times, work at the disciplines and practices of our faith, if we wish to mature in Christ's glory. Paul describes this happy effort as running a race to win, to get a prize. No matter the analogy, though, we should celebrate the theme of 1 Corinthians that Christ welcomes our striving, without requiring anything of us but our confession and belief, to receive his full grace.

Author. The letter attributes Paul as its author, about which scholars also show strong consensus. Read more about Paul in the above section on his letter to the Romans. Paul wrote 1 Corinthians around A.D. 55, on his third missionary journey. Paul wrote the letter from Ephesus, near the end of three years that Paul had served another church in that prominent city located on Asia Minor's westernmost coast across the Aegean Sea from Greece.

Audience. Paul wrote 1 Corinthians to the church in Corinth, a large and rich port city on the southern coastline of the eastern part of Greece (Achaia), not far from Athens. Paul had founded the church in Corinth on his second missionary journey. The church in Corinth to whom Paul addressed 1 Corinthians was navigating an especially idolatrous and sexually corrupt culture. Rampant immorality threatened to undermine the spiritually immature church. Paul had already written one letter to the church at Corinth, lost to history. This next letter, one that we nonetheless call 1 Corinthians, refers to that earlier lost epistle. Evidently, Paul's first letter raised more questions, some in a letter from friends in Corinth to which 1 Corinthians 7:1 refers, and some by oral report, that Paul sought to answer in 1 Corinthians. Here, Paul sought to fortify the church's faith with specific answers to the church members' practical questions about how to conduct themselves in the face of temptation, confusion, and opposition.

Structure. Paul begins 1 Corinthians by stressing that the believers should remain unified around the faith's gospel tenets. Church leaders have specific roles that they should undertake with maturity. Paul then addresses how the church should treat immoral members, the letter denouncing in the strongest terms the sexual sin that beset the church. Paul next addresses how to preserve and strengthen the weakened marriages typical in the corrupt culture. Paul's spectacular love chapter, chapter thirteen, breaks through other sections answering specific questions of conduct on worship, women, communion, and spiritual gifts. The long and rich letter next discusses death and the resurrection body, often quoted at memorials, followed by parting thoughts, greetings, and benediction. First Corinthians remains a weighty and highly practical tool for preserving unity within a body of believers and instructing believers in how to relate to one another while resisting surrounding corruption. It also reveals priceless inspiration and comfort on death and the resurrected body.

Application. We do need to strive. We need to show some discipline and commitment. Christ's good news is one of grace, but its heartfelt receipt should produce an earnest desire to do as Christ invites. We do not find that desire in hoping to obey rules to achieve his full measure of grace. That response would not be to recognize and accept his grace. Instead, we run the race joyfully, knowing Christ's welcome and prize at race's end. Christ did not come to further burden an already heavily burdened religious class. He came to free the lost, to unburden his followers, and to offer the sanctifying, purifying, and uplifting work of his Holy Spirit. We run in that Spirit, toward the full embrace of a glorious Christ.

Memory Verses. 1:18: For the message of the cross is foolishness to those who are perishing, but to us who are being saved it is the power of God. 6:9-10: Do not be deceived: Neither the sexually immoral nor idolaters nor adulterers nor men who have sex with men nor thieves nor the greedy nor drunkards nor slanderers nor swindlers will inherit the kingdom of God. 6:19: Do you not know that your bodies are temples of the Holy Spirit, who is in you, whom you have received from God? You are not your own; you were bought at a price. 10:13: No temptation has overtaken you except what is common to us all. And God is faithful; he will not let you be tempted beyond what you can bear. But when you are tempted, he will also provide a way out so that you can endure it. 13:4: Love is patient, love is kind. It does not envy, it does not boast, it is not proud. 15:50: I declare to you, brothers and sisters, that flesh and blood cannot inherit the kingdom of God, nor does the perishable inherit the imperishable.

2 Corinthians

He has made us competent as ministers of a new covenant—not of the letter but of the Spirit; for the letter kills, but the Spirit gives life. 3:6.

Theme. The theme of 2 Corinthians is apostleship. We look for apostles, those who establish, lead, and guide in the Holy Spirit, spreading and nurturing a bold and pure faith. What does apostleship look like, and what does it take? How do apostles think, and how do they courageously act? What do apostles experience in strength, weakness, and brokenness? This letter shows the great apostle Paul in bold action, relying wholly on the Spirit, while giving both spiritual and practical counsel to a body of believers in whom the apostle had invested intensely. Read 2 Corinthians not just for its counsel but for its model of apostleship.

Author. This next letter 2 Corinthians, like 1 Corinthians, also attributes Paul as its author, about which scholars likewise show strong consensus. Read more about Paul in the above section on his letter to the Romans. Paul wrote 2 Corinthians around A.D. 56, about a year after his prior letter 1 Corinthians. Paul wrote the letter from Ephesus, across the Aegean Sea from Corinth on the peninsula of Greece (Achaia).

Audience. Paul wrote 2 Corinthians to the same church in Corinth that he had written 1 Corinthians and a prior lost letter, largely in response to how the church had received his prior letter 1 Corinthians. The maturation of faith involves communication, indeed back-and-forth conversation. The two letters 1 and 2 Corinthians, and their lost predecessor, show an apostle's deep concern and willingness to carry on that conversation.

Structure. Paul gives 2 Corinthians a three-part structure, beginning in the first seven chapters with a description of suffering and comfort. In 2 Corinthians, Paul commends those who had taken to heart his 1 Corinthians counsel, thus maturing in their still-developing faith. Yet Paul then felt compelled to defend himself against slanderous attacks of others, a small but dangerous number of false teachers, who had rejected his 1 Corinthians counsel. The letter is thus more personal than 1 Corinthians and plainly more painful for Paul to write. Paul had in effect to brag to establish his authority, which worked against Paul's godly humility. Paul not only defends himself in 2 Corinthians but also attacks false teachers. The next two chapters exhort to share God's grace in generous giving, supplying practical counsel like that of 1 Corinthians, here though on how to collect money for the poor. The final four chapters return to the theme of suffering, Paul declaring in 12:9 that God's grace is enough, having made our own power perfect in our weakness. The letter shows how intensely one ought to love the church and its members, and struggle for the truth, not in one's own strength but in weakness and the Spirit's power. No doubt, 2 Corinthians will forever remain an inspired witness to the striving of an apostle.

Application. Paul makes an enormous contribution to the adherent who, though striving, only feels weak. When Paul shares verse 12:9, "But he said to me, 'My grace is sufficient for you, for my power is made perfect in weakness,'" Paul teaches us that we need not feel strong nor rely on our strength. We need only rely on the Spirit's power, God working best, indeed to perfection, in our weakness. Perhaps Paul is saying that our strength, the strength that we draw from our self-confidence and self-interest, simply gets in God's way. We should be confident in God, not in ourselves, and interested in God's desires, not our own, for God is a God of compassion and comfort. When we rely on him in our brokenness, we can also help others in their own brokenness. God then continues to deliver us from our weakness and give us his strength. Plumb the depths of verse 12:9, to rely more and more on the Spirit's power, while recognizing that we are weak.

Memory Verses. *3:18: And we all, who with unveiled faces contemplate the Lord's glory, are being transformed into his image with ever-increasing glory, which comes from the Lord, who is the Spirit. 5:17: Therefore, if anyone is in Christ, the new creation has come: The old has gone, the new is here! 5:21: God made him who had no sin to be sin for us, so that in him we might become the righteousness of God. 6:14: Do not be yoked together with unbelievers. For what do righteousness and wickedness have in common? Or what fellowship can light have with darkness? 12:9: But he said to me, "My grace is sufficient for you, for my power is made perfect in weakness." Therefore, I will boast all the more gladly about my weaknesses, so that Christ's power may rest on me.*

Reading Guide

Groups

We tend to think of reading as individual pursuit, which to a large degree it is. But reading the Bible with others, whether in pairs or small or large groups, can be an especially fruitful activity, more so, at times, than reading the Bible alone. The Bible encourages us to listen carefully to others, especially wise teachers but also the spiritually mature. That counsel holds true for what we discern from the Bible. The Spirit can speak to the mind alone, but the Spirit also certainly speaks to the mind through others. Reading Bible books and passages together with others creates opportunities to learn what others are discerning. Those others may speak to you, and you may speak to them, about what you discern. Multiple views can help correct interpretation errors, just as much as they can help confirm correct interpretation. The views of others who are reading the same thing that you are reading from the Bible can also raise questions that you hadn't considered. Even reading the Bible aloud to one another can, through oral emphases, prod the mind into hearing better what the Bible author was relating.

Reading the Bible with others has another benefit. Few activities have, or perhaps no activity has, quite the same value to a relationship as sharing God's word. Preaching at another may not foster relationship. But when two or more read God's word together, they not only learn from one another but also enjoy closer relationship around the preeminent shared affinity. Nothing has greater value than one's relationship to God. Finding others who share in that relationship, and share through reading God's word, enriches one's own life while enriching the lives of those others. You don't have strong friends? You can't find friends who enjoy doing what you enjoy doing? Then try finding a companion or joining a small group to read the Bible together. You may not initially think that much of one another's company. But over time, God's word has a way of fostering relationship.

Galatians

It is for freedom that Christ has set us free. 5:1.

Theme. The theme of the letter to the Galatians is freedom. Righteousness, Galatians 2:21 explains, does not come through rule-keeping, not through religious law or practice, because if it did, then Christ died without purpose. Instead, Galatians 2:20 explains, we, too, died, crucified with Christ, for the purpose of living by faith in Christ, set free. We need not meet a measure, satisfy a standard, nor keep up with the holy devout. We need only meet Christ, embrace him, die with him on the cross, and then rise again as he rose, to live free for him in his kingdom paradise. These things that sound like we might have to achieve, he has already achieved for us, making us free in Christ.

Author. Galatians attributes Paul as its author, about which scholars likewise show strong consensus. Read more about Paul in the above section on his letter to the Romans. Paul wrote Galatians while in Antioch in central Asia Minor, just before Paul returned to Jerusalem in 50 A.D. for a council to settle an issue, one that Paul addressed in Galatians and elsewhere. Paul was thus very much in the thick of guiding the church's spread, even as, with the Spirit's help, the church discerned sound doctrine.

Audience. Paul wrote the letter Galatians to the churches that Paul had founded on his first missionary journey through Galatia, a region in south-central Asia Minor. Because Paul did not address the letter to any specific church, he plainly intended that the Galatian churches circulate the letter among them. Those churches would have shared similar culture giving rise to similar challenges even if they also likely faced differing specific issues.

Structure. Galatians has a three-part structure, beginning in its first two chapters with Paul's statement on the authenticity of the gospel that he preached. The letter's second part, comprised of the next two chapters, asserts the superiority of the gospel arousing out of Judaism, to Judaism without Christ. As an early letter, Galatians addressed an issue that divided the early church, having to do with the relationship between Jewish and Gentile converts. Jewish leaders known as the Judaizers were advocating that Gentile converts to the new Christian faith must keep Jewish laws and traditions. To the Judaizers, faith in Christ was not enough. New Gentile converts must also comply with burdensome laws including those for circumcision. In Galatians, Paul rejected that position, opposing the apostle Peter, and advocating vigorously that faith in Christ was enough. The letter's third and last part, comprised of the last two chapters, asserts the new faith's liberating effect. The new faith-based covenant was one of life and liberty, whereas the old law-based covenant was one of demand and enslavement. Galatians is a spectacular testimony that the gospel is authentic, superior, and enough.

Application. The import of Galatians is that we embrace and experience the liberty that comes with Christ. That liberty is not to licentiousness, for which we have no desire in any case, Christ having liberated us from sin's bondage. Rather, our liberty is to love him and, as we do so, love our brothers and sisters in Christ. Christ frees us from the worry of death and, before death, demands to conform. Live as Christ made you, in his image and yet unique in him. Look on Christ, listen to his Spirit, and live your life in such joy that your love overflows to others, who may then likewise receive his Spirit. Know the fruit of that Spirit, which Galatians 5:22 tells us is love, joy, peace, patience, kindness, goodness, faithfulness, gentleness, and self-control. Our freedom is to pursue these things without limit.

Memory Verses. 2:20: *I have been crucified with Christ and I no longer live, but Christ lives in me. The life I now live in the body, I live by faith in the Son of God, who loved me and gave himself for me. 3:28: There is neither Jew nor Gentile, neither slave nor free, neither male nor female, for you are all one in Christ Jesus. 5:1: It is for freedom that Christ has set us free. Stand firm, then, and do not let yourselves be burdened again by a yoke of slavery. 5:16: So I say, walk by the Spirit, and you will not gratify the desires of the sinful nature. 5:22-23: But the fruit of the Spirit is love, joy, peace, forbearance, kindness, goodness, faithfulness, gentleness, and self-control. Against such things there is no law. 6:7: Do not be deceived: God cannot be mocked. People reap what they sow.*

Ephesians

Praise be to the God and Father of our Lord Jesus Christ, who has blessed us in the heavenly realms with every spiritual blessing in Christ. 1:3.

Theme. The theme of the letter to the Ephesians is God's blessings through the church. God wants believers to flourish, to experience the joy of the Spirit and fullness of life. God knows that we do so through united and holy community, not in isolation, alone with our thoughts. Our radical transformation from anxious souls worried over the next meal while fearing a looming death, to joy-filled spirits confident in God's provision and looking forward to joining him in paradise, happens within a mature body of believers, supporting one another's growing faith. We all desire blessing. We all need hope and relief. Ephesians points us toward the sure path upward with fellow believers.

Author. Ephesians attributes Paul as its author, supported by other letters indicating that the trusted Tychicus, accompanied by the runaway slave Onesimus, delivered this letter to its recipients along with delivering other letters known as Colossians and Philemon to other places. Paul would have written Ephesians around 60 or 61 A.D., when Paul was imprisoned in Rome for the first time, marking Ephesians as one of the prison epistles, along with Philippians, Colossians, and Philemon. Ephesians shows how joyfully Paul could write even from prison. See the above section on Romans for more details about Paul's life.

Audience. Ephesians addresses itself both to the churches at Ephesus, on the western coast of Asia Minor across the Aegean Sea from Athens on the Greek peninsula, and to believers everywhere. Ephesus was a strategic, regional port city on the high order of Syria's Antioch and Egypt's Alexandria, while also on the main route between Rome and the East including Jerusalem. Paul resided in Ephesus for three years, serving the local churches, as Acts 18:18-21 and 19:1-41 amply records, supporting that the letter addressed family and friends in the faith, although the letter's joyful encouragement serves believers everywhere.

Structure. Paul wrote Ephesians in three parts, with a beginning greeting comprised of chapter one. Paul's second part, comprised of the next four-plus chapters, articulate how God was fulfilling his plan through the churches. God had raised people spiritually from life to death, reconciled Jews and Gentiles through the cross, and formed the church as one body in Christ. God was also maintaining unity in the church, fostering corporate maturity through God's gifts to the church, and attaining Christ-like morality through radical transformation. Paul's last part closes with a reminder of the battles we must face and with words of encouragement. Ephesians thus does not address specific issues but instead supplies general guidance and encouragement, instructing believers in the church's nature and role. Its main message is that Christ unites believers in his life-giving body, which is the church, in one Spirit, under one God and Father over all. That broader perspective makes Ephesians' message universal and the letter a bright jewel in the King's crown, a treasure to believers everywhere.

Application. Check yourself: have you matured in the faith? And if you can look back seeing your own growth, then are you still maturing, or have you stalled? Ephesians encourages us to examine our spiritual growth in the context of how united we are with a vital body of believers ardently following Christ. Do we love our fellow believers, serving and encouraging them? Are we living holy lives, apart from society's desultory influences? Are we sharing the gifts that God so generously gave us, to build up the body of Christ? And are we reaching beyond our church to witness to the community around us? We must embrace these blessings to enjoy the fullness of life in Christ.

Memory Verses. 2:1-2: As for you, you were dead in your transgressions and sins, in which you used to live when you followed the ways of this world and of the ruler of the kingdom of the air, the spirit who is now at work in those who are disobedient. 2:8: For it is by grace you have been saved, through faith – and this is not from yourselves, it is the gift of God.... 6:10-12: Finally, be strong in the Lord and in his mighty power. Put on the full armor of God, so that you can take your stand against the devil's schemes. For our struggle is not against flesh and blood, but against the rulers, against the authorities, against the powers of this dark world and against the spiritual forces of evil in the heavenly realms.

Philippians

> In all my prayers for all of you, I always pray with joy because of your partnership in the gospel from the first day until now.... 1:4-5.

Theme. The theme of the letter to the Philippians is joy. We desire and accept the joy of the Lord, aided and inspired by Christ's Spirit. Yet we also want to share that joy with the body of believers with whom we celebrate our salvation in Christ. This letter does so. It is not a critique but a celebration of the love that its author and recipients had for one another. We should share that joy with our own church, our own faith community, as we witness to the glory of knowing our Lord and Savior Jesus Christ, anticipating joining him in his paradise kingdom.

Author. Philippians credits Paul with its authorship, as do a strong consensus of scholars. Paul wrote Philippians around 61 A.D., as the last of his three prison letters, this one near the end of his first Roman imprisonment. Epaphroditus had brought Paul an offering from the church in Philippi, to which Paul wished to respond in thanks by Epaphroditus's return trip, except that Epaphroditus fell ill, delaying the letter, as the letter itself describes. Like the letter before it, Ephesians, Philippians shows the joy with which Paul could write, even from a Rom prison. See the above section on Romans for more details about Paul's life.

Audience. Paul founded the church at Philippi on his second missionary journey, after a vision had sent him to Macedonia. With Philippi located on the Aegean Sea's northern coast, outside of Asia Minor, the church was the first on the European continent. The church may have formed under the auspices of the businesswoman Lydia, who welcomed Paul and his co-workers into her home, and perhaps also the Philippian jailer whom Paul converted after a miraculous earthquake had set Paul free. The church plainly held Paul in the highest regard because it had sent a gift for Paul, whom Rome then held in prison. Paul wrote to thank the church for the gift and encourage the church's members, and believers everywhere, in deepening their faith.

Structure. Paul offers a clear, chapter-by-chapter structure in his letter to the Philippians. In the first chapter, Paul shows that Jesus is our life, the second chapter that Jesus is our model, the third chapter that Jesus is our goal, and the final chapter that Jesus is our contentment. Paul's one passion was to know Christ more for that opportunity's surpassing greatness, against which everything else, including all earthly riches, was loss. Hardship meant nothing to Paul. Philippians is thus a letter of love, joy, and celebration, overflowing with the glorious Holy Spirit. The letter is a favorite of many believers, made even more encouraging by the fact that Paul was enduring such prison hardship while writing it.

Application. Philippians 2:14-16 urges that we do everything without complaining, instead holding onto the word of life. Why shouldn't we do so, Philippians 3:8-10 asks, knowing that everything is loss, beyond knowing the power of Christ's resurrection? We must thus forget what is behind us and instead strain toward the prize that is ahead in heaven in Christ Jesus, Philippians 3:13-14 exhorts us. We should rejoice, rejoice always, rather than be anxious about anything, instead praying with thanksgiving and requests to God, putting what we have learned into practice, Philippians 4:4-9 concludes. Philippians is a joyful witness to our celebration life in Christ.

Memory Verses. *1:6: Being confident of this, that he who began a good work in you will carry it on to completion until the day of Christ Jesus. 2:5: In your relationships with one another, have the same attitude of mind Christ Jesus had.... 4:4: Rejoice in the Lord always. I will say it again: Rejoice! 4:6: Do not be anxious about anything, but in every situation, by prayer and petition, with thanksgiving, present your requests to God. 4:8: Finally, brothers and sisters, whatever is true, whatever is noble, whatever is right, whatever is pure, whatever is lovely, whatever is admirable – if anything is excellent or praiseworthy – think about such things. 4:13: I can do all this through him who gives me strength.*

Colossians

The Son is the image of the invisible God, the firstborn over all creation. 1:15.

Theme. The theme of the letter to the Colossians is that Christ is supreme, enough on his own, not approached or surpassed by any other. We look for what is best for us and our community, having the natural desire to succeed, to excel. And so, we try this bit of religion and that bit of philosophy or expertise, creating what we believe to be an effective concoction from the best of each thing that we sample. Yet somehow, we find little help from that self-made mix. Colossians thus carries the theme that faith in Christ is enough on its own. To mix lesser things with Christ is not to improve over faith, but to distort and diminish it. Look, Colossians says, to Christ as supreme, superior, and sufficient alone. One does no better than to trust in Jesus Christ.

Author. Colossians is another letter that credits Paul as its author. Paul wrote Colossians during his first Rome imprisonment, making it another one of his four prison letters, this one, like Ephesians and Philemon, delivered by his trusted Tychicus, accompanied by the runaway slave Onesimus. Paul would have written the letter around 60 A.D.

Audience. Paul addresses the letter Colossians to a church in Colosse, located inland in the southwestern part of Asia Minor. Paul did not found or visit Colosse's church, which Epaphras, and others whom Paul's missionary preaching converted, seem instead to have founded. The letter indicates that misguided believers in Colosse's church were mixing their precious Christian faith with pagan and secular beliefs in a sort of religious relativism, the contemporary equivalent of which may be *cultural Christianity*. The letter thus directs its instruction to the sufficiency of faith in Christ alone. Given Christ's fullness and lordship, Christ *and* anything else is less than Christ and thus a loss and dangerous heresy. Colossians confronts that heresy with the truth that Christ is God and the head of the church, we are in Christ, and therefore we have no need for the world's legalism, philosophy's asceticism, or another

226

world's mysticism. Christ has all power and authority. Colossians offers a timeless and precious grounding in the deepest reaches of our faith.

Structure. Paul gives Colossians a two-part structure. Chapters one and two show the faith's foundation in *who Jesus is*. Jesus is preeminent, both the world's creator with his Father and the world's gift recipient, through his Father's grace in allowing Jesus to become human within creation. Jesus, as John 1:11 states, came to that which was his own, the Son as visible manifestation of his invisible Father. Paul's second part, comprised of chapters three and four, shows the first part's application in *who we are to be*. How we comprehend Christ determines who we are. When we accept Christ as all-sufficient Savior, we become like him in the way he created us to be. Paul in Colossians connects the theological with the practical. Theology, meaning here our understanding of Christ and his mission on earth, becomes highly practical, as the experience of the Colossians proved. Paul set that proof straight.

Application. Jesus, we should learn from Colossians, holds everything together, as if a cosmic glue, when we acknowledge him. We then must accept his holding everything together, rather than searching for other mixtures to add to his glue. We then must apply what we learn from his Spirit, rather than apply other mixtures that do not hold like his glue. Christ not only holds us together but holds the church together, too. As Christ's body, the church grows when each member does the part Christ made the member to do. We thus learn to work corporately, adding our gifts to the gifts of others that the body may grow.

Memory Verses. 1:15: The Son is the image of the invisible God, the firstborn over all creation. 1:16: For in him all things were created: things in heaven and on earth, visible and invisible, whether thrones or powers or rulers or authorities; all things have been created through him and for him. 3:1: Since, then, you have been raised with Christ, set your hearts on things above, where Christ is seated at the right hand of God. 3:12: Therefore, as God's chosen people, holy and dearly loved, clothe yourselves with compassion, kindness, humility, gentleness and patience. 3:16: Let the message of Christ dwell among you richly as you teach and admonish one another with all wisdom through psalms, hymns and songs from the Spirit, singing to God with gratitude in your hearts.

Reading Guide

Commentaries

Bible readers inevitably reach questions about the text that they cannot answer with any confidence from further study of the text itself but about which the Spirit leads them to investigate further. Commentaries are one source for that research. A commentary represents the considered view of an author, often a theologian or scholar but also preachers, academics, and others, claiming some expertise or at least a deep interest in the Bible. Commentaries come from all perspectives, recent or long ago, mainstream or radical, denominational or nondenominational, spiritual or literary, and believing or disbelieving, among many others. Readers can find hundreds of commentaries, many of them covering all books of the Bible, verse by verse, each suggesting a specific meaning or alternative meanings.

Exploring commentaries can be invigorating and informative, or distracting and daunting. Readers are wise to be cautious in their confidence in commentaries. A good way to look at the question of reliability is that the Bible is *the* commentary on all other thinking and writing. Indeed, reading commentaries while already holding a sound, Spirit-supported and Spirit-inspired understanding of Bible meanings tends to reveal the interests, perspectives, and even biases of the commentators more so than the Bible's meaning. God's word appraises us, not the other way around. That insight is one good way to evaluate commentaries, which is not to credit commentators who claim greater authority than the God of the Bible. Humility is always a primary attribute of a sound interpreter. Consider investigating commentaries, especially on verses or passages that don't yet fit for you with your understanding of the Bible's purpose and good-news message.

1 Thessalonians

Now about your love for one another we do not need to write to you, for you yourselves have been taught by God to love each other. 4:9.

Theme. The theme of 1 Thessalonians is fellowship. The letter at its verse 3:12 prays that our love would increase and overflow for one another within the church. We desire loving fellowship, where others accept us as God made us and encourage us as one of their own. God made us for caring community, to be kind and considerate, and to help one another with instruction, encouragement, provision, and service. We are in some sense incomplete as persons until we find a community to call our fellowship home. First Thessalonians shows the reader how we share such fellowship in the hope of Christ's soon return.

Author. First Thessalonians credits Paul as its author, as scholars agree. Paul wrote 1 Thessalonians around A.D. 51, months after leaving the church to which he wrote. Acts 17:2 indicates that Paul preached on three consecutive sabbaths there, although scholars find other indications of a longer stay, perhaps three months, from the multiple offerings the church received while Paul was there, from Philippi. Paul's letter, then, would be the sort of communication a pastor might make to a local body that he knew, but perhaps whose members he did not know so well. See more about Paul in the section above on the letter to the Romans.

Audience. Thessalonica, to whose church Paul wrote, was along an important land trade route and seaport located at the northern head of the Aegean Sea. Paul had founded the church on his second missionary journey. The letter came shortly later, to encourage the new believers in their growing faith. Indeed, Paul sent Timothy to encourage the church and confirm the members in their new faith. First Thessalonians thus carries ardent messages of assurance, exhortation in the faith, and comfort in coming resurrection. Only toward the letter's end does Paul challenge the church to avoid sexual immorality while living righteously in a sinful world. Paul concludes the letter with specific counsel on preparing for Jesus's return, helping one another remain strong, and testing all teaching against the true gospel message, followed by benedictions and requests for prayer. First Thessalonians remains solid reassurance, especially to new believers needing encouragement in faith.

Structure. In 1 Thessalonians, Paul offers a two-part structure. The letter's first three chapters look back, from a pastor's yearning heart, for the new church. One can see the longing that Paul had that his new church in Thessalonica would survive and prosper. The letter's second part, comprised of its last two chapters, looks ahead. Here, Paul gives the church specific guidance in how to conduct themselves, as verse 5:6 says, alert and self-controlled, so that the church would not stumble but instead grow as Paul so strongly desired.

Application. While 1 Thessalonians is a corporate epistle, reflecting a pastor's deep concern for his new little church, readers find plenty of lessons for the individual within it. One of those lessons is that in all we do, we should be expecting Jesus to come. Because of that great expectation that Jesus will return to take us to be with him forever, we must not grieve like those who lack this hope. That hope is what keeps our faith from growing stale. Instead, the closer we draw to joining Jesus, the stronger our faith grows in anticipation of that day. Holding fast to that hope, we see its evidence in our growing morality, peace, perseverance, and mercy and grace shown toward others, as 1 Thessalonians 4:3-7 confirms. We also show respect for others with whom we are in peaceful fellowship, as we pray without ceasing, giving thanks in all things, 1 Thessalonians 5:12-23 attests.

Memory Verses. *4:13: Brothers and sisters, we do not want you to be uninformed about those who sleep in death, so that you do not grieve like the rest, who have no hope. 4:16: For the Lord himself will come down from heaven, with a loud command, with the voice of the archangel and with the trumpet call of God, and the dead in Christ will rise first. 5:6: So then, let us not be like others, who are asleep, but let us be awake and sober. 5:18: Give thanks in all circumstances; for this is God's will for you in Christ Jesus. 5:21-22: [H]old on to what is good, reject every kind of evil.*

2 Thessalonians

So then, brothers and sisters, stand firm and hold fast to the teachings we passed on to you, whether by word of mouth or by letter. 2:15.

Theme. The theme of 2 Thessalonians is resolve. Anything that we hope to achieve in the world requires a degree of resolve. Things of faith, though, often require more resolve than things of the world. The world opposes faith, challenging and persecuting its followers. Persecution has but one response, which is to forge ahead in resolve. Resolve, toughness, perseverance, and trust go hand in hand to equip the follower to hold fast to the faith. We need to hear of this resolve. The alternative, quitting and failure, isn't pretty.

Author. Second Thessalonians credits Paul as its author. Paul wrote the letter from Corinth around 51 A.D., as little as a few months after he wrote 1 Thessalonians to the same church. The brevity and content of 2 Thessalonians make clear that Paul wrote the letter to address confusion, or, much worse, deliberate distortion, about the timing of Christ's return that his prior letter 1 Thessalonians, and the church's continuing persecution, had raised. See more about Paul in the section above on the letter to the Romans.

Audience. Paul's letter shows in greater detail that some in the church had either innocently misconstrued or, as false teachers, deliberately distorted, his statement in 1 Thessalonians that Christ could come at any moment. Readers of that earlier letter were using it as an excuse for idleness. They had also misconstrued their persecution as evidence that the Lord's day was indeed quite near, as an excuse for not pursuing more of the Lord's good work. Paul in 2 Thessalonians corrected the church, indicating that while Christ's return could be quite near, an expectation that is fully appropriate, his imminent return was no excuse for idleness. The church will first see the lawless man revealed before Christ returns. The Lord indeed desires patient and expectant waiting but also desires that the Lord's ministers, which includes all believers, should work as he desires. Evil will increase in the last days, bringing with it the believers' increased persecution, but those signs are simply greater reason to spread the gospel message, doing the Lord's commissioned work.

Structure. Paul gave 2 Thessalonians a three-part structure, each comprised of a single chapter. Paul's first part exhorts the letter's recipients to remain strong in the faith in the face of trials and persecutions, as the church had so far done. Paul next advises the church to stand firm in belief, trusting what the members had trusted initially. The church had received Paul's reliable teaching, on which its members must continue to stand. Finally, Paul exhorts the church's members to keep working while praying. They must never tire of doing right. Paul makes 2 Thessalonians a good reminder during challenges to press forward in faith.

Application. Paul uses 2 Thessalonians to teach the church discipline, self-control, and focus. We must not grow tired, nor lax and lazy, nor turning to our comforts while seeking further luxuries. The world offers us these things, but the offers pale in comparison to the riches of faith. We must look again to Christ, seeing how he pressed on through worse suffering, while knowing that he comes. Our Savior will stand on the earth. We must be ready to welcome him. Return to our Savior, rest in him, and never tire of following the faith.

Memory Verses. 2:3: Don't let anyone deceive you in any way, for that day will not come until the rebellion occurs and the man of lawlessness is revealed, the man doomed to destruction. 2:13: But we ought always to thank God for you, brothers and sisters loved by the Lord, because God chose you as firstfruits to be saved through the sanctifying work of the Spirit and through belief in the truth. 3:6: In the name of the Lord Jesus Christ, we command you, brothers and sisters, to keep away from every believer who is idle and disruptive and does not live according to the teaching you received from us.

1 Timothy

I am writing you these instructions so that ... you will know how people ought to conduct themselves in God's household.... 3:14-15.

Theme. The theme of 1 Timothy is leadership. Godly leaders are necessary, even critical, to the health, mission, and growth of the church. Jesus spent three full years training the disciples, who were about to become the leaders of his church. And so, we see in Paul's pastoral letters, of which 1 Timothy is the first, Paul's concern that the young leaders he was training exhibit Christ-like leadership. Sound leaders produce sound followers who soon become sound leaders for other sound followers. Read 1 Timothy with its lessons for leaders in mind. At some level and at some point, we are each a leader within Christ's church.

Author. Paul wrote 1 Timothy later in his ministry, around 64 A.D., just before his final Rome imprisonment. The book of Acts shows that Paul had met the respected young Christ-follower Timothy in Lystra, in Asia Minor, a decade earlier. Writing 1 Timothy so late in his life, Paul exhibits a more-reflective tone, showing greater care for how others will lead than for his own leadership the end of which was so near. Read more about Paul in the above section on his letter to the Romans.

Audience. In 1 Timothy, Paul addresses his young protégé, the son and grandson of godly Jewish women who had accepted Christ, raising Timothy in the faith as among the first of the second-generation Christians. Timothy, though young, had substantial responsibility as the pastor of the church that Paul had served at Ephesus. When Rome released Paul from his first imprisonment, likely in 62 A.D., Paul had traveled to the church in Ephesus, soon placing Timothy in leadership there. Ephesus was a challenging place to build a church, as the home of one of the seven wonders of the world, an enormous temple to the mother goddess known to the Romans as Diana and to the Greeks as Artemis. That temple was a place of extraordinary sexual indulgence. Timothy thus faced considerable challenges both within the body of believers, to maintain the body's morality and unity, and from without, to resist the surrounding culture's pressure while helping the members endure popular persecution. These challenges made Paul's advice in 1 Timothy especially worthwhile counsel for those whose first concern is with leadership within the church.

Structure. Paul offers a three-part structure in 1 Timothy, beginning in chapter one with *what* a leader should teach. Paul gives Timothy fatherly counsel first confirming Timothy in the faith but then warning him about the peril of false teachers, a warning that Paul amplifies later in the letter. The next part of Paul's letter, comprised of chapters two and three, articulates *how* a leader should teach, in prayer and modesty, while living a disciplined life pleasing to God. Paul's third part, comprised of chapters four through six, articulates the *heart* of godly leadership, in which the leader puts hope in the living God, Christ the Savior. During these leadership lessons, Paul instructs in orderly and unified public worship, and counsels on the qualifications of church elders and deacons. Paul thus coaches Timothy in how to build and maintain character among leaders and order in the church body. The letter includes substantial advice on pastoral care before concluding with exhortations to encourage the young pastor in his own motives, character, ministry, and faith. The letter remains core counsel for church leaders, surely as important of a witness to the Holy Spirit today as it was for the young Timothy.

Application. Paul exhorts Timothy, in verse 4:13, to devote himself to public reading of scripture, and to preaching and teaching. That advice is key for any leader, that they share and adhere to God's word. No leader is sound without God's word at the fore of the leader's thought, talk, and action. Sound doctrine forms a core for sound leadership. Then, as leaders, we should follow that doctrine ourselves, in self-control and discipline. Leaders must not stray while keeping the flock on its narrow path. Finally, we should do those things—teach and preach, and maintain good personal conduct—because we hope in Christ Jesus. Leadership has no mystery to it. Leadership depends on the same thing that other good conduct depends, which is the heart of Christ.

Memory Verses. 2:1: *I urge, then, first of all, that petitions, prayers, intercession and thanksgiving be made for everyone.... 2:5: For there is one God and one mediator between God and human beings, Christ Jesus, himself human.... 3:1: Here is a trustworthy saying: Whoever aspires to be an overseer desires a noble task. 3:16: Beyond all question, the mystery from which true godliness springs is great: He appeared in a body, was vindicated by the Spirit, was seen by angels, was preached among the nations, was believed on in the world, was taken up in glory. 4:1: The Spirit clearly says that in later times some will abandon the faith and follow deceiving spirits and things taught by demons.*

2 Timothy

I have fought the good fight, I have finished the race, I have kept the faith. 4:7.

Theme. The theme of 2 Timothy is endurance. Endurance implies forging ahead although circumstances make doing so hard. Endurance implies toughness, perhaps a thick skin and strong heart. No one leads a life without recognizing at times the need to endure. Pastors, certainly, must endure as they lead their congregation through its own disorder and outside persecution. Paul emphasizes in 2 Timothy that he had endured to the end of his race, as Timothy should endure. Yet pastors are not the only ones who must endure through spiritual challenges. All who follow Christ should expect persecution and thus must, like Paul, also endure. We must above all draw strength from the Holy Spirit, who brings us God's power and word. Second Timothy emphasizes both the need to endure and the source of our endurance.

Author. Second Timothy credits Paul as its author. Paul wrote 2 Timothy just a couple of years after penning 1 Timothy, around 66 or 67 A.D., during his second, short Rome imprisonment before execution, making the letter Paul's latest, in chronology his last. One can barely imagine enduring all that Paul endured, to write such an encouraging letter from his execution prison. Second Timothy makes a perfectly fitting latest Pauline letter. Read more about Paul in the above section on his letter to the Romans.

Audience. Paul's last letter constituted a passing of the torch from the apostolic generation, who met and knew the Lord, to those like Timothy who would carry the church forward based instead on witness and faith. In 2 Timothy, Paul expressed the deep love the apostles had for their faith children like Timothy, on whose commission the gospel message would now depend. Paul urged Timothy to remember his calling and hold fast to the truth as he exercised his gifts to prepare the next generation's leaders. The letter warned again of deceivers and the word's power to expose them and stand against them. Paul used his own life as an example, relating in verse 4:7 that he had fought the good fight to finish the race in faith. Paul concluded with a final commission for Timothy to preach to the end, closing with a poignant request for some personal items and information. The letter stands as timeless testament to the strength of character and depth of love with which the Holy Spirit blesses enduring faith leaders.

Structure. Paul's second letter to Timothy has a three-part structure referring to the past, present, and future. Chapter one urged Timothy and, by extension, other church leaders to guard the treasure of the past, with the Holy Spirit's help. That treasure is a good deposit entrusted to church leaders, who someday must pass it on like Paul was doing in 2 Timothy. Chapters two and three then exhorted Timothy to endure the present hardships like the good soldier in Christ that Timothy was. Chapter four concludes the letter with an assignment for the future, to preach the word in season and out of season.

Application. Second Timothy reminds us that we must endure as Paul endured, he expected Timothy to endure, and the other apostles endured. Paul writes in verse 1:12 that whatever came, he refused to be ashamed of the gospel because he knew in whom he had believed, Christ Jesus, who would guard what Paul had entrusted to him. He also wrote, in verse 3:12, that everyone trying to live godly in Christ Jesus suffers persecution. We must expect similar persecution and, when it comes, endure as Paul endured and Timothy must also have endured.

Memory Verses. 1:7: For the Spirit God gave us does not make us timid, but gives us power, love and self-discipline. 2:15: Do your best to present yourself to God as one approved, a worker who does not need to be ashamed and who correctly handles the word of truth. 3:1: But mark this: There will be terrible times in the last days. 3:16: All Scripture is God-breathed and is useful for teaching, rebuking, correcting and training in righteousness. 4:2: Preach the word; be prepared in season and out of season; correct, rebuke and encourage – with great patience and careful instruction.

Titus

These, then, are the things you should teach. Encourage and rebuke with all authority. 2:15.

Theme. The theme of the letter to Titus is teaching. Paul exhorts his protégé Titus to encourage and rebuke with authority. Teaching is a critical role within the church, for as Paul reminds Titus at verse 3:14, they must teach their people to do good, leading productive lives that provide for their urgent needs. Teaching is important because its effect is practical. People do not eat when they are not taught. God's word warns, stops, turns, and guides the path forward to productive life, flourishing life. Sound doctrine is important. It makes for better life.

Author. The letter to Titus credits Paul as its author. Paul wrote the letter to Titus around 64 A.D., between his two Rome imprisonments and about the time that Paul wrote 1 Timothy, late in Paul's life. Paul was in Nicopolis when he wrote the letter to Titus. Read the above section on Paul's letter to the Romans for more on Paul's life.

Audience. Paul's letter was to his special representative Titus, who oversaw the churches on the island of Crete, where Titus and Paul had preached and ministered together, on a visit lasting weeks, before Paul left to Titus to finish their work. Titus was Paul's Greek protege whose faith Paul had long nurtured. Galatians, for instance, records Titus meeting with the leaders of the Jerusalem church as evidence of the Holy Spirit's work among Gentile believers. Indeed, Titus served as Paul's ambassador in other work. Paul's letter to Titus is another, and likely last, step in Paul's careful development of another outstanding servant of the faith, like Timothy. In the letter, Paul counsels Titus on church affairs, much like Paul had counseled Timothy. Paul's counsel on how to treat different age groups of believers is a touching example of the care with which Paul urged his pastors to shepherd the flock. While the letter to Titus includes precious counsel, its greater witness may be to the care that established faith leaders should take in identifying and developing the next generation of leaders. In that day, missing one generation in leadership could have caused the church to have disappeared. The same remains true today, that the church is always only one generation from severe setback. Paul thus confirms the Holy Spirit's enduring power and purpose in his letter to Titus.

Structure. Paul's letter to Titus follows a three-part structure centered around teaching. Paul first exhorts Titus, in verse 1:5, that he had left Titus in Crete to straighten out what Paul had left unfinished. Churches, in their local condition, are not always straight, sound. Sometimes, they have unfinished business that sound teaching will straighten out. Paul then turns in chapter two to what Titus must teach his church, which was sound doctrine that says "no" to ungodliness. Paul was concerned with the conduct of the church's members, that they reflect the holiness of Christ. Paul ends the letter with a third part in which he urges Titus to remind the people to do good, giving a list in verses 3:1-2 of specifics. Paul embeds three statements of Jesus's incarnation as God in Christ, at verses 1:1-4, 2:11-14, and 3:4-7, within this practical, three-part message. Paul's letter to Titus is thus both deeply spiritual and practical in nature, and so must have heartened its reader with the clarity of its doctrine.

Application. We, too, like Titus, must both do good ourselves and teach others to do good. Paul's list includes to obey, be subject to ruling authorities, be peaceable and considerate, and show humility to all. What, though, motivates us to do good? Have we found our purpose in Christ? God will some day ask us what we did with his Son Jesus Christ, whether we confessed, trusted, loved, and obeyed. He will also ask us what we did with the life that he gave us. Let God's desire and Christ's love be our motivation.

Memory Verses. 1:2: *In the hope of eternal life, which God, who does not lie, promised before the beginning of time.... 1:6: An elder must be blameless, faithful to his wife, a man whose children believe and are not open to the charge of being wild and disobedient. 1:9: He must hold firmly to the trustworthy message as it has been taught, so that he can encourage others by sound doctrine and refute those who oppose it. 3:5: He saved us, not because of righteous things we had done, but because of his mercy. He saved us through the washing of rebirth and renewal by the Holy Spirit. 3:14: Our people must learn to devote themselves to doing what is good, in order to provide for urgent needs and not live unproductive lives.*

239

Philemon

> Perhaps the reason he was separated from you for a little while was that you might have him back forever—no longer as a slave, but better than a slave, as a dear brother. 1:15.

Theme. The theme of the letter to Philemon is forgiveness. We all need forgiveness, and at one time or another we all also owe it. The letter to Philemon gives an extraordinary example of both receiving Christ's forgiveness, and then realizing what that receipt might require in forgiving others. We cannot receive Christ's forgiveness, in which he releases us from a due debt that he paid at ultimate expense, without letting go of what we hold over others. Forgiveness is at the gospel's core, as this brief but profound letter reminds us.

Author. Philemon credits Paul as its author, making the letter the last of the Bible's thirteen Pauline letters. Paul had ministered in Ephesus for two years on his third missionary journey, seeing great success. One of those Ephesus successes was in reaching this letter's recipient Philemon with the gospel. Paul and Philemon had apparently then worked in ministry at Ephesus together, as reference in this letter suggests. Read the above section on Paul's letter to the Romans, for more detail about Paul's life.

Audience. Paul wrote this letter to the wealthy slaveowner Philemon from Paul's Rome prison, in about A.D. 60. Fortuitously, Philemon's runaway slave Onesimus, who had escaped to Rome to hide there, met Paul, accepting Jesus in response to Paul's instruction. Paul then wrote this letter to Philemon, addressing Onesimus's meeting and status. Paul's letter would have been extraordinary for the time, in calling Philemon's slave Onesimus, then in Paul's service but a thief-and-slave runaway from Philemon, Philemon's brother in Christ. In the letter, Paul makes a plea that the slaveowner take the runaway slave back free, as a brother, because as Paul so tactfully puts it in the letter, the slaveowner owed his own life to Paul. All are dead apart from Christ, while all are free together in Christ. The short and spare letter's profound implications for the equality of all in Christ thus go far beyond the letter's simple plea that Philemon take Onesimus back as a faith brother. Paul's letter to Philemon testifies that Christ removes all legal, economic, social, and other barriers among believers, uniting all in freedom as members of the one body of Christ.

Structure. Paul structures his two-part letter to Philemon first by introducing its three characters, Paul the apostle, Philemon the co-worker slaveowner convert, and Onesimus the runaway slave. The second part of Paul's brief letter turns to who in this situation holds the authority. Paul writes that he could order Philemon to release Onesimus but instead appeals in love. Paul wanted to do nothing without all consenting, preferring to preserve their unified spirit around a bond of peace. In this way, Paul invokes the gospel, which is Christ's forgiveness at perfect expense, but that compels believers to likewise forgive.

Application. Philemon teaches that forgiveness is not optional. Once God reconciles us to him through his sacrificed and resurrected Son Jesus, we must reconcile with one another, which means to forgive. Examine yourself: whom do you need to forgive? Ask yourself: whom do you need to ask for forgiveness? The gospel requires both acts, to forgive one another even as we humbly beg Christ's forgiveness.

Memory Verses. 1-5: I always thank my God as I remember you in my prayers, because I hear about your love for all his holy people and your faith in the Lord Jesus. 8-9: [A]lthough in Christ I could be bold and order you to do what you ought to do, yet I prefer to appeal to you on the basis of love. 15-16: Perhaps the reason he was separated from you for a little while was that you might have him back forever—no longer as a slave, but better than a slave, as a dear brother.

241

Hebrews

[T]he ministry Jesus has received is as superior to theirs
as the covenant of which he is mediator is superior to the old
one 8:6.

Theme. The theme of the letter to the Hebrews is superiority,
specifically that of Jesus Christ over all others. We live in a world and
time when many claim superiority, prominence, and preeminence. The
world hosts one grand competition in which personages, corporations,
governments, religions, and brands claim to be first and best. Many
things compete for our allegiance and, beyond that, our devotion,
tempting us to make idols of those things. In that din, we look for true
superiority. We know that the universe has an order, and so we sense that
something, someone, somewhere must in fact be superior. Hebrews tells
us that the superior being with the superior offer is our Lord and Savior
Jesus Christ.

Author. Scholars disagree enough over who wrote Hebrews,
assuming anyone of whom we know, that calling the letter anonymous
may be best. Anonymity does not mean lack of prominence or
credibility. Scholars speculate that Hebrews' author could have been
Paul, Luke, Barnabas, Apollos, Clement, or Priscilla, among prominent
others. While we should all appreciate the extraordinary experiences that
these known persons had, we should also appreciate that the anonymity
of any author makes no difference to writings that the Holy Spirit
inspired. If God can talk through a donkey, as he did to the diviner
Balaam, then God can talk to us through an anonymous author of an
exquisitely crafted letter like Hebrews. Hebrews' author, even if
anonymous, had profound experiences, knew and interacted with
historical figures, and above all heard and obeyed God's Holy Spirit.
Thus, have no concern over anonymous or uncertain authorship, even as
you take a healthy interest in known authors and their experiences. The
Bible, including each of its letters, is the inspired word of God.

Audience. The letter to the Hebrews, probably written around 70
A.D. just before the Temple's destruction, addressed Jews who were

examining Christianity or had converted to Christianity but questioned how the new faith related to the previously all-important Jewish law and traditions. That Jewish-Christian community may have been in Rome. This important but precarious Jewish-Christian audience faced double challenges, opposition and persecution from both Jews who rejected Christ while demanding adherence to the religious laws and from Romans who perceived threats to their rule from the new faith. Hebrews thus addresses at length the supreme authority and complete sufficiency of Christ. Hebrews also stressed the freedom that Christian faith brings from strict observance of religious practices and traditions, while respecting that the same God instituted both the old and new covenants, out of one overarching design. Hebrews resolves critical theological issues in ways that preserve Christian liberty, while respecting the essential role of the old-covenant laws in preparing the ground for Christian faith. Hebrews must have been enormously heartening to Jewish converts who wondered at the seeming delay in Christ's return and who endured terrible persecution.

Structure. Hebrews has a three-part structure showing first (in chapters one to four) that Jesus is above all others, then (in chapters five to ten) that Jesus is our great high priest, and finally (in chapters eleven to thirteen) that Jesus is greater for our lives. Hebrews first affirms at great length Jesus's superiority to angels, leaders, and priests, his new covenant's superiority to the old covenant, his body's superiority to the old Temple, and his sacrifice a better sacrifice than that of the priests. The Son radiates God's glory, as God's exact representation, the Son's word sustaining all things. The letter then examines the faith's practical implications including to hold onto one's confession and encourage one another in faith, while waiting patiently for Christ's return. Hebrews then confirms the contrasting consequences, whether punishment or reward, of rejecting or persevering in the faith. The letter includes a rousing review of faith heroes that, again, must have deeply encouraged the letter's Jewish-Christian readers and hearers. The letter's high tone and sermon-like construction make it unique among the letters, a priceless message guaranteed to confirm and inspire Christian believers in every age, everywhere.

Application. Hebrews has but one primary lesson, which is to ensure that we make Jesus Christ first in everything. We are, verse 12:2 tells us, to fix our eyes on Jesus, who authors our faith. One wonders, even, if saying to put Jesus first is enough. Perhaps we should instead agree to make Jesus our only one. Do not make Jesus compete with anything. The competition is long over, and Jesus won.

Memory Verses. *1:3: The Son is the radiance of God's glory and the exact representation of his being, sustaining all things by his powerful word. 4:12: For the word of God is alive and active. Sharper than any double-edged sword, it penetrates even to dividing soul and spirit, joints and marrow; it judges the thoughts and attitudes of the heart. 4:15: For we do not have a high priest who is unable to empathize with our weaknesses, but we have one who has been tempted in every way, just as we are – yet he did not sin. 11:1: Now faith is being sure of what we hope for and certain of what we do not see. 11:6: And without faith it is impossible to please God, because anyone who comes to him must believe that he exists and that he rewards those who earnestly seek him. 12:1: Therefore, since we are surrounded by such a great cloud of witnesses, let us throw off everything that hinders and the sin that so easily entangles. And let us run with perseverance the race marked out for us.... 12:2: Fixing our eyes on Jesus, the pioneer and perfecter of faith. For the joy set before him he endured the cross, scorning its shame, and sat down at the right hand of the throne of God. 13:8: Jesus Christ is the same yesterday and today and forever.*

James

Show me your faith without deeds, and I will show you my faith by my deeds. 2:18.

Theme. The theme of the letter James is authenticity. Its author showed himself concerned with hypocrisy arising in the church. No one admires the hypocrite. Those who profess one thing but do another are easy to dislike because their words are a fraud. We want people to be consistent in their words and actions, calling that consistency *integrity* and valuing integrity highly. What one says in public should be what one does in private. Those who must conceal their actions to maintain a false front do not deserve respect but instead deserve exposure. Authenticity is a rare attribute in persons, one that we rightly value highly. See how this extraordinary letter teaches about authenticity.

Author. Tradition holds that Jesus's brother James wrote the letter bearing that name, even though the letter itself refers to James only as a servant of God and of the Lord Jesus Christ, not expressly Jesus's brother. Some readers prefer to call James a *half* brother of Jesus, holding that Jesus and James would have shared only Mary as their mother. The Holy Spirit came on Mary when she conceived Jesus, while Mary's husband Joseph would have been James's father and the father of Mary's other children. Others prefer to treat James and his other siblings as Joseph's children from a prior marriage ending in his wife's death, and thus Mary's adopted children, or simply as cousins to Mary's Son Jesus, Mary thus maintaining her virginity. In any case, biologically related to Jesus or not, James until his death around 62 A.D. was a prominent leader in Jerusalem of the community of believers that the apostles formed and influenced. In dozens of places, the letter's text shows that its author was familiar with Jesus's sayings, before repetition spread and tradition fixed those sayings. Jesus's brother James could well have been the letter's author.

Inference finds it easier to rule out as the letter James' author, others bearing the James name. Jesus's two apostles James the son of Zebedee and James the son of Alphaeus were less likely the letters' author,

Zebedee's son because of his early martyrdom (as the book of Acts records) and Alphaeus's son because of his lack of prominence in the biblical record. The letter implies that the James who wrote the letter was prominent, as Jesus's brother James surely was. Paul's letters described James, the brother of the Lord, as one of three church pillars. Jude, the author of another letter by that name, referred to himself not only as a slave of Jesus Christ, as James likewise did in his letter, but also as a brother of James, again taken by some as further evidence that Jesus's brother wrote the letter.

If indeed, Jesus's brother James, the early Jerusalem church's leader, wrote the letter by his name, then we have an extraordinary witness to the Holy Spirit's testimony. John's Gospel records that Jesus's brothers did not believe in Jesus, and so James' conversion likely followed the resurrection. Paul in 1 Corinthians records that the resurrected Lord appeared to his brother James. Confirming James's prominence, some historians identify Jesus's brother James as James the Just, James of Jerusalem, and the Bishop of Jerusalem. James, Peter, and Paul each played leading roles in the early church. The Jewish historian Josephus records outside the biblical record that James, Jesus's brother, had the Pharisees' respect for his pious observance of the law, despite that enemies had James put to death in 62 A.D. in a brief period between local Roman governors.

The three great witnesses James, Peter, and Paul certainly knew and supported one another, if at times also contesting in the faith, as the book of Acts records Paul doing openly in Peter's presence. Acts also records Paul receiving in Antioch a messenger from James carrying an instruction to local believers that Paul rejected. Yet Acts also records Peter leaving a message for James and the other apostles when Peter was preparing to leave Jerusalem, much as Acts mentions Paul's visiting James on Paul's last time in Jerusalem. James clearly supported both Paul and Peter. In Galatians, Paul notes his visit to Peter and James in Jerusalem after Paul's conversion and a second visit to Peter, James, and John, whom Galatians records Paul regarding as the church's pillars. So again, in Jesus's brother James, the letter would have an extraordinary author. Yet whoever wrote the letter James, we know from its inclusion in the Bible and the profound quality of its text that we have a most-extraordinary witness writing in the Holy Spirit.

Audience. James wrote his letter from Jerusalem around 49 A.D., just before the Jerusalem council the next year, to Jewish Christians who had migrated outward from the Jerusalem church into surrounding

Gentile areas. His Christian audience faced persecution, although the letter's content suggests that their greater threat may have been from their own hypocritical tendencies and poor behavior. James thus writes as their stern and authoritative former senior pastor, free to give frank counsel because of their close relationship and strong bond. James begins by telling them how Christians should live and act among others, next suggesting how faith moves into action. Faith, to be worthwhile, must make a difference in a believer's life. Behavior matters. James next cautions to hold one's tongue and warns against false earthly wisdom. James wants his former church members to avoid temptation in favor of godly living. He concludes the letter with encouragement to respect, support, and pray for one another. The letter James remains today an extraordinarily practical and direct manual for sound Christian living, invaluable to anyone earnestly practicing the faith.

Structure. James has a three-part structure that debunks, one at a time, three myths. The first debunked myth is that trials are bad, when James instead teaches that trials build character, making us depend on God. Trials will end, James comforts, while distinguishing trials from temptations. The second myth that James debunks, beginning at his chapter two, is that faith is merely what one believes in one's mind. James teaches that faith also involves action, contrasting beliefs held by Satan with beliefs put into action by a list of faith heroes. The last myth that James debunks is that faith is only a private matter, when instead faith has to do with our public words, attitudes, and actions. James is in every sense a straightforward, practical writer, whose insight and wisdom have the power to shape a life.

Application. James hammers home that our faith must produce actions if we are to regard it as genuine. We cannot say that we love God if we do not love our neighbor, and we cannot say that we love our neighbor if we do nothing to meet our neighbor's needs in loving care. In verse 2:18, James states that if you show him your faith without deeds, he will show you his faith by his deeds. James demands action of us. His primary lesson is to walk the walk as you talk the talk. Do not merely profess the faith but show your faith by your actions. Religion without deeds is dead. Even Satan believes God. Our actions must prove our belief.

Memory Verses. 1:2: *Consider it pure joy, my brothers and sisters, whenever you face trials of many kinds.... 1:5: If any of you lacks wisdom, you should ask God, who gives generously to all without finding fault, and it will be given to you. 1:17: Every good and perfect gift is from above, coming down from the Father of the heavenly lights, who does not change like shifting shadows. 1:19: My dear brothers and sisters, take note of this: Everyone should be quick to listen, slow to speak and slow to become angry.... 1:22: Do not merely listen to the word, and so deceive yourselves. Do what it says. 1:27: Religion that God our Father accepts as pure and faultless is this: to look after orphans and widows in their distress and to keep oneself from being polluted by the world. 2:14: What good is it, my brothers and sisters, if people claim to have faith but have no deeds? Can such faith save them? 2:18: Show me your faith without deeds, and I will show you my faith by my deeds. 2:19: You believe that there is one God. Good! Even the demons believe that—and shudder. 4:7: Resist the devil, and he will flee from you. 5:16: The prayer of a righteous person is powerful and effective.*

1 Peter

For Christ also suffered once for sins, the righteous for
the unrighteous, to bring you to God. 3:18.

Theme. The theme of 1 Peter is hope, especially hope during
suffering. The hardest time to hope is when under the greatest challenge.
When someone is attacking, persecuting, and destroying one's peace,
reputation, and prosperity, hope seems far away. Who can hope when all
one sees is death and destruction? Yet hope does exactly that, taking the
first step toward believing that the unseen rescue is more powerful and
enduring than the seen enemy. Hope precedes faith, which is action
without evidence. Hope feeds faith, giving faith cause to act. In the
darkest hour, we wish for hope, and wishing for hope, hope answers.

Author. The letter 1 Peter credits its author Peter, at the letter's
beginning. We know a great deal about Peter's life from the four gospel
books and the book of Acts. We also know from external accounts
(amplified by tradition) a little bit about his final imprisonment and
death. Luke's gospel book tells us that Peter's original name was Simon,
a Galilean fisherman brother of another disciple Andrew. Luke suggests
that Peter and Andrew were the first two disciples whom Jesus called,
both leaving their fishing boats and nets on Jesus's invitation to be
fishers instead of men. The gospel books portray Peter as an outspoken
and often-erring leader of the disciples in their interaction with Jesus.
Thus, at the last supper, Peter initially refused Jesus's offer to wash his
feet but then impulsively asked Jesus to wash his entire body. Peter,
though, was the first to call Jesus the Son of the living God, the Messiah,
on occasion of which Jesus renamed Simon as Peter, meaning *the rock*,
as on confession of Christ all else stands. Peter witnessed Jesus's
transfiguration and miracles, and was with Jesus as Jesus prayed at
Gethsemane, along with John and his brother James, the three
comprising an inner circle of disciples.

At Jesus's last supper, Peter professed willingness to die with Jesus
but then promptly denied Jesus three times outside the high priest's
courtyard at Jesus's trial, as Jesus had predicted. Peter was nonetheless

one of the two disciples who ran to the empty tomb immediately after Jesus's reported resurrection. Peter thereafter resumed a leading role among the disciples, after Jesus restored Peter along the Sea of Galilee's shores, three times telling Peter to feed Jesus's sheep. Peter preached boldly in Jerusalem at Pentecost, when the Spirit descended, and thousands confessed Christ. Peter and John also preached boldly when brought before the Sanhedrin, for having healed another at the temple gate, and later suffered imprisonment before release by an angel. Peter was one of the three pillars of the early church in Jerusalem, along with John and Jesus's brother James. A vision brought Peter to eat with the gentile Cornelius, the event, with Paul's intercession, helping to enlarge Christianity's reach beyond Jewish converts to Gentiles. Peter left Jerusalem carrying the gospel to other regions including likely Rome, where external accounts and tradition hold (consistent with Jesus's prophecy at Peter's restoration) that Peter suffered death by crucifixion. Indeed, tradition holds that Emperor Nero granted Peter's wish to die crucified upside down, in humility to Jesus's glorious cross-borne victory. Tradition and external accounts further hold that Peter converted his jailers and dozens of others to Christ in the months before his death around 67 A.D., despite enduring horrible torture. Peter, like Paul, James, and John, was an extraordinary witness to author letters under the Holy Spirit.

Audience. Peter wrote his first letter around 62 to 64 A.D., possibly from Rome, just before Nero's persecution of Christians that included Peter's execution. Like James, Peter was writing to Jewish Christians whom persecution had driven from Jerusalem. Roman torture and execution of Christians throughout the empire was driving the Christian faith outward rather than extinguishing it. Peter's Jewish-Christian audience for his first letter had dispersed north into Asia Minor. The letter's purpose was to bolster the fleeing Christians' faith against horrible persecution.

Structure. The widely read letter opens with the revelation that persecution simply proves faith genuine, bringing not shame but rather, on Christ's return, glory and honor. God's blessings are what Christians seek, not human praise and honor. Peter's letter instructed the suffering believers in how to conduct themselves under terrible trial and how to guide other suffering believers. The comforting themes of 1 Peter include salvation as precious gift, persecution proving victory, the family of believers, and God's ultimate judgment. The letter continues to reveal to believers today the great weight of their coming glory.

Application. Peter, who accompanied Jesus for three years and later led the Jerusalem church through opposition and tumult, before his arrest, removal to Rome, and execution, had the experience and authority to write a letter saying to bear up under persecution. How, though, do we accept what we do not deserve? Peter's lesson is to look at the larger picture. In verse 2:9, Peter calls the followers of Christ a "royal priesthood, holy nation, [and] God's special possession," exhorting us then to declare his praises, even in darkness as in his wonderful light. We must look beyond our circumstances to who we are in Christ Jesus. Peter also, in verse 3:18, reminds us of Christ's own suffering, "the righteous for the unrighteous," to bring us to God. Who, Peter seems to say, are we to complain about unjust suffering, when Jesus suffered most unjustly and did so for us? Once again, look to our Savior, not to our circumstances. And don't underestimate the Savior's power in the worst of circumstances. One has only to look to the forgiving martyr Stephen and evangelizing martyr Peter for evidence of that power.

Memory Verses. *2:9: But you are a chosen people, a royal priesthood, a holy nation, God's special possession, that you may declare the praises of him who called you out of darkness into his wonderful light. 3:15: Always be prepared to give an answer to everyone who asks you to give the reason for the hope that you have. 3:18: For Christ also suffered once for sins, the righteous for the unrighteous, to bring you to God. He was put to death in the body but made alive in the Spirit.*

2 Peter

> Therefore, dear friends, since you have been forewarned,
> be on your guard so that you may not be carried away by the
> error of the lawless and fall from your secure position. 3:17.

Theme. The theme of 2 Peter is warning. Cheerful banter is nice, and specific encouragement is nicer. Warning? Not so much. Yet warning is far better than banter or encouragement, when warning speaks of that which it knows. We should far rather have warning of a dire event from which preparation can save us, than to have only fair-weather forecasts. Give us warning, or in lack thereof we may find death. Second Peter fulfills the writer's duty to be frank as to what lies ahead.

Author. Some hold that the prominent disciple Peter also wrote 2 Peter, as he wrote 1 Peter. Others note differences in the letters' styles. Indeed, 2 Peter's style seems closer to the following letter Jude, causing some scholars to attribute 2 Peter to the same author who wrote Jude. One theory holds that the author's reference in Jude to desiring to write another letter when needing instead to urgently write the letter Jude, was a reference to 2 Peter. That theory would then make the reference in 2 Peter to an earlier letter already sent, a reference to the letter Jude rather than, as many assume, a reference to 1 Peter. In any case, if Peter did not write 2 Peter, then readers can still have confidence that 2 Peter's author knew Peter, his experiences, and his teaching well. If Peter was the author of his credited second letter, rather than another author attributing Peter, then Peter wrote it around 67 A.D., shortly after his first letter and at the very end of his life, just before his execution.

Audience. The audience for Peter's second letter was the universal church, believers everywhere, rather than those of a certain ancestry, local church, locale, or region. The assurances of 1 Peter are largely absent from 2 Peter, replaced in 2 Peter with warnings against false teachers, a call to diligent action, a challenge to grow in faith, and an assurance of Christ's return in judgment against non-believers. The challenges that 2 Peter addresses are not external, such as Roman persecution, but internal, against heresy and spiritual malaise. Believers need comfort from suffering, but they also need reminders that faith involves moving forward confidently and responsibly, as 2 Peter continues to admonish.

Structure. Peter's second letter follows a three-part structure. Chapter one urges the letter's readers to make their calling and election sure, under the prophecy of scripture. Jesus, Peter argues, has given us everything we need for a godly life. We need only make every effort to add godly qualities to our faith. Jesus authors our faith, but we must strive to develop godly qualities through that faith. Peter's second chapter warns against the destruction of false teachers. Peter's third and final chapter is a warning that the day of the Lord will come so suddenly that we must make every effort to hold onto our secure position with him. Conduct remains important, Peter reveals, and so we should be blameless when Christ returns.

Application. The day of the Lord will come like a thief, Peter tells us, meaning when least expected, perhaps when night has lulled our faith asleep. Second Peter's warning theme gives the reader two applications. First, as Peter's first chapter exhorts, be sure of your salvation. Confirm your calling and election. Get right with Jesus. Confess him publicly and believe in his resurrection privately. Second, as Peter's last chapter alerts, because the day of the Lord when Jesus returns to judge will be upon us when we least expect it, always live a holy and godly life. Be on guard against all lawlessness.

Memory Verses. *1:3: His divine power has given us everything we need for a godly life through our knowledge of him who called us by his own glory and goodness. 1:5-7: [M]ake every effort to add to your faith goodness; and to goodness, knowledge; and to knowledge, self-control; and to self-control, perseverance; and to perseverance, godliness; and to godliness, mutual affection; and to mutual affection, love. 3:8: But do not forget this one thing, dear friends: With the Lord a day is like a thousand years, and a thousand years are like a day. 3:9: The Lord is not slow in keeping his promise, as some understand slowness. Instead he is patient with you, not wanting anyone to perish, but everyone to come to repentance. 3:10: But the day of the Lord will come like a thief. The heavens will disappear with a roar; the elements will be destroyed by fire, and the earth and everything done in it will be laid bare.*

1 John

Anyone who claims to be in the light but hates a brother
or sister is still in the darkness. 2:9.

Theme. The theme of 1 John is fellowship, meaning deep love for
one another. We crave the company of others who are for us. God clearly
made us to show others that they matter to us and created us to need that
affirmation. Fellowship is a bond beyond friendship to the point of
knowing we can trust and why we can trust. Where do we find
fellowship? In verse 1:7, John's letter tells us that we find fellowship in
the community of believers in Jesus Christ.

Author. Jesus's beloved disciple John, who wrote the gospel of that
name, very likely wrote the letters under his name, too. As the above
section on John's gospel indicates, John and his brother James, also a
disciple of Jesus, were sons of Zebedee, the three of them working as
unschooled and ordinary fishermen on the Sea of Galilee, when Jesus
called John and James to discipleship. John, his brother James (not
Jesus's brother James), and Peter were Jesus's inner circle of disciples
who witnessed Jesus's transfiguration, saw Jesus raise Jairus's dead
daughter, and accompanied Jesus (but slept) while Jesus prayed just
before his arrest at Gethsemane. Some inference exists that John's
mother was Salome, who could have been a sister of Jesus's mother
Mary, which, if so, would have made John a cousin to Jesus.

John was close to Jesus in other ways. Mark's gospel account
records that Jesus nicknamed John and his brother James the Sons of
Thunder for their outspoken quick tempers. On the cross, Jesus appointed
John to care for Jesus's mother Mary. John was the one to recognize the
resurrected Jesus the moment of the miraculous catch of fish. Because
John in his gospel account referred to himself in the third person, John
may also have been the disciple who knew the high priest and thus
accompanied Jesus into the high priest's courtyard for Jesus's trial, and
who ran with Peter to the empty tomb. The book of Acts records that
John was with Peter for the lame man's healing at the temple, to preach
before the Sanhedrin about Jesus's crucifixion and resurrection, and for

arrest, miracle release by an angel, and later flogging. In Galatians, Paul identifies John with Peter and Jesus's brother James (not John's brother James, whom King Herod Agrippa I beheaded around a decade after Jesus's resurrection) as a pillar of the early church in Jerusalem. John, like Paul and James, was plainly an extraordinary witness to author his letters, under the Holy Spirit.

Audience. John wrote the letter 1 John from Ephesus on the western coast of Asia Minor, likely between 85 and 90 A.D. The late date of John's letters would mean that Rome had already destroyed Jerusalem's temple, Nero had already sought to rid Rome of its Christians, and the other disciples had probably already been executed, leaving John as the sole survivor. By then, Christians had followed the Jewish diaspora out of Jerusalem in all directions. John was probably writing not to any specific church or region but to believers everywhere, carrying the faith into the future.

Structure. John's letter has four parts, depicting first the joyful life (1:4), then a clean life (2:1), the discerning life (2:21), and finally a loving life (3:1). The letter opens without addressing itself to any audience, beginning instead with John's claim to have seen the Lord's incarnation. John portrays God as light and urges believers to walk in that light, obeying Christ and embracing the faith family while resisting antichrists who oppose the gospel's truth. The letter next portrays God as love, irresistible and familial. God makes us his children, while we reveal our family relationship with God through our good deeds. Again, John repeats, we must reject deceivers. The letter concludes with John portraying God as life, that life found in our relationship with his Son Jesus Christ. The letter's clarity and succinctness beautifully reflect John's gospel, making the letter a pearl of incalculable value.

Application. John wanted us to love one another. In verse 4:12, he writes that although no one has ever seen God, God lives in us *if we love one another.* We must love one another for God to join us in our lives. In so urging, John refers to his gospel's verses 13:34-35, where he recorded Jesus's new command to love one another "as I have loved you," so that others will know that we follow Jesus. John not only tells us what to do but how to do it. In his letter's verse 3:16, he reminds us that Jesus laid down his life for us, and so we should do the same for one another. Love is sacrificial, acting for others' benefit. Verse 2:15 further reminds us not to love the world or things in the world, which draw us away from the Father's love. Love like Jesus, John's letter teaches us.

Memory Verses. *1:7: [I]f we walk in the light, as he is in the light, we have fellowship with one another, and the blood of Jesus, his Son, purifies us from all sin. 1:9: If we confess our sins, he is faithful and just and will forgive us our sins and purify us from all unrighteousness. 2:15: Do not love the world or anything in the world. If you love the world, love for the Father is not in you. 3:1: See what great love the Father has lavished on us, that we should be called children of God! And that is what we are! 4:1: Dear friends, do not believe every spirit, but test the spirits to see whether they are from God, because many false prophets have gone out into the world. 4:7: Dear friends, let us love one another, for love comes from God. Everyone who loves has been born of God and knows God.*

2 John

Watch out that you do not lose what we have worked for,
but that you may be rewarded fully. **8**.

Theme. The theme of 2 John is discernment. To discern is to distinguish, especially to separate good from evil, right from wrong. Somewhere along the way in our lives, we realize that we need to know how to act. We thus look for guidance, some of us in all the wrong places. We need a wise source from which to draw our discernment. This brief letter reminds us of both where to look, toward the Lord Jesus, and what to do for discernment, which is to obey his words. Discern by drawing from the source.

Author. Jesus's beloved disciple John very probably wrote 2 John. John uses a distinct title *elder* for himself at this brief letter's start, without mentioning his name, giving some scholars pause to believe that an unknown different author wrote the letter. But earliest second-century church tradition has associated the letter with the disciple John, as have generations since, making appropriate the confident attribution of the letter to the disciple. See the above section on 1 John and the section on the gospel of John for more detail on John's life. John wrote his very short second letter near the date of his first letter, probably around A.D. 90, around the time of his exile from Ephesus to the island of Patmos.

Audience. John's second letter differs from his first in that he directs it to a *chosen lady* and her children, which might mean a member of a local church but could just as well mean a certain church and its members, or the broader church and believers everywhere. The church is Christ's bride, hence making the church Jesus's chosen lady. Readers wisely take John's second letter as an address to the church and to themselves.

Structure. John's second letter differs from his first letter in its instructional emphasis. His first letter had more of an inspirational emphasis. John's first letter celebrated the fellowship that we have as followers of Christ. John's second letter warned that false teachers can rob us of that fellowship. In his second letter, John firmly confirms that faith means following Christ, which is to obey his words. The letter both challenges and lifts readers. We must walk in obedience to Christ's commands, the primary one of which is to love one another. Christ is truth carried out in sacrificial love. We must also be on guard against wicked deceivers, false teachers who deny the truth. John's second letter, like the first, lifts the face and opens the heart toward the glory of Christ, while adding stern warnings against false teaching, making the key to distinguish.

Application. The way to recognize a false teacher is that the teaching contradicts the commands of Christ. We must love one another, John's second letter says, like his first letter urged, but to do so we must avoid false teachers who would have us do otherwise. We must then obey Christ. Know the difference between good and evil. Good loves as Christ loves. Evil does not. Reject evil, love good, and obey Christ.

Memory Verses. *4: It has given me great joy to find some of your children walking in the truth, just as the Father commanded us. 5: And now, dear lady, I am not writing you a new command but one we have had from the beginning. I ask that we love one another. 6: And this is love: that we walk in obedience to his commands. As you have heard from the beginning, his command is that you walk in love. 7: Many deceivers, who do not acknowledge Jesus Christ as coming in the flesh, have gone out into the world. Any such person is the deceiver and the antichrist. 8: Watch out that you do not lose what we have worked for, but that you may be rewarded fully.*

3 John

We ought therefore to show hospitality to such people so
that we may work together for the truth. 8.

Theme. The theme of 3 John is hospitality. Where do we find some
comfort, some welcome, a place we can drop by for a moment's respite
and perhaps some kind repast? Hospitality is a generous gift because it is
not something earned or owed. Hospitality implies offering a refreshing
place when one has no obligation to do so. Those who are hospitable
have the heart of Christ. Welcome people everywhere, showing the heart
of Christ.

Author. Jesus's beloved disciple John very probably wrote 3 John,
based on the same inferences drawn in the above section as to 2 John.
Here, too, in 3 John, the author uses a distinct title *elder* for himself at
this brief letter's start, without mentioning his name, giving some
scholars pause to believe that an unknown different author wrote the
letter. But earliest second-century church tradition has associated the
letter with the disciple John, as have generations since, making
appropriate the confident attribution of the letter to the disciple. See the
above section on 1 John and the section on the gospel of John for more
detail on John's life. John wrote his very short second letter near the date
of his first letter, probably around A.D. 90, while in exile on the island of
Patmos.

Audience. John addresses his very short third letter to a dear friend
Gaius to thank him for his hospitality. John and other traveling church
leaders depended on believers like Gaius for food and shelter as they
visited to preach to and instruct local congregations. Gaius led a church
or churches in Asia Minor, where a certain Diotrephes, of whom we
know nothing else, was apparently causing Gaius troubles. John meant
his letter to guide Gaius in dealing with Diotrephes, even as John
encouraged Gaius for his generous fellowship.

Structure. In his third letter, John praises Gaius and another
hospitable believer for their service and support, while disparaging

259

another believer who had refused any hospitality and instead tried to commandeer and control the local church for his own benefit. John's letter thus serves as a brief reminder to care for leaders who serve the church faithfully, while the letter warns against false leaders who would instead have the church serve them. True to John's teacher's heart, though, the brief letter slips in a few short instructions to avoid evil, do good, and thus see God. John lets God's light shine even in a brief thank-you letter and reminder to support church leaders.

Application. Hospitality is a difficult grace to extend unless one has the heart of Christ. Do not be self-involved. Do not put yourself first. Put others first, as Christ put us first, so that you welcome all but the false teachers against whom John warns. Especially, welcome people into the church. Circumstances may discourage you from welcoming others into your home, but show them the hospitality of Christ, the joyful welcome, into his church.

Memory Verses. 3: It gave me great joy to have some believers come and testify to your faithfulness to the truth, telling how you continue to walk in it. 4: I have no greater joy than to hear that my children are walking in the truth. 11: Dear friend, do not imitate what is evil but what is good. Anyone who does what is good is from God. Anyone who does what is evil has not seen God.

Jude

[K]eep yourselves in God's love as you wait for the mercy of our Lord Jesus Christ to bring you to eternal life. 21.

Theme. The theme of Jude is perseverance, to press on through challenge, over obstructions in our path. We must all, at times, persevere. Indeed, perseverance is something that we must do daily. Sometimes the challenges are greater, and sometimes they are less, but challenges always exist. Those challenges are both internal, in our own health, attitude, and disposition, and external, directed at us intentionally by those who oppose our way or coming to us naturally out of circumstance, without obstructive intention. Given our many challenges, perseverance is a prime attribute. We need to persevere.

Author. The author of the letter Jude states that he is a brother of James, possibly intending the James, brother of Jesus, who wrote the epistle by that name. Jude may be another of the Lord Jesus's brothers (or half-brothers or stepbrothers, if you prefer), son of Joseph and possibly also of Mary. If that is so, that Jude was, like James, a member of Jesus's natural family, then Jude, like James, would not have been a follower of Jesus until after Jesus's resurrection, for the same reasons and based on the same accounts mentioned above as to James. The biblical record and other accounts give little more information about Jude, the brother of James and half-brother or stepbrother of Jesus, other than a reference in 1 Corinthians that the Lord's brothers and their wives made missionary trips. The author Jude, if the Lord's brother, would thus have served and traveled as a missionary like Paul, Peter, and James and would, like those others, have been an extraordinary gospel witness.

Alternatively, the author Jude may, when writing that he is a brother of James, have meant that he was a spiritual rather than biological brother of James. The author Jude may also have referred to a different James entirely, rather than the Lord's brother. If so, then the biblical record includes several other Jude-brother candidates named James, although the record suggests no one candidate over another. Some believe that Jude could have been Jesus's disciple Judas (not the betrayer

Judas Iscariot), Jude being an equivalent name commonly substituted for Judas after the betrayal. If a disciple, then Jude would indeed have been an extraordinary gospel witness. Given the questions over authorship and the little information that we have about any candidate author, the letter Jude is hard to date but probably followed Peter's writing 1 Peter around 65 A.D. and could have been between 67 and 80 A.D.

Audience. The short letter Jude addresses itself simply to those whom God called and whom Jesus kept, thus to believers everywhere. The whole of the letter urges that believers contend for the faith, making the letter's universal appeal even clearer.

Structure. The letter's first section documents the mendacious methods and corrupt characteristics of false teachers whom believers must identify, oppose, and reject. The letter's second section urges believers to fight for truth, persevere through trials, and stand firm in the faith. The letter ends with a stirring doxology to the God and Savior who keeps us and purifies us to present us to himself as witness to his glory. Jude's brevity, simplicity, and urgency make it a more-than-fitting conclusion to the letters, in anticipation of the Bible's concluding masterpiece Revelation.

Application. Press on, press on, press on, Jude's letter seems to tell us, and with good reason. Unless you press forward today, today is lost. Tomorrow hasn't yet come, and yesterday is over, so today is the day to persevere. Perseverance may not be an attribute, a quality that we either possess or don't possess. It may instead simply be a behavior, that we either move forward or we don't. And so, Jude's lesson is to hold fast to the faith, and let that holding be enough whether you feel like it or not. Press forward in faith, and let that pressing on be enough, whether you think you have the quality or not. God rewards those who run the race to the end, along the way contending for the faith.

Memory Verses. 2: *Mercy, peace and love be yours in abundance.* 3: *Dear friends, although I was very eager to write to you about the salvation we share, I felt compelled to write and urge you to contend for the faith that the Lord has once for all entrusted to us, his people.* 4: *For certain individuals whose condemnation was written about long ago have secretly slipped in among you. They are ungodly people, who pervert the grace of our God into a license for immorality and deny Jesus Christ our only Sovereign and Lord.* 24: *To him who is able to keep you from stumbling and to present you before his glorious presence without fault and with great joy....*

Vision of the Future

Humans need some vision of the future, indeed of the future's end, if the world is to end. How many times through the course of a life do we reflect on the world's course? Every age has its apocalyptic vision. Those visions change as threats, trends, and technologies change. In the first half of the last century, apocalyptic visions were of world wars, ever-greater weapons threats, and nuclear annihilation. At other times, the end-times visions have been of ice ages, incinerating meltdowns, famines driven by over population, and world pandemics and plagues. Some foresee meteor crashes ending life as we know it, while others see visiting aliens taking over the world. Some just picture the universe slowly dissipating into a cold, lifeless, steady-state entropy.

In the single book of Revelation, the Bible meets head-on the human urge for end-times or next-times definition, discovering instead that the world does not end but instead transforms. The book of Revelation is a fitting conclusion to the Bible. Given the astoundingly broad, varied, ancient, and deep nature of the Bible record to this point, the Bible's last book would have to be extraordinary, other-worldly, jaw-dropping, which Revelation every bit is. Revelation takes work in interpretation, given its heavy symbolism. That work is worthwhile because Revelation lays it all out. Revelation, together with the rest of the Bible on which Revelation draws, answers every fundamental question having to do with civilization's future, with the future of humankind, and the world's future. Enjoy Revelation's singular, deeply satisfying, though everywhere challenging, view of what God holds for our future.

Revelation

[T]he voice I had first heard speaking to me like a trumpet said, "Come up here, and I will show you what must take place after this." 4:1.

Theme. The theme of the book of Revelation is unveiling, unfolding, as in to reveal or disclose. As curious humans, we want to know what's behind the curtain and, more so, what's coming. We don't like secrets unless they are secrets that we know. We constantly investigate, and we constantly conjecture and predict, out of our urge to know the future. God, though, we should know reveals. The Bible's innumerable prophecies prove God's prophetic presence. God knows not only the past and present but the future. And God lets us see just enough of the future to benefit us the most. Too much disclosure, and we'd give up. Too little disclosure, and we'd give up, too. In Revelation, God gives us just what we need to know.

Author. Revelation shares its author's name, John, three times at the beginning of its first chapter and a fourth time at the book's end. From the early church forward, tradition has soundly credited the disciple John, author of the fourth gospel book, as the John who wrote Revelation. In his later years, John left Jerusalem, where he had helped to lead the emerging church, to serve Asia Minor's churches. The book of Revelation and external sources record John's exile to the island of Patmos in the Aegean Sea, as punishment for preaching the gospel. John's exile likely took place around 95 A.D., near the end of the persecutor Dominian's reign. Dominian's assassination a year later likely enabled John to return to Asia Minor to die there, probably near Ephesus, around 98 A.D., with his reputed tomb in the ruins of St. John's Church at Selcuk in modern-day Turkey. If that history is correct, then John may well have been the only one of the twelve disciples to die of natural causes, as the end of his gospel account suggests, and as tradition also holds. Read more about John in the sections on his gospel book and his letters.

Context. Revelation's canonical context is that it serves as the Bible's last book, well after the four gospel books and at the end of the New Testament's twenty-one letters. Somehow, some way, the Bible must capture and project forward everything that went before the Bible's last book. Revelation splendidly fulfills that difficult role. The author paragraph just above indicates the book's historical context. Following Jesus's resurrection, the church had emerged from Jerusalem, spreading from the Jews to the Gentiles, north and west all the way to Rome, where it had recently met with cruel persecution. Persecution in Jerusalem had sent the church outward to Rome, but Rome had responded with its own wave of persecution. Rome had also destroyed the temple in Jerusalem, responding to Jewish rebellion. The world had changed since Jesus's resurrection, in ways that Jesus had prophesied. John thus wrote to a maturing church, one that was moving from excitement over its establishment and growth, toward wonder at what its future held.

Structure. Revelation structures its extraordinary narrative around seven emerging visions, each symbolic or allegorical for future historic developments involving Christ and the church. The first vision, comprised of chapters one to three, shows Jesus standing among seven golden lampstands, then addressing seven specific churches, each church representative of patterns that followers would find among the churches. Revelation's second vision, comprised of chapters four to seven, begins a chronological narrative. John, taken heavenward, sees God's throne and several seals, each to be broken. Revelation's third vision, in chapters eight through eleven, involves seven trumpets announcing successive judgments. The fourth vision, in chapters twelve through fourteen, shows a symbolic Christ figure set against a mighty dragon. The fifth vision, in chapters fifteen and sixteen, depicts God pouring out seven successive bowls of wrath. The sixth vision, in chapters seventeen to nineteen, depicts the fall of Babylon, in symbols involving a woman and beast. The final vision, in the concluding chapters twenty to twenty-two, shows the new heaven and new earth, after which John concludes with a brief epilogue. Whether John used allegory to protect his writing from the scrutiny of persecutors, or whether the allegory is simply a better way to serve his communication purpose, Revelation's extraordinary imagery leaves the reader fully satisfied as to God's complete vision for our next-times future.

Key Events. Key events give further structure to John's remarkable vision. The first such event was God's instruction to John, who was in the Spirit on the Lord's day on Patmos, to write God's vision on a scroll.

John recorded, in chapter one, his simultaneous vision of the resplendent Lord. After John recorded the Lord's words to the seven churches, God then called John to heaven, as the fourth chapter records, where John saw elders and creatures worshipping God on his throne. The fifth chapter records an angel asking who would open a scroll, when John saw a slain Lamb, the Lord Jesus, step forward to take the scroll, at which millions of angels encircled God's throne to praise the Lamb. Revelation then has the Lamb open the seven seals, one by one, extraordinary events in heaven proceeding from each of them. Great woes on earth proceed out of the seven successive trumpets, during which John receives a measuring rod for the temple. Chapter twelve records a war in heaven between Michael and his angels, and the dragon Satan, who in losing, God casts to earth with his evil angels. In figurative language, Satan pursues Christ's church on earth. Beasts on earth, perhaps representing kingdom and nation powers, arise to join Satan. But the Lamb stands on Mount Zion with his followers. Seven angels bring plagues to earth, pouring out God's wrath. Babylon, representing earth's powers, finally falls, giving way to Christ's thousand-year reign on earth, at the end of which Satan gains release from prison only to be thrown into an eternal fire. God on a great white throne judges the dead at book's end, just before the Holy City, a new Jerusalem, God's dwelling place and the bride of the Lamb, descends from heaven. God restores Eden, his paradise garden.

Key Locations. Revelation's two key locations include God's throne in heaven, around which array worshipping elders and creatures, and gather throngs of celebrants, and earth, on which Satan and his beasts and demons pursue the church but suffer destruction from heaven. At Revelation's end, God joins those two locations when his Holy City, the New Jerusalem, descends to earth, restoring the Eden garden into which God had placed humankind at his creation. Revelation also mentions the location Patmos from which John wrote, and the location of the seven churches around Asia Minor to whom Jesus spoke. Yet Revelation's dominant theme is of the final battle that heaven wages on earth to rid it of Satan's presence, to restore humankind to God's presence. Revelation's last two chapters are quite clear as to the full benefit to humankind of Eden's restoration, that God's throne and Lamb will be in the Holy City, healing the nations, where humankind will find no more death, mourning, crying, or pain.

Revelation of Christ. The book Revelation finally fully reveals Christ the slain Lamb in his glory both in heaven and on earth. No other

Bible book gives as complete and detailed a picture of Christ's authority, including his worship by angels, creatures, and millions of followers. No one can read Revelation without recognizing Christ's absolute power to conquer all evil, destroy all curse, and restore the earth to its original, pristine, garden condition, as God intended earth to be for humankind. John ends Revelation with the only fitting tribute to Jesus as the loving, creating, conquering God, which is to celebrate that he is coming soon.

Application. Revelation both challenges us to ensure our commitment to Jesus as Savior and comforts us that Jesus will indeed save, in every possible aspect. We need only come to him, taking, as Revelation 22:17 says, his gift of the water of life. Take from Jesus as he offers. Live in the sure knowledge that he is removing from us every pain, especially the pain of death. See in Revelation a fully worthy Savior who has a paradise place for each of us. Let Revelation stun you into the greatest admiration, greatest humility, and fullest worship of the one Lord and Savior Jesus Christ.

Memory Verses. *1:7: "Look, he is coming with the clouds," and "every eye will see him, even those who pierced him"; and all peoples on earth "will mourn because of him." 3:20: "Here I am! I stand at the door and knock. If anyone hears my voice and opens the door, I will come in and eat with them, and they with me." 7:9: After this I looked, and there before me was a great multitude that no one could count, from every nation, tribe, people and language, standing before the throne and in front of the Lamb. 12:9: The great dragon was hurled down – that ancient serpent called the devil, or Satan, who leads the whole world astray. He was hurled to the earth, and his angels with him. 19:11: I saw heaven standing open and there before me was a white horse, whose rider is called Faithful and True. With justice he judges and makes war. 20:11: Then I saw a great white throne and him who was seated on it. The earth and the heavens fled from his presence, and there was no place for them. 21:1: Then I saw "a new heaven and a new earth," for the first heaven and the first earth had passed away, and there was no longer any sea. 22:18: I warn everyone who hears the words of the prophecy of this scroll: If any one of you adds anything to them, God will add to you the plagues described in this scroll.*

Conclusion

How fitting that the Bible ends not with the world's end but instead with the world's beginning. The Bible is not ultimately a story about the end of the world, nor the destiny of any of us within it. Oh, we have individual destinies, the Bible is clear. Yet the Bible is God's story of his purpose for the world, of which we are only a part within it, even if the most-important part as to ourselves and God's love interest collectively. We can read the Bible through a lens of self-interest. Why not? Is anyone more important to you than you? Yet God did not inspire the Bible to satisfy the intensely individualistic modern American soul. God inspired the Bible to tell his story, not ours, even though our stories are the major part of his. Indeed, collectively, we are, meaning humankind is, God's greatest concern, as he demonstrated by giving us himself. His story, though, is of his intention for all of us, in fact all creation including plant, animal, or inanimate objects around us.

The Bible's ultimate point, played out through the pages of Revelation, is that God's story does not end. The Bible reveals something critical, through the knowledge of which we must read the Bible. Read it again: *God's story does not end.* From Genesis forward to Revelation, we must read the Bible knowing that God's story is always beginning, meaning eternal, ongoing, without end. As the way, truth, and life, as *being itself,* the great I Am, God continues moment to moment to write his glorious future with his image-bearing creation. The Bible reveals God in ways that should stop our downward course, arrest us in our tracks, as God arrested the murderous Pharisee Saul, in an instant turning him into the most-extraordinarily loving, discerning, generous, and gifted apostle Paul. All that God did in that moment, Paul admits in his letter to the Galatians, is to give Paul a glimpse, a flash of light, the briefest revelation, of who he truly is in the Lord Jesus.

That, friends and fellows in Christ, is why and how we read the Bible, to catch that fleeting glimpse of our Lord Jesus. We who read the Bible intensely, searching each page for a glimpse again of our precious Lord, have caught a fever for his transformation. We wish to die to our former selves, those selves so enslaved to our limited view of God and his world, and thus enslaved to sin. We who read the Bible for another glimpse of Jesus wish birth again, that Jesus would make us new. And in our newness, we wish then to share this glorious life in God's kingdom. We thus read the Bible backward, from the last stunning page of Revelation, when God's Holy City descends, bringing God's full presence among us again, in the paradise for which he initially created us, light each page of the Bible. The Bible reveals who God is, from whom we learn who we are. Read the Bible in that Holy Spirit of revelation.